Back from an attack on Berlin, the crewmen of a U.S. B-24 Liberator bomber head for a debriefing session at their base in England. The plane's prankish name, painted on its side, was "Arise My Love and Come with Me."

THE AIR WAR IN EUROPE

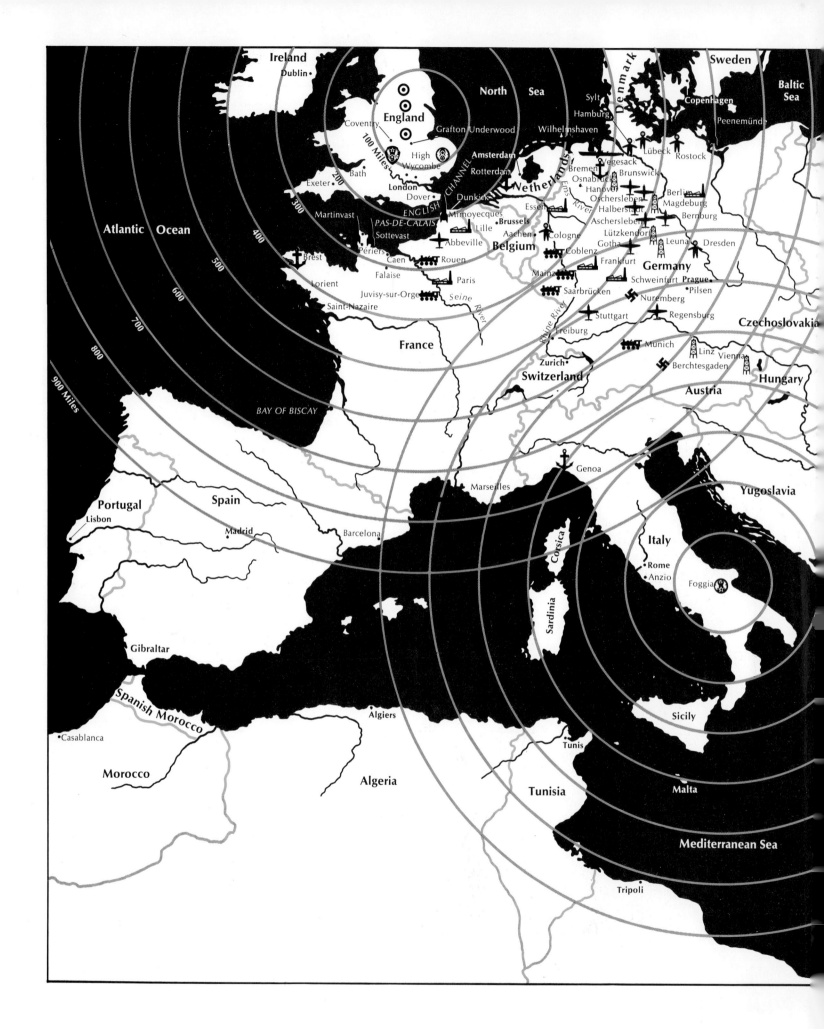

THE AIR WAR IN EUROPE: 1940-1945

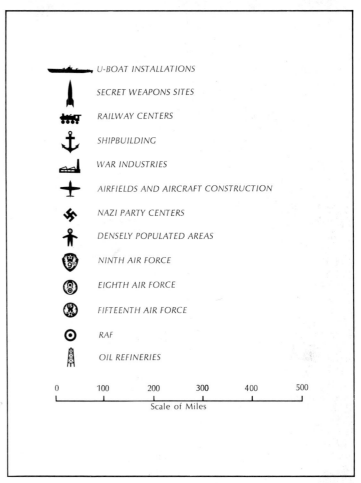

	U-BOAT INSTALLATIONS
	SECRET WEAPONS SITES
	RAILWAY CENTERS
	SHIPBUILDING
	WAR INDUSTRIES
	AIRFIELDS AND AIRCRAFT CONSTRUCTION
	NAZI PARTY CENTERS
	DENSELY POPULATED AREAS
	NINTH AIR FORCE
	EIGHTH AIR FORCE
	FIFTEENTH AIR FORCE
	RAF
	OIL REFINERIES

0   100   200   300   400   500

Scale of Miles

In the air war over Europe, RAF and U.S. Eighth Air Force bombers flew long distances (indicated by the concentric circles on the map) from their bases in England to attack not only industrial and military targets but also cities, in a concerted effort to undermine Germany's ability to carry on the war. Other bomber groups, flying from bases in North Africa, hit targets in southern Europe, and starting in 1943 the U.S. Fifteenth Air Force staged raids to the north and east from bases around Foggia.

TIME
LIFE ®
BOOKS

Other Publications:

THE EPIC OF FLIGHT
THE GOOD COOK
THE SEAFARERS
THE ENCYCLOPEDIA OF COLLECTIBLES
THE GREAT CITIES
HOME REPAIR AND IMPROVEMENT
THE WORLD'S WILD PLACES
THE TIME-LIFE LIBRARY OF BOATING
HUMAN BEHAVIOR
THE ART OF SEWING
THE OLD WEST
THE EMERGENCE OF MAN
THE AMERICAN WILDERNESS
THE TIME-LIFE ENCYCLOPEDIA OF GARDENING
LIFE LIBRARY OF PHOTOGRAPHY
THIS FABULOUS CENTURY
FOODS OF THE WORLD
TIME-LIFE LIBRARY OF AMERICA
TIME-LIFE LIBRARY OF ART
GREAT AGES OF MAN
LIFE SCIENCE LIBRARY
THE LIFE HISTORY OF THE UNITED STATES
TIME READING PROGRAM
LIFE NATURE LIBRARY
LIFE WORLD LIBRARY
FAMILY LIBRARY:
    HOW THINGS WORK IN YOUR HOME
    THE TIME-LIFE BOOK OF THE FAMILY CAR
    THE TIME-LIFE FAMILY LEGAL GUIDE
    THE TIME-LIFE BOOK OF FAMILY FINANCE

Previous World War II Volumes:

Prelude to War
Blitzkrieg
The Battle of Britain
The Rising Sun
The Battle of the Atlantic
Russia Besieged
The War in the Desert
The Home Front: U.S.A.
China-Burma-India
Island Fighting
The Italian Campaign
Partisans and Guerrillas
The Second Front
Liberation
Return to the Philippines

WORLD WAR II · TIME-LIFE BOOKS · ALEXANDRIA, VIRGINIA

BY RONALD H. BAILEY
AND THE EDITORS OF TIME-LIFE BOOKS

THE AIR WAR IN EUROPE

Time-Life Books Inc.
is a wholly owned subsidiary of
TIME INCORPORATED

Founder: Henry R. Luce 1898-1967

Editor-in-Chief: Henry Anatole Grunwald
Chairman of the Board: Andrew Heiskell
President: James R. Shepley
Editorial Director: Ralph Graves
Vice Chairman: Arthur Temple

TIME-LIFE BOOKS INC.

Managing Editor: Jerry Korn
Executive Editor: David Maness
Assistant Managing Editors: Dale M. Brown
(planning), George Constable, George G. Daniels
(acting), Martin Mann, John Paul Porter
Art Director: Tom Suzuki
Chief of Research: David L. Harrison
Director of Photography: Robert G. Mason
Senior Text Editor: Diana Hirsh
Assistant Art Director: Arnold C. Holeywell
Assistant Chief of Research: Carolyn L. Sackett
Assistant Director of Photography: Dolores A. Littles

Chairman: Joan D. Manley
President: John D. McSweeney
Executive Vice Presidents: Carl G. Jaeger,
John Steven Maxwell, David J. Walsh
Vice Presidents: Nicholas Benton
(public relations), Nicholas J. C. Ingleton (Asia),
James L. Mercer (Europe/South Pacific),
Herbert Sorkin (production), Paul R. Stewart
(marketing), Peter G. Barnes, John L. Canova
Personnel Director: Beatrice T. Dobie
Consumer Affairs Director: Carol Flaumenhaft
Comptroller: George Artandi

WORLD WAR II

Editorial Staff for *The Air War in Europe*
Editor: Gerald Simons
Picture Editor/Designer: Raymond Ripper
Text Editor: Henry Woodhead
Staff Writers: Dalton Delan, Brian McGinn,
Tyler Mathisen, Lydia Preston,
Teresa M. C. R. Pruden
Chief Researcher: Oobie Gleysteen
Researchers: Kristin Baker, Loretta Y. Britten,
Josephine Burke, Mary G. Burns, Charlie Clark,
Jane Edwin, Nancy Friedman
Art Assistant: Mary Louise Mooney
Editorial Assistant: Connie Strawbridge

Editorial Production
Production Editor: Douglas B. Graham
Operations Manager: Gennaro C. Esposito,
Gordon E. Buck (assistant)
Assistant Production Editor: Feliciano Madrid
Quality Control: Robert L. Young (director),
James J. Cox (assistant), Daniel J. McSweeney,
Michael G. Wight (associates)
Art Coordinator: Anne B. Landry
Copy Staff: Susan B. Galloway (chief),
Patricia Graber, Peter Kaufman, Victoria Lee,
Celia Beattie
Picture Department: Alvin L. Ferrell

Correspondents: Elisabeth Kraemer (Bonn);
Margot Hapgood, Dorothy Bacon, Lesley Coleman
(London); Susan Jonas, Lucy T. Voulgaris (New
York); Maria Vincenza Aloisi, Josephine du Brusle
(Paris); Ann Natanson (Rome). Valuable assistance
was also provided by: Martha Mader (Bonn);
Carolyn T. Chubet, Miriam Hsia, Christina
Lieberman (New York); Mimi Murphy (Rome).

The Author: RONALD H. BAILEY is a freelance author
and journalist who was formerly a senior editor of
LIFE. He is the author of two volumes in TIME-LIFE
BOOKS' Human Behavior series, *Violence and Ag-
gression* and *The Role of the Brain,* and two earlier
volumes in the World War II series, *The Home
Front: U.S.A.* and *Partisans and Guerrillas.* He has
written a photography book, *The Photographic Illusion: Duane Michals,* was a contributor to *The
Unknown Leonardo,* a book about the inventive
genius of Leonardo da Vinci, and is now a contributing editor for *American Photographer* magazine.
While at LIFE he edited a book of Larry Burrows'
war photographs, *Larry Burrows: Compassionate
Photographer.* He and his wife and four children
live on a farm in New York State.

The Consultants: COLONEL JOHN R. ELTING, USA
(Ret.), is a military historian and author of *The
Battle of Bunker's Hill, The Battles of Saratoga* and
Military History and Atlas of the Napoleonic Wars.
He edited *Military Uniforms in America: The Era
of the American Revolution, 1755-1795* and *Mili-
tary Uniforms in America: Years of Growth, 1796-
1851,* and was associate editor of *The West Point
Atlas of American Wars.*

ALFRED GOLDBERG received his Ph.D. from Johns
Hopkins University. A historian with the Eighth Air
Force and the U.S. Strategic Air Forces in Europe
during World War II, he later served as chief of the
Current History Branch, U.S. Air Force Historical
Division. He edited *A History of the U.S. Air Force,
1907-1957,* co-authored seven volumes of *The
Army Air Forces in World War II* and contributed
to *D-Day* and *The War Lords.* He taught at the
University of Maryland and the University of
Southern California.

Library of Congress Cataloguing in Publication Data

Bailey, Ronald H.
  The Air War in Europe.

  (World War II; v. 16)
  Bibliography: p.
  Includes index.
  1. World War, 1939-1945—Aerial operations. 2. World
War, 1939-1945—Germany. 3. Germany—History—1933-
1945. I. Time-Life Books
II. Title. III. Series.
D785.B26   940.54'21   78-2937
ISBN 0-8094-2496-7
ISBN 0-8094-2495-9 lib. bdg.

For information about any Time-Life book, please write:

Reader Information
Time-Life Books
541 North Fairbanks Court
Chicago, Illinois 60611

CONTENTS

FORGING A MIGHTY WEAPON

Practicing the art of formation flying, a group of British biplanes passes over London's Hendon Aerodrome in a rehearsal for an air show held there in 1935.

AIR POWER: THE PAINFUL BIRTH OF AN IDEA

At the weary close of World War I, air power was just a gleam in the eyes of a few farsighted men, notably British Chief of the Air Staff Hugh Trenchard and the assistant chief of the U.S. Army's Air Service, William "Billy" Mitchell. The wartime air forces had been novelties, and to most strategists of the day they seemed to have no military future. As French Marshal Ferdinand Foch put it, "Aviation is good sport, but for the Army it is useless."

Trenchard proclaimed otherwise to anyone who would listen, but he found his hands full merely defending the independent status of the Royal Air Force, then under attack by cost-cutting officials who saw no need for an air arm separate from the Army and Navy. In a strong, terse statement made public in December 1919, Trenchard argued for a small, well-trained RAF, adaptable to future needs and uninhibited by the tradition-bound military branches, which used planes "simply as a means of conveyance, captained by chauffeurs." Thanks largely to Trenchard's paper, the RAF remained unfettered. He said, "I have laid the foundations for a castle: if nobody builds anything bigger than a cottage on them, it will at least be a very good cottage."

In the United States, the visionaries of air power faced tougher going: the commanders of both the Army and the Navy, jealous of their prerogatives, successfully opposed the formation of a coequal air force. But Billy Mitchell's powerful opponents could not prevent him from demonstrating the terrible potential of what he termed "bombardment aviation." In a series of tests conducted in 1921 and 1923 off the Atlantic Coast, Mitchell's Martin MB-2 bombers sent to the bottom three warships confiscated from Germany and three more obsolete U.S. warships.

Neither Mitchell nor Trenchard worked miracles. In 1925 Britain still could not claim a single home-based squadron of bombers or fighters, and the U.S. had yet to produce a successor to its obsolescent Liberty engine, which dated to World War I. But as planes were improved by new technology, the idea of air power gained strength and followers.

Hugh Trenchard, British prophet of air power, stumps for the RAF at a 1934 ceremony opening the Hampstead headquarters of the 604th Bomber Squadron.

A 100-pound phosphorus bomb, dropped by a biplane in Billy Mitchell's September 1921 test, scores a direct hit on the crow's nest of a target warship.

Climbing to a record 33,113 feet with the aid of a newly developed supercharger, a La Pere biplane soars over McCook Field in Dayton, Ohio, in 1920. At that altitude the atmosphere was thin and the temperature −67° F., but the pilot wore an oxygen mask of his own design and also an electric, fur-lined flying suit.

TAKING THE GUESSWORK OUT OF FLYING

"A good pilot doesn't depend on his instruments," flight instructors warned their students in the 1920s. The admonition was a wise one, for navigational instruments available to pioneer aviators were dangerously inaccurate. The standard altimeter of the time was typical: it registered altitude 10 seconds late—obviously hazardous for planes flying in fog or low clouds.

Engines were not a lot better; they failed at a discouraging rate. Between 1918 and 1925, mechanical failures caused U.S. airmail planes to make some 1,600 emergen-

cy landings. After one pilot had to put his plane down in a crowded cow pasture, his headquarters in Washington received this cheerless telegram: "Engine quit. Only place to land on cow. Killed cow. Wrecked plane. Scared me. Smith."

Year by year, trailblazing engineers extended the limits of aircraft performance. During the 1920s designers improved both the liquid-cooled and the air-cooled radial engine and introduced superchargers that pumped air into the engine, enabling it to function at high altitudes. And the barriers of clouds and darkness were penetrated by the appearance of many new navigational aids, including gyroscopic instruments and radio direction finders.

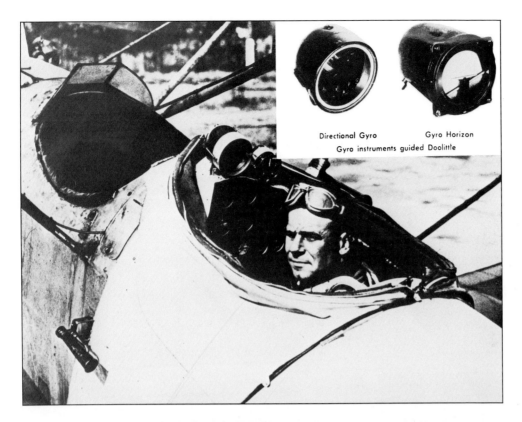

Directional Gyro   Gyro Horizon
Gyro instruments guided Doolittle

The Wright Whirlwind, the first dependable radial engine, was cooled by air flow rather than by the circulating liquid that was used for in-line engines. It powered Charles Lindberg's celebrated plane, the Spirit of St. Louis.

U.S. aviator Jimmy Doolittle, the first pilot to fly blind from takeoff to landing, looks out from the cockpit of his Consolidated biplane in 1929. Doolittle—flying under a canvas canopy, but with another pilot keeping watch— depended upon two gyroscopic devices (inset) invented by Elmer Sperry: a directional gyro (left), used to keep the plane on a straight course, and a so-called artificial horizon, which registered any deviation from level flight.

Before making a high-altitude research flight in 1934, U.S. aerial innovator Wiley Post takes a seat beside his Lockheed Vega "Winnie Mae" while assistants pump up his protective garb–a modified rubber diving suit. Post's plane was fitted with two superchargers: one for the engine, the other to pressurize his suit.

13

The barnstormers' indestructible Curtiss JN-4D—widely known as the Jenny—also saw duty as an Air Service trainer until the late 1920s. Light and maneuverable, the 90-hp Jenny needed only 1,000 feet to take off or land.

An early De Havilland Moth biplane, its wings conveniently folded, could easily be towed and stored in a garage. Forerunner of the Tiger Moth military trainer, the little craft could flutter to a landing at only 45 mph, and it consumed just a few gallons of gas per hour.

"BARNSTORMERS" AND "WHISTLING PIGS"

The men who first showed that airplanes could be reliable were not engineers but itinerant pilots who christened themselves "barnstormers" after the touring theatrical troupes. Flying cheap war-surplus Curtiss Jennys, they took countless thousands of thrill-seeking passengers on brief joy rides for a few dollars each.

Barnstormers' uncanny ability to keep their crates flying with scavenged parts did not persuade the military to invest heavily in airplanes. But convincing technological advances came thick and fast. Wood and cloth biplanes gave way to monoplanes made of light and durable aluminum alloy. Wooden propellers were replaced by metal blades—improved models of a crude prototype whose strange whirring sound earned it the nickname "whistling pig." Deicing equipment and wing flaps became standard. These and other developments produced, in 1933, a small but sure sign that air journeys were becoming as safe as surface travel: British Imperial Airways lowered its flight insurance premium from 12 shillings to one shilling per £1,000.

The first all-metal passenger plane, Germany's Junkers F-13 boasted a tough corrugated skin. Engineers soon discovered, however, that corrugation caused air friction, and later designs called for a smooth "stressed skin."

France's Latécoère-300, flown by the famous Jean Mermoz, provided regular air-mail service across the South Atlantic. Though flying boats were among the world's safest aircraft, Mermoz disappeared on his 24th ocean crossing, apparently a victim of engine failure.

At Calshot, England, a modified Supermarine S.6 seaplane is rolled out of the hangar for a speed trial. The plane was driven by a 2,300-hp Rolls-Royce engine—the forerunner of the Merlin engine of World War II fighters.

Daredevil Howard Hughes shows off his H-1 racer, with which he set a landplane speed record of 352 mph in 1935. Three years later, in a Lockheed Super Electra, he circled the globe in 91 hours, halving Wiley Post's record.

Jimmy Doolittle's speedy Gee Bee Super Sportster housed a huge 800-hp engine in a short, squat body.

IN HOT PURSUIT OF SPEED

"I have yet to hear of anyone engaged in this work dying of old age," wrote veteran flier Jimmy Doolittle after retiring from professional racing. Speed did kill: Doolittle had won the 1932 American Thompson Trophy race in a barrel-nosed Gee Bee; all of the seven Gee Bees built eventually crashed and killed six pilots. But speed like the Gee Bee's 250-plus miles per hour held a powerful fascination for everyone—especially the military.

The best aircraft designers were in the forefront of racing, and the innovations built into their streamlined planes were refined for aircraft of World War II. The British Supermarine S.6 racing plane gradually became the Spitfire fighter. And the German Messerschmitt-209, which set a speed record of almost 470 mph in 1939, influenced the development of some of the prominent German fighters of the War.

In addition to racing around measured courses, pilots set—and broke—innumerable speed records in flights from city to city and country to country. In 1933 Wiley Post caused an international sensation by circling the globe alone in less than eight days. Three years later Hollywood playboy Howard Hughes streaked east across the continent to Newark, New Jersey, in just over nine hours. All such flights included stops for refueling, however. The advocates of air power realized that speed alone was not enough, that military aircraft needed sufficient range to overfly enemy territory and return without landing.

The world's fastest prewar plane, the German Me-209, designed by Willy Messerschmitt, owed its speed to a compact 1,550-hp Daimler-Benz engine and a trim aerodynamic body.

The four-engined Curtiss NC-4 flying boat was the first plane to cross the Atlantic. The epic 1919 journey took the plane from Newfoundland to Lisbon via the

A World Cruiser, on a 1924 round-the-world flight for the U.S. Army's Air Service, passes a ship in Tokyo Bay.

The huge ANT-25, an experimental Russian

Striving for distance in a piggyback relay, the large Short-Mayo flying boat launches its light seaplane Mercury (top). The Mercury's airborne takeoff saved fuel and enabled it to set a distance record of 5,998 miles in 1938.

Azores and then on to England—all in 15 days.

bomber, comes to rest near San Jacinto, California, after a record 1937 flight over the Pole from Moscow.

REACHING FOR GREATER RANGE

Aircraft engineers' quest for range showed promise as early as 1919, when the U.S. Navy Curtiss NC-4 flying boat crossed the Atlantic Ocean by stages. Just eight years afterward, Charles Lindbergh stunned the world with his solo, nonstop transatlantic hop from New York to Paris. The U.S. Army Air Corps did not neglect the challenge of distance. The year 1935 saw the first flight of a plane that newspapers dubbed "the deadliest air weapon in the world." The aircraft was the prototype of a plane that could fly 3,300 miles unloaded, or nearly 2,300 miles packing 2,500 pounds of bombs; it went into production in 1936— as the B-17 Flying Fortress.

The need for a long-range transport was filled at about the same time. The Douglas Aircraft Company, creator of the renowned World Cruiser (*far left*), produced the DC-3, with a maximum range of more than 2,100 miles. This work horse eventually transported 70 per cent of the total Allied air cargo.

ELEPHANTS OF THE AIRWAYS

"More likely to antagonize the air than pass through it," was how one observer described the U.S. Army's 21-ton Barling bomber, a huge, six-engined triplane that could lumber no more than 170 miles before it had to land for refueling. Although the only Barling made was scrapped in 1925, designers continued trying to construct immense, capacious planes whose great weight inevitably made them awkward, slow and short in range.

The largest aircraft of all were the flying boats, which carried dozens of passengers. Germany's enormous Dornier Do X made its formal debut in 1929 carrying 150 passengers, 10 crew members and nine stowaways. Though its ostensible purpose was commercial, the Do X was actually designed to study the feasibility of a warplane capable of both long-range reconnaissance and mine laying.

The mammoth planes posed all sorts of specialized problems for their builders and users. The British Tarrant Tabor triplane had to be assembled in a great balloon shed and then rolled out sideways on rails. And none of these early giants proved to be worth their weight in gasoline, which the Do X guzzled at the extravagant rate of 400 gallons per hour.

The RAF's huge Handley-Page Heyford biplane, built in the mid-1930s, proved to be the last big bomber with more than one wing. But by then the better qualities of these behemoths were being incorporated into smaller, more efficient bombers.

Its design inspired by the RAF's call for a "bloody paralyzer" that could bomb Berlin, the tall Tarrant Tabor prepares for its first, and last, run in 1919. While taxiing, the behemoth nosed over, crushing its three officers.

The largest aircraft of its day, the Dornier Do X takes aboard passengers for its maiden flight. Powered by six pairs of back-to-back engines, it boasted three elaborate decks. The "X" in its name represented "unknown quantity."

Flanked by two fighters, Russia's colossal 92,000-pound ANT-20 soars over a 1935 military parade in Moscow's Red Square. Named the Maxim Gorky by the Russians, but dubbed the "Maximum Gawky" by sensible fliers, the plane was kept aloft—briefly—by eight engines and a wingspread of 207 feet. One day an accompanying fighter smashed the Gorky's wing; the craft plummeted to destruction.

Britain's Handley-Page Heyford was able to carry one and a half tons of bombs—but only for some 900 miles at a rate of 140 mph.

Prototype of the Bristol Blenheim bomber, the 1935 "Britain First" could fly 285 mph with a full load. The plane also had an effective range of 1,000 miles.

Europe-bound travelers at Port Washington, New York, board one of the half dozen Boeing-314s that were used by Pan American Airways in its regular prewar transatlantic flights to Lisbon and Southampton.

PUTTING IT ALL TOGETHER

By the late 1930s, two decades of experiment and experience had begun to produce specialized but efficient and well-balanced airplanes. Instruments were now more than adequate: the first airborne radar system, which could spot a ship 10 miles away, was installed in a British Avro Anson in 1937. The Bristol-142, prototype of the Blenheim bomber, could fly nearly 50 mph faster than the fastest fighter the RAF then had. Pan American Airways' Boeing flying boats began commercial transatlantic service just in time to bring out hundreds of European refugees in 1939.

The two leading apostles of air power, Hugh Trenchard and Billy Mitchell, lived to see the U.S. adopt the B-17 bomber in January of 1936. Six and a half years later, the first wave of B-17s joined the British air assault on Germany and roared 200 miles from England to bomb enemy targets in occupied France. By then Mitchell's unlikely dream of "strategic aviation" was already an inescapable reality.

In an awesome display of accuracy in long-range navigation, a pair of war-ready

B-17 Flying Fortresses intercept and make a practice bombing run on the Italian oceanliner Rex as it steams along approximately 700 miles out into the Atlantic.

1

In the waning hours of September 3, 1939, the rumble of engines resounded at a Royal Air Force base at Linton-on-Ouse in northern England. That day Great Britain had declared war on Germany for invading Poland, and now 10 Whitley bombers began rolling down the flare-lit runway, primed to strike the RAF's first blow against the foe.

As the little force lumbered aloft and turned east in the darkness, it was singularly lacking in the discipline as well as the magnitude of the armadas that by 1944 would fill the air over Germany. The pilots made no pretense of flying in formation, but simply headed for their targets by whatever route each chose.

The Whitley was an ungainly plane with an angular fuselage and twin engines canted slightly upward so that it struggled along blunt nose down, like a comic-strip stork. Only five years off the drawing board, it was already considered obsolete. It had a cruising speed of less than 200 miles per hour and a ceiling limit of 17,000 feet. "The Whitley," remarked one pilot who flew it, "was not the sort of vehicle in which one should go to pursue the King's enemies."

The Whitleys' assault that night was aimed at the key German ports of Bremen and Hamburg and at half a dozen cities of the Ruhr Valley *(map, page 61),* Germany's industrial heartland. The Ruhr was so heavily defended by antiaircraft guns that RAF crews would in time flippantly dub it "Happy Valley." Just the previous month, Luftwaffe chief Hermann Göring, commander of Germany's air and ground defenses, had boasted: "We will not expose the Ruhr to a single bomb."

Before daybreak, the Whitleys had reached their targets, dropped their loads and turned for home. All got back safely except one bomber that was forced to land in friendly France because of heavy ice on its wings and propellers. But Göring's boast still stood: neither the Ruhr nor Bremen nor Hamburg had been exposed to British bombs. The entire 13-ton payload carried by the Whitleys, and stamped "Secret" to keep crewmen from prying, had consisted of nothing more lethal than 5.4 million pieces of paper—propaganda leaflets warning the Germans that no matter how long the War lasted, the Allies would eventually prevail.

To the men of RAF's Bomber Command, the leaflet raid came as a shattering anticlimax. For years they had been steeped in a radical concept of modern warfare, strategic

BRITAIN GOES IT ALONE

bombing, that now offered them their only way to hit the Germans at home. However, instead of bombs RAF planes were dropping clouds of paper politely urging the Germans to get rid of their Führer, Adolf Hitler. "The only thing achieved," said one crusty RAF officer of this and subsequent leaflet raids, "was largely to supply the continent's requirements of toilet paper for the five long years of war."

Certainly, the air marshals who ran the RAF would have preferred to pepper the Third Reich with bombs. But two important considerations held them back. The first was a concern for the opinion of other nations—particularly that of the United States, from which Britain was seeking aid in the struggle against Germany. The British were adhering to President Franklin D. Roosevelt's request—issued when Germany moved into Poland on September 1—that all combatants refrain from bombing civilian targets.

The RAF's second reason for holding back was even more compelling. Bomber Command simply was not ready. It could muster only 17 squadrons of bombers capable of making the round trip to and from the heart of Germany. Moreover, of the total of 209 aircraft on hand—Whitleys plus the newer twin-engined Wellingtons and Hampdens— many were not operational. And of those that were serviceable, only 80 per cent could be provided, on any given day, with crews. Additional planes were in production, but bigger, four-engined bombers were still in the planning stage. So were the expanded organization required to train new crews and the technology to help them find their targets.

Bomber Command's entry into the War as a paper tiger was more than a little ironic. Since the 1920s, the British had been the world's foremost proponents of strategic bombing. The military establishments of other countries were more familiar with tactical bombing, which was intended to support an army or navy in the immediate area of combat. The new strategic doctrine was far broader; it held that the way to defeat an enemy lay beyond the battlefield, in destroying the ultimate sources of his power—his arms factories, his economic strength, his very will to fight.

One of the reasons for Britain's early embrace of the doctrine stemmed from recent experience. During World War I the Germans had sent their twin-engined Gothas and their huge lighter-than-air Zeppelins to drop nearly 400 tons of bombs in a series of air attacks on London and other English cities. The raids killed about 1,400 people. But the attacks were intended more to inspire terror than to destroy strategic targets, and the Germans themselves failed to recognize the potential for future conflicts. When their defeated and dismantled air force was reborn in the early 1930s as the Luftwaffe, its primary function was foreseen as tactical bombing, specifically in support of ground forces.

But a few farseeing individuals in Britain and elsewhere drew on the lesson of the German air raids of World War I to help shape the new theory of strategic bombing. One of the concept's major prophets was an Italian military thinker, General Giulio Douhet, who published his views in 1921 in a book entitled *Command of the Air*. Douhet argued that aerial attackers should give priority to industrial rather than military objectives, and that they should inflict a "merciless pounding" upon the enemy's cities as well. "The time would soon come," he wrote, "when, to put an end to horror and suffering, the people themselves, driven by the instinct of self-preservation, would rise up and demand an end to the war—this before their army and navy had time to mobilize at all!" Douhet's notions were anathema to most of the world's generals and admirals for a special reason of their own: he insisted that strategic bombing required an air force that was independent of an army and navy and that would, in fact, make them obsolete.

This heresy was shared by many airmen—and most particularly by a pugnacious American who was assistant chief of the U.S. Army's fledgling Air Service: Brigadier General William "Billy" Mitchell. Not only did Mitchell irk the Army by demanding that the Air Service be removed from Army control and made a separate entity, he also enraged the Navy by asserting that the bomber spelled doom for sea power. In bombing tests off the Atlantic Coast in the early 1920s, Mitchell's planes sank three obsolete American battleships and three German prizes of World War I, including the supposedly "unsinkable" battleship *Ostfriesland*.

Despite Navy protests that results would have been otherwise had the ships not been anchored, unarmed and unmanned, Mitchell's demonstration provided a dramatic glimpse of air power's potential. But his habitual bluntness proved his undoing. A statement in which he accused the War and Navy Departments of "criminal negligence" and near treason led, in late 1925, to his court-martial for insubordination. Suspended from duty for a term of five years, he chose, instead, to resign, and continued his crusade as a civilian, slowly but surely gaining converts to his cause.

By then, the British military had accepted the doctrine of strategic air power. Britain's military leaders knew that they lacked the manpower to maintain a large army; huge numbers of their soldiers and the officers who led them had fallen on the battlefields of France. Yet the British still had a far-flung empire to protect. In past centuries they had relied on sea power. Now, however, they could no longer be sure of the battleships that were the mainstay of their fleets; in an era of bombers, the worth of the big ships was questionable. Added to these broad considerations was the lingering memory of the German air raids of World War I. The British needed no lengthy convincing about the damage that an enemy could deal from the skies. Even before that war's end, Britain had taken the first step that theorists of strategic air warfare deemed vital to the nation's success in future wars—the setting up of an independent air arm.

In April of 1918 the Army's Royal Flying Corps and the Royal Naval Air Service were merged into the new Royal Air Force, separate from and coequal with the Army and Navy. For a nation known to be wary of change, the break with the past was all the more remarkable. A scant few years earlier, British military doctrine had held that the chief role of aircraft was as spotters for land and sea forces, and many an irate pilot had been required to hone his powers of observation by spending tedious hours in a tethered balloon over some English village, sketching its lanes and counting the cows on its green.

The RAF's first postwar exercise in strategic bombing seemed almost as ludicrous to many thoughtful Britons. During the 1920s, bombers were used to help police warring tribes in Iraq and other Middle Eastern areas under British control. If a tribe seized its neighbors' cattle and women, an RAF plane would drop a warning message to the offending chief, giving his people a chance to evacuate their village. Then, if the chief failed to come to terms with the civil authorities, the bombers would swoop in. Theoretically, the bombs were aimed only at the chief's dwelling; actually, a good deal of the village was chewed up. In England and other countries, the pacifist sentiment of the postwar period saw such episodes as revolting excess. RAF pilots, on the other hand, felt that their early warning and specific targeting of the tribal chief were gentlemanly gestures, and one wing commander stoutly defended the practice as "perhaps the most humane method of warfare which has yet been discovered."

British confidence in the bomber between the wars was embodied in the RAF's first chief, Hugh Trenchard. Known as "Boom" for his big voice, Air Chief Marshal Trenchard also had big ideas. In World War I he had commanded the Army's Flying Corps in France and had also led bombing raids on Germany in retaliation for the attacks on England. His experience had convinced him that the appalling casualties of trench warfare could be avoided through proper use of air power. He believed that the bomber—with only a little help from the Army and Navy—could win wars.

The man who was to lead Germany's air force, Hermann Göring, matched Trenchard in supreme self-assurance. But in presiding over the birth of the Luftwaffe in the early 1930s, Göring made what was to prove to be a costly decision. While Trenchard preached the gospel of strategic bombing, Göring and his associates put their faith in tactical air forces, including a new kind of plane to be employed in direct support of ground forces—the dive bomber.

In 1937 the future antagonists met at a lavish banquet hosted by Göring in Berlin. To cap the evening, Göring staged a mammoth fireworks display, which was climaxed by a deafeningly overamplified recording of his dive bombers screaming earthward.

"That's German might for you," Göring shouted at Trenchard above the din. "I see you trembled."

"You must be off your head," Trenchard boomed back. "I warn you, Göring, don't underestimate the RAF!"

It would never have occurred to Trenchard that he might be overestimating the RAF. Nor did he or his associates harbor any doubts about the major premise on which the doctrine of strategic air warfare was based—bombing's essential effectiveness. Leading Englishmen outside the military, including Britain's Prime Minister in the mid-1930s, echoed their certainty. As Stanley Baldwin placidly put it: "The bomber will always get through."

And once the bomber got through, its champions assert-

ed, the result was bound to be little short of Armageddon. In 1938 the scientist J. B. S. Haldane, basing his calculations on the effects of German bombing attacks on Barcelona during the Spanish Civil War, predicted that in the next war each ton of bombs would cause 20 deaths—hence, that 500 planes each carrying two tons of bombs could be expected to kill 20,000 people in a single raid. Haldane was so awed by his own findings that he likened the blast of a large bomb to the Biblical "last trumpet, which literally flattens out everything in front of it."

During the first eight months of World War II—the period of feint-and-counterfeint known as "the phony war"—Britain and Germany seldom engaged each other in direct action except at sea. Meanwhile, RAF Bomber Command seized the opportunity to test one of the basic tenets of its prewar planning for strategic air warfare—and found it decidedly unreliable.

The plans had called for daylight attacks by formations of bombers that were unprotected by fighter planes but sufficiently well-armed to defend themselves. But a series of daytime attempts to attack German warships off the North Sea port of Wilhelmshaven proved disastrous. Even the best of the British bombers, the Wellington, which was armed with three power-operated gun turrets, was no match for the much faster German interceptors. In the most costly of the daylight raids, on December 18, 1939, no fewer than 12 Wellingtons of a force of 24 were shot down by German fighters—Messerschmitt-109s and 110s. In the hopelessness of such attacks, one RAF marshal saw a grim parallel to "the charge of the Light Brigade," in which British cavalrymen in the Crimean War in 1854 had ridden into the Russian enemy's lines knowing that they faced virtual annihilation.

Clearly, daytime attacks presented inordinate risks, and so Bomber Command decided to test night bombing. On March 19, 1940, in retaliation for a Luftwaffe attack on Scapa Flow, the home base of Britain's fleet in the Orkney Islands, RAF bombers raided a German seaplane base on the island of Sylt, off the coast of Schleswig-Holstein. Like the German attack on Scapa Flow, the counterblow caused no substantial damage; Sylt suffered little more than a hole in a hangar roof. Bomber Command drew a measure of satisfaction from the fact that for the first time in the War

British bombs had fallen on German soil. But the loss rate of the bombers was even more gratifying—of the 50 on the raid, only one failed to return.

In comparing this result with the devastating losses off Wilhelmshaven, Bomber Command's chiefs had to take into account the far weaker enemy opposition at Sylt. But they had another set of statistics to strengthen the argument for turning to night forays: the leaflet missions over Germany after dark were incurring a loss rate of only 2.8 per cent.

While the phony war lasted, Bomber Command continued to mull over the figures and to concentrate its missions largely on propaganda-dropping. The men on the missions, for their part, continued to be assailed by a sense of futility. To vent their frustration, the crews would sardonically sing "Roll Out the Barrel" as they dumped their bundles of leaflets through a special chute underneath the fuselage. Some airmen, hoping the sheer weight of the bundles might make a dent in the enemy's home front, did not untie them.

Still, the leaflet raids served as useful rehearsals. Gradually, the crews learned to exercise more care in the extreme cold of high altitudes; removing a glove for only a minute could result in a frostbitten hand. The men also learned that weather changes could often pose a more formidable problem than the Germans' antiaircraft batteries. One bomber's

Flying in its characteristic nose-down attitude, a gawky but dependable Whitley Mark V bomber sets off on an RAF mission in 1940. The Whitley was one of Britain's earliest long-range bombers, and the RAF's first to feature turreted defensive armament and retractable landing gear. But the plane's slab-sided fuselage and broad wings drew derisive comments from RAF pilots, who dubbed the Whitley "The Flying Barn Door."

Italy's General Giulio Douhet, an early apostle of strategic bombing, shocked civilians and even military men with the publication of Command of the Air in 1921. In the book, Douhet advocated air attacks against an enemy's urban and industrial centers—particularly aircraft factories. He argued that it was "not enough to shoot down all birds in flight if you want to wipe out the species; there remain the eggs and the nests."

experience was typical. In the course of a single mission it was hit first by an electrical storm, then by a blizzard.

But after mid-May of 1940 the bomber crews no longer needed to endure such trials in the service of mere pieces of paper. On May 10 the phony war ended; Germany launched its blitzkrieg against Belgium, Holland and France. On the same day Britain's air-power advocates rejoiced as their staunch friend Winston Churchill succeeded Neville Chamberlain as Britain's Prime Minister.

Churchill had been fascinated by flying even before the First World War. He had taken lessons, giving them up only after the crash of his trainer, from which he was lucky enough to walk away. As Secretary of State for War and Air after World War I, he had helped beat back attempts to deprive the RAF of its separate identity, and in subsequent Cabinet posts he had consistently pushed its interests.

Among the dilemmas that Churchill immediately faced as Prime Minister was the need to speed the production of RAF fighter planes. With the Germans imminently in control just across the Straits of Dover, and an assault on England clearly in the cards, a stepped-up output of fighters to cope with the Luftwaffe's inevitable attacks was crucial. But even as Churchill put Britain's aircraft builders on a seven-day, round-the-clock work week, he kept his characteristically long view. As he was to put it: "The fighters are our salvation, but the bombers alone provide the means of victory."

Churchill lost no time warning the Germans that any air raids on civilian areas would bring an "appropriate" response. Coincidentally, on the very day he took office bombs fell on the city of Freiburg in southwestern Germany, killing 57 people and provoking an outraged charge by Hitler that the British were guilty of "inhuman cruelty." But it turned out that the offending bombers were German—Heinkel-111s that had lost their way in heavy clouds en route to an attack on a French air base.

Five days later, however, RAF Bomber Command went into action. On May 14 the Germans bombed Rotterdam, killing more than 800 civilians. The following night, 99 RAF bombers dispatched at Churchill's order roared over the Ruhr Valley's oil refineries and railways. This time the planes carried not leaflets but bombs, and Göring's boast about the Ruhr's impregnability was belied.

The strategic air offensive against Germany had begun at last. It would go on for almost precisely five years and constitute, in the words of Bomber Command's official history, "probably the most continuous and grueling operation of war ever carried out." At the moment, with the Germans rapidly pushing the British expeditionary force back to the beaches of Dunkirk and out of France, it was Britain's only means of hitting at the enemy.

With the memory of the disastrous daylight raids still fresh, RAF Bomber Command now decided that the air strikes at Germany would, with only occasional exceptions, take

place at night. To many of the men aboard the planes, the very act of dropping bombs was a new and strange experience, but doing so at night magnified the strangeness. A daytime mission, if low enough, might afford glimpses of people on the ground—friendly, if furtive, waves in occupied Holland, clenched fists of anger in Germany. At night, however, the life below was unseen, eerily suggested only by the faintest glimmers of light.

A perceptive young Whitley pilot named Leonard Cheshire often thought about the night bomber's remoteness from earthbound reality. Flying home at dawn from a mission in June of 1940, he wondered about the British troops still fighting somewhere below him in France. "I was going back to a warm bed and breakfast, but what had they to look forward to? Felt a curious sense of detachment: almost unreal, like being at a cinema."

Cheshire, who was to become one of the RAF's most decorated heroes, was flying missions four nights out of five that summer. He later recalled marking the tiresome six-hour round-trip passages by a succession of coastlines: "English coasts and Dutch coasts and German coasts coming and going, not once but often: sometimes in the brilliant light of the moon, sometimes lurking in the virginity of darkness. And in coasts such a wealth of meaning. If hostile, the expectancy of wondering whether it is the right landfall, the thrill of knowing at last the fight is on. And then, if friendly, the thought: 'God, how friendly?' Never shall I forget the warmth of those dawn receptions. One day, just out to sea, a bird escorted us home to the coast. I do not know what sort of a bird it was: I never shall know. I only know it was soft and fluffy and that it flew along just beside the port wing-tip."

Like many other bomber pilots, Cheshire went into the air war with an overblown image of himself as "a fully-groomed operational pilot wanting but a short experience of gunfire to be complete." Soon, however, he was caught up in the practical problems of preparing himself for his new combat role. Between missions he would sit in the grounded plane wearing a blindfold and grope about the cockpit "until I could lay my hands on everything without the use of eyesight." He also learned every task of his three-man crew, from loading the guns to setting the bombsight. Cheshire came to realize that "bombing is technical, a matter of knowledge and experience, not of setting your jaw and rushing in."

As one observer noted, the men of Bomber Command and Fighter Command were "two very different breeds, different both by temperament and by virtue of their jobs." About all they had in common was their slang: a crash was a "prang"; something that failed to work was "U.S.," for unserviceable; a dead pilot had "got the chop"; a coward had "LMF," or lack of moral fiber.

A natural rivalry sprang up between the "Bomber Barons" and the "Fighter Glamour Boys," and it was exacerbated late in the summer of 1940 by the fact that the Barons had to take second place in public esteem to the Fighter Boys, who were daily engaged in defending England against Luftwaffe attacks. Moreover, the two knew little about each other's job. The bomber pilots, catching up on their sleep during the day, seldom saw the fighters in action. And because the short range of the fighter planes precluded their escorting the bombers to Germany and back, the Fighter Boys never saw the Whitleys, Wellingtons and Hampdens in action.

The rivalry became acute only when both groups invaded the same pub on the same night. One squabble that began over tankards of ale led to a bizarre, if bloodless, private war. Three Hampden pilots touched it off by zooming low over a fighter base and dropping a cascade of toilet tissue and old propaganda leaflets. The Fighter Boys responded by landing at the bomber base, kidnapping the wing commander, flying him back to their own base and forcing him to pick up all the litter. Only the intervention of higher authorities—and the reminder that there was a real war going on—kept the feud from escalating to even more imaginative levels.

The top-priority targets of the strategic air offensive during that first summer were Germany's aircraft factories, synthetic oil plants and railway marshaling yards. But in August, when Luftwaffe raids on England began to mount, the British public's desire for revenge claimed precedence. It was intensified by London's baptism of fire on the night of August 24. The bombing was, in fact, unintended, and was contrary to Hitler's current standing order to the Luftwaffe to avoid London; two German pilots, on their way to another destination, had strayed off their assigned course and

Encircled by their planes, British airmen of the 216th Bomber Transport Squadron turn out for a parade in 1937 on the runway at Heliopolis, an RAF base in Egypt. In prewar years, about two dozen squadrons manned British air bases from Suez to Hong Kong. They were occasionally called into action to suppress intertribal fighting or to quell local uprisings. But the fliers logged much more air time delivering smallpox vaccine to remote areas and searching for parties lost in deserts or jungles.

had decided to unload their bombs before heading home.

Churchill knew opportunity when it knocked. Swift retaliation would help satisfy the growing British thirst for vengeance. It would undoubtedly spur reprisal raids on London. But these, in turn, were bound to fire up the American sympathy and support that Churchill urgently needed.

And so, on the night following the London episode, 81 British bombers made their first appearance over Berlin. Though ostensibly the targets were industrial, the intent was simply to hit back at the Germans. As Churchill later phrased it to prolonged cheers in the House of Commons: "On every side is the cry, 'We can take it,' but with it there is also the cry 'Give it them back.'"

The raid on Berlin caused little damage; the cloud cover over the city was unusually thick that night. But the audacity of the British in striking at the German capital stunned Berliners. "They did not think it could ever happen," the American correspondent William L. Shirer recorded in his diary the next day. Shirer had been arguing that very point with a censor in the German Propaganda Ministry minutes before the air-raid sirens sounded; the censor had flatly declared it impossible that any enemy bombers could get at the proudest city of the Third Reich.

The RAF bombing of Berlin—repeated three more times in 10 nights—cheered the British as much as it shocked the Germans. Indeed, the boosting of morale on the home front was a cardinal function of the strategic air offensive. However, government propaganda and press accounts exaggerated the importance of every raid, and false optimism took hold. Even within Bomber Command itself, officers who

Aboard a Whitley bomber over enemy territory in 1940, an RAF crewman waits for the signal to drop propaganda leaflets through a specially adapted photoreconnaissance flare chute. The paper bombardment, prepared within the Political Intelligence Department of Britain's Foreign Office, attempted to drive a wedge between the German people and their Nazi leaders. Said the leaflet at right: "The Gestapo ravage entire lands and call it peace. Is that the Lebensraum that you are fighting for?"

should have known better tended to accept uncritically any encouraging news that leaked out of Germany via secret agents and neutral businessmen. According to one intelligence report, industrial output in the Ruhr plummeted by more than 30 per cent during the summer of 1940. This estimate was based on reasoning that was equally erroneous: the RAF's night raids, the report asserted, had kept the Ruhr's workers from getting any sleep, and thus had lowered their productivity.

The truth was that the bombing had little more than nuisance value. Britain did not yet have enough bombers to do a bigger job, and many in the existing force had to be diverted to attack the barges massing across the English Channel for Operation *Sea Lion*, Hitler's projected invasion of England.

Bomber Command rarely could dispatch more than 100 planes to Germany in any one night. Moreover, the fuel required to get there and back meant that each plane could carry no more than a ton of bombs, and the biggest bomb in Britain's arsenal in mid-1940 was a 500-pounder. And the bombs were seldom concentrated on a single target but were distributed among half a dozen or so. A typical raid in August of 1940 had to spread its impact over two synthetic oil plants, a power station, a naval armaments factory, two aircraft plants, a storage facility for aircraft parts, two railway yards and a metal castings factory.

The individualistic approach that had characterized the early leaflet raids still pervaded the air offensive. Bombers still flew to their objectives separately rather than in formation. Over the target, each plane's captain selected the time and the altitude for dropping its bombs. Even the takeoff time was left to his discretion. One pilot, Guy Gibson, recalled delaying takeoff for a mission against oil tanks in Hamburg simply because he and a crew member wanted to attend a movie that night.

Fortunately for the British, Germany's defenses were also in their infancy. They relied almost entirely on 450 heavy antiaircraft batteries that were clustered around such key industrial areas as the Ruhr. The guns fired 22-pound shells that exploded into 1,500 fragments of shrapnel. But in the 25 seconds a shell was on its way, a bomber could take evasive action.

Defenders and attackers acquired a special language. The Germans called their antiaircraft guns *Fliegerabwehrkanonen,* then mercifully shortened this to *Flak* to signify the fire that the guns spewed up at the rate of 15 to 20 rounds per minute. The British called it "ack-ack," derived both from antiaircraft and from the sound itself. They also invoked a venerable English word, "jinking," a kind of artful dodging, to describe the rapid turning-and-weaving that was used to confuse the enemy's aim.

As an American military observer later noted, a heavy bomber in the process of jinking "suggested an elephant trying to waltz on roller skates." Moreover, bombs released during evasive action were likely to miss their target. The Germans, in fact, regarded this as a secondary purpose for their flak: if the antiaircraft failed to hit the attacker, it could at least reduce his accuracy. To some RAF pilots, however, the very act of trying to dodge the enemy shells became an exciting, if deadly, interlude in an otherwise long, dull flight. Cheshire called it "the gripping, priceless attraction of night-bombing."

At first, the Luftwaffe's vaunted fighter planes were even less of a peril than the exploding shells. Though the speedy Me-109 was a terrible threat to the occasional British plane attempting to bomb in daylight, it proved unsuitable as a night interceptor. It lacked the endurance necessary to track a target at night, and because of its short radio range, it could not travel far afield without risking the loss of vital information supplied by ground control. The pilot, the Me-109's sole occupant, had his hands full just flying the plane in darkness—let alone hunting down an unseen bomber.

During the summer of 1940, the Me-109 was being replaced as a night interceptor by the Me-110. Dubbed "The Destroyer," the twin-engined Me-110 had failed to live up to the name in the role for which it was originally designed, as a bomber escort. In the Luftwaffe's raids on England, it proved far too slow to cope with Britain's Spitfire interceptors. But its speed—approximately 300 miles per hour—was adequate to overtake the lumbering British bombers, and it possessed special advantages for night fighting. The Me-110 could remain in the air for as long as three and a half hours without refueling; moreover, it carried two men. The crewman could operate the radio and handle navigation while providing the pilot with a second set of eyes for the difficult task of spotting enemy bombers in the dark.

The Me-110 crews disliked being relegated to defense of the home front. It seemed too humdrum an assignment compared with fighting the air war over England. They also grumbled that it was impossible to see in the dark, and they gobbled quantities of vitamin pills and yellow turnips in a vain attempt to improve their night vision. In their first few weeks on the job, they managed to bring down just one plane—one of their own. The Me-110's twin-finned tail closely resembled that of the Whitley bomber.

On the night of July 20, 1940, one of the loudest complainers, a 29-year-old former banking apprentice named Werner Streib, was at the controls of his Me-110 over the Ruhr. He and his squadron mates had been alerted by a radar station on the German coast. The Germans' radar—

named Freya for the mythological Teutonic goddess who looked after the souls of dead warriors—had a range of 75 miles. Though it could determine the direction in which an intruder was flying, it could not fix the altitude. But the night of July 20 was clear and moonlit, and as Streib and his crewman looked around, they suddenly glimpsed the shadowy outline of another plane. To make sure it was a Whitley and not another Me-110, Streib crept in until he was flying practically wing tip to wing tip with the enemy bomber. Then he turned and came in from behind. At 250 yards the Whitley's tail gunner opened fire.

Streib countered with two short bursts from the machine guns and cannon mounted in the Me-110's nose. He then pulled away to await the foe's next move. "His starboard engine was burning mildly," Streib later reported. "Two

In a crowded shop, English metalworkers knock brass and iron fittings off aluminum kettles, pots and pans—a fraction of the thousands of tons of cookware contributed by citizens after an appeal by the government. Once the fittings had been removed, the pots were melted down and the aluminum sent in ingots to aircraft manufacturers, who needed more than 15,000 pounds of aluminum for a typical heavy bomber.

dots detached themselves and two parachutes opened out and disappeared into the night. The bomber turned on a reciprocal course and tried to get away, but the plume of smoke from its engine was still clearly visible even by night. I attacked again, aiming at the port engine wing, without this time meeting counterfire. Two more bursts and engine and wing immediately blazed up."

German night fighters had made their first score. Two nights later, Streib bagged another bomber. By the middle of October, he had accounted for eight more, including three Wellingtons that he managed to shoot down in the space of just 40 minutes.

Streib's successes and those of his comrades heralded a stiffening of the Reich's defenses. But the small British losses were considered tolerable by Bomber Command's leaders. What bothered them more than flak or night fighters was the basic problem of how to find and hit the target. The darkness that enabled the bombers to fly over Germany with relative impunity also hid the targets from them. The problem was succinctly summed up by one RAF group commander as "a never ending struggle to circumvent the law that we cannot see in the dark."

In time, improved airborne radar would help to solve the difficulty, but in the autumn of 1940 airborne sets were in limited use even by the fighters that were defending England itself; they relied instead on ground-based radar, which directed them to Luftwaffe attackers with great precision. In this respect, Britain's night interceptors enjoyed an advantage over Germany's night interceptors. Conversely, however, the German bombers had the advantage over the British bombers in night raiding; the German bombers were guided to their targets in England by a system of intersecting radio beams known as *Knickebein* (crooked leg), while the British bombers had to try to make their way to their targets in Germany by the hit-or-miss method that the mariners of old had employed when they could not go by the stars—dead reckoning.

Navigation by dead reckoning was so undependable that Bomber Command later labeled it getting there "by guess and by God." Using elementary tools—map and compass—the navigator would plot a course based on the speed of the aircraft and the predicted wind velocity en route. Theoreti-

cally, this course would take the plane to the target in a given number of hours.

But things almost never worked out that way. Any disturbance could throw the plane off course—flak or a shift in the winds over the Continent, which were notoriously unpredictable. On the 600-mile trip to Berlin, for example, an unexpected side wind of 20 miles per hour could blow a Wellington off course by as much as 66 miles.

Navigators constantly tried to correct the course en route to the target. There were several ways of doing this, none of them easy. Bearings broadcast by radio from ground stations in England could provide a fix on the plane's precise position, but only for the first 200 miles from home base. Farther along, if the moonlight was bright enough—the so-called bomber's moon—the navigator could try to get a visual fix on some identifiable feature, such as a river or forest, that appeared on his map. But dipping low enough to see the ground brought the plane perilously close to the Germans' antiaircraft guns.

If the sky was clear, the navigator could shoot the stars with a sextant. But this required the aircraft to be flown level for several minutes—an extremely difficult feat. And once he had gathered all the necessary information about wind speed and direction, the location of the stars, and the speed and direction of his plane, the navigator had to do a series of complex mathematical calculations to determine where he was—or where he had been when he began. As one navigator described this nerve-racking exercise: "It was rather like sitting in a freezing cold stair cupboard with the door shut, the Hoover running, and trying to do calculus."

Reaching the general area of the target—coming within 20 miles was regarded as first-rate navigation—was only half of the problem. The navigator now had to try to spot either the target itself or a recognizable landmark that was nearby. He would attempt to do so by the unreliable light of the moon or the stars, or perhaps by the light of a dropped flare—although this would reveal the bomber's presence. It was not uncommon for a bomber to spend a precious half hour or more cruising around trying to locate its assigned target.

The German ground defenses, like those in England, did their best to complicate the task of an enemy navigator by means of decoy targets. A decoy could be as simple as a brushwood fire, deliberately ignited to persuade the navigator that preceding bombers on the mission had already set the target ablaze. Other elaborate decoys, placed in the countryside, were constructed to suggest entire towns. They had *papier-mâché* buildings, fake lighting systems and even sparking devices to simulate the flashes of moving trolley cars. RAF pilot Guy Gibson remembered one decoy so improbably sophisticated in its design that it became a familiar landmark for the British, serving to point them to their actual objective nearby.

After the navigator had spotted the target, or something plausibly approximating it, his work was not done. He had to double in brass as the bombardier—in RAF parlance, the "bomb aimer." Having spent three or four hours poring over his lighted charts, he now had to recover his night vision, issue careful instructions to the pilot throughout the final bomb run, and then release his load at precisely the right moment.

Not surprisingly, a navigator would sometimes get so hopelessly confused that his plane would drop its bombs on a dummy city, the wrong city or even, occasionally, on an RAF base back in England. In one notorious instance, a Whitley plowed through an overcast sky, unloaded its bombs on an airfield below, then ran out of gas and crash-landed in a cabbage patch. All four men aboard scrambled out safely and set fire to the plane to keep it from falling into enemy hands. Then, hoping to make a getaway by daylight, they hid in a nearby barn. They were confronted

During a 1938 gathering of the enthusiastic aeronauts in the Oxford University Air Squadron, young Leonard Cheshire, who became the most decorated British bomber pilot of the War, signs his flight plan before taking off in a Hart Trainer airplane. Cheshire and many other RAF airmen piloted their first planes as members of one of the dozens of flying clubs that promoted aviation in England between the Wars. Although Cheshire later flew more than 100 combat missions over Europe, he confessed: "I've always been terrified of heights; even in a plane."

there a few minutes later by an apoplectic RAF group captain who had watched the whole affair through binoculars from his own control tower.

For all the mishaps that marred the strategic air offensive in the fall of 1940, its leaders continued, even in private, to express confidence that Bomber Command was finding and hitting its targets. With virtually no evidence except the rosy reports brought back from the raids on Germany, they went on assuming a theoretical average bombing error of only 300 yards—a figure that was derived from prewar experiments conducted in broad daylight and unhampered by enemy flak or fighters.

In December of 1940 the climate of optimism began to change. Prime Minister Churchill himself contributed to the new mood. Though he had not questioned the RAF estimate of the accuracy of the night bombing, the tonnage figures of the bombs dropped on Germany worried him: the figure for December—992 tons in all—was less than the Luftwaffe had dropped in just five nights over England.

An urgent message bearing a bright red sticker marked "Action this day" was sent off to Chief of the Air Staff Sir Charles Portal. The gist of the message was blunt and Churchillian: "I am deeply concerned at the stagnant condition of our bomber force."

Doubts about the bombers' performance were beginning to penetrate even Bomber Command. Among the growing skeptics was Air Vice-Marshal Robert Saundby, the senior staff officer. One day at Bomber Command headquarters he stood studying an impressive wall map checkered with red and black squares. As the officer in charge of the map explained it, the red squares represented Germany's synthetic oil plants, the black squares those plants that had been flattened by British bombs. The officer was certain that the plants marked in black had been destroyed. It had been shown statistically, he said, that 100 tons of bombs would destroy half of an oil plant; hence, 200 tons would do the whole job. By such reasoning, in fact, one civilian expert had concluded that Germany's synthetic oil production had been reduced by fully 15 per cent.

Saundby patiently heard out his subordinate, then politely set him straight. "You have not dropped 200 tons of bombs on these oil plants," he said. "You have *exported* 200 tons of bombs, and you must hope that some of them went near the target."

As it happened, Bomber Command was just starting, at the end of 1940, to employ a new device that could demonstrate conclusively how many—or how few—bombs fell near or on a target. The device was the aerial reconnaissance camera, and it had entered the RAF's arsenal by a somewhat circuitous route.

Back in 1939, with war clearly threatening the British Empire, an Australian civilian named Sidney Cotton had undertaken to find out everything he could about what was going on in Germany. He was aware of the hazards of spying, but he was an adventurous man, and RAF intelligence gave him its blessing. As a cover, Cotton set up a business he called Aeronautical Research and Sales Ltd., whose ostensible activities included the marketing of color film in Germany. Cotton made frequent trips there at the controls of an American-built plane, a Lockheed-12A, which had three cameras concealed in the cabin floor.

For months before the outbreak of war, Cotton roamed the skies over Germany, making aerial photographs of arms factories and military installations. On one occasion, scarcely five weeks before hostilities began, he brashly dropped in on a Nazi air rally in Frankfurt. Curious Luftwaffe colonels and generals clustered around his unusual aircraft, which was painted a duck-egg green to make it harder to detect at higher altitudes. Cotton genially took the Luftwaffe officers for a ride. Even as they enjoyed the view, he casually flicked an inconspicuous switch, activating the cameras to click away at future targets of the RAF.

In November of 1940, Bomber Command formed its own Photographic Reconnaissance Unit. One of the unit's first assignments was to photograph the effects of a major raid on the city of Mannheim in southwestern Germany. The raid took place on the night of December 16, under unusually favorable conditions. The moonlight was perfect and the bomber force one of the biggest of the period—134 planes. To make the task of hitting the target even easier, the crews were not assigned to pinpoint specific industrial plants, but were instead instructed simply to aim at the center of town.

Five days later, a Spitfire succeeded in photographing Mannheim by daylight. The photographs revealed that although there was considerable damage, many bombs landed wide of the main target.

These and later photographs that showed less damage to other targets did not in themselves prove that the bombers were failing badly. Conceivably, the Germans were repairing or camouflaging the damage with lightning speed. To check out this possibility, special photographic systems were installed in the bombers themselves. The system consisted of a camera and a flash—itself a small bomb—synchronized so that the ground would be illuminated at the instant the bombs hit. The resulting photographs, when matched against preraid pictures of the target, would show precisely where the bombs fell.

The bomber crews disliked the new gadgetry. It was like having a snooper along on their missions. Moreover, the cameras were conveying messages that clearly spelled out the failure of some of the missions. Many crewmen refused to believe the photographs, and so did some higher-ups. But there were other officers in Bomber Command who were sufficiently disturbed over the photographic evidence to show it to an aide of Lord Cherwell, Churchill's scientific adviser, in the hope that Cherwell would mention it to the Prime Minister.

The ploy worked; Churchill ordered a full-scale investigation. Cherwell's aide, David Bensusan-Butt, was set to analyzing some 650 photographs taken in June and July of 1941 in the course of 100 missions over France and Germany, involving a total of 4,065 sorties. He compared the bombing photographs not only with prior photographs of the target areas but also with the claims of the crews.

The Butt report, presented on August 18, shocked even those who were already inclined to take Bomber Command's claims with a grain of salt. Of all the planes in the bombing photographs, only one in five came within five miles of the target. In the case of the Ruhr Valley, where smoke and the glare of searchlights compounded the attackers' difficulties, the news was still worse. Only one in 10 of the crews that claimed to have hit the target there actually dropped their bombs within five miles of it.

After reading these dismal conclusions, Churchill could not resist taking a sarcastic poke at Bomber Command. "It is an awful thought that perhaps three quarters of our bombs go astray," he wrote in a note to Chief of the Air Staff Portal.

"If we could make it half and half, we should virtually have doubled our bombing power."

Churchill's enthusiasm for the strategic air offensive was beginning to fade. Fully a year had passed since he had predicted that Britain's bombers alone would provide "the means of victory." And since that rousing declaration, made on the first anniversary of Britain's entry into the War, he had gone out on another large limb. With the German invasion of Russia on June 22, 1941, he had promised his new ally, Soviet dictator Josef Stalin, that British aid would include an intensified punishment of the Reich from the air—"a heavier discharge of bombs, making the German people taste and gulp each month a sharper dose of the miseries they have showered upon mankind."

At the end of September of 1941, Churchill gave notice that his ardor for strategic air warfare had cooled to the chilling point. Before him was a new RAF plan to destroy "beyond all hope of recovery" 43 German cities with a total population of 15 million. The proposal envisioned the need for a minimum of 4,000 British bombers—approximately 10 times the number that was currently available for operations over Germany.

"It is very disputable whether bombing by itself will be a decisive factor in the present war," Churchill wrote in response. "On the contrary, all that we have learnt since the war began shows that its effects, both physical and moral, are greatly exaggerated. The most we can say is that it will be a heavy and I trust a seriously increasing annoyance."

Churchill had further cause for his change of attitude. Not only was the RAF having a hard time finding its targets, the bombers were not always getting through to Germany. The Luftwaffe, though it had been fought to a standoff over England, was demonstrating a new ferocity over the western approaches to Germany.

German air defenses were now in large part deployed in occupied France, Belgium and Holland. To reach the Reich, British bombers had to run a gauntlet of searchlights and night fighters stretching from Denmark in the north to the French-Swiss frontier in the south (map, preceding the title page). Many bombers were being knocked down en route.

The gauntlet was known as the Kammhuber Line, after its designer, Major General Josef Kammhuber. Formerly com-

THE LUFTWAFFE'S SPANISH PROVING GROUND

In July of 1936, Hitler seized an opportunity to test his fledging Luftwaffe in combat. At the request of Spanish insurgent leader Francisco Franco, he supplied planes to transport Franco's Nationalist forces from Morocco to Spain to battle the Republicans in the Civil War. Soon afterward, he made a more direct contribution, sending Franco some 6,000 Luftwaffe airmen who fought under an impressive name invented for the occasion: the Condor Legion.

For nearly three years, the men of the Condor Legion honed their skills in strikes against military and industrial targets, cities and towns. German engineers drew on the lessons of combat to improve planes that would long be Luftwaffe mainstays—the Messerschmitt-109, Heinkel-111, Dornier-17 and Stuka Ju-87 dive bomber.

The Condor Legion won its practice war handily, downing 277 Republican aircraft against just 96 losses. More significant, the airmen gained the experience and confidence that would pay big dividends in Hitler's blitzkrieg and the air war.

Triumphant Condor Legionnaires parade through Berlin in 1939.

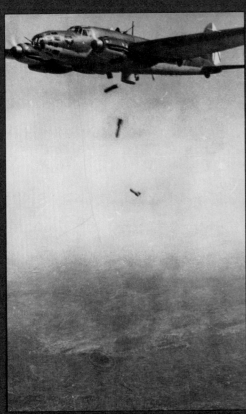

A Heinkel-111 showers bombs on Valencia Harbor.

A German pilot climbs into a Messerschmitt.

mander of a bomber wing, Kammhuber had taken charge of his country's night air defenses in July of 1940 at the order of Göring himself. Göring was no longer in a mood to boast about Germany's defenses; he now frankly described them as his country's "Achilles' heel." Kammhuber was an excellent choice for his new job. Though he had a taste for good living—he installed himself in a handsome 17th Century castle near the Dutch city of Utrecht—he had a great gift as an organizer. Methodically, he began building a massive barrier against the British bombers.

First, he had the powerful German searchlights moved west, away from the gun-encircled German cities, and positioned them in a belt up to 20 miles wide. Here, his Me-110 night fighters would have no fear of being shot down by German flak when they engaged enemy bombers that were caught in the searchlights' glare. And the glare was unending; one searchlight would pick up a bomber in its beam, then follow the plane until another searchlight took over. One British tail gunner reported that it was like being "in the center of an enormous lighted but empty circus, waiting for the unknown." Then the Me-110 interceptor would appear, "a faint ghostly shape entering the circle of light."

Kammhuber's searchlight barrier became even more effective in 1941 with the introduction of a radar-controlled master light. This would lock onto a bomber automatically and hold it in a pale blue beam until the manually operated searchlights picked it up.

The searchlights were only part of Kammhuber's arsenal; if the British got past them, they were greeted by radar-directed gun batteries. Kammhuber also had at his disposal some 30 light bombers—Junkers-88s and Dornier-17s that had been converted for use as night fighters. Their function was to head for England and shoot up the RAF bombers just as they were taking off for a raid and before they had attained sufficient air speed to evade the intruders. The German planes launched their mission upon an alert by specially trained radio operators in Holland who tuned in on RAF frequencies. When the eavesdroppers heard a whistling and chirping, they knew that the radio operators in the bombers at the RAF bases had switched on their sets to check them out before takeoff.

Kammhuber's intruders would also hit the air bases in England just as the bombers were returning from a raid, sometimes boldly queuing up with the Whitleys and Well-

An array of seven towers forms one of 20-odd radar installations that guarded England's east coast in 1939. Aerials on the three 350-foot towers at left transmitted microwave signals, which bounced off aircraft up to 110 miles away and returned to antennae on the shorter towers at right. The course of the approaching planes was plotted by a radar technician, and the RAF dispatched fighters to intercept the intruders.

ingtons as they waited to come in for a landing. "If I want to smoke out a wasps' nest," Kammhuber explained, "I don't go for the individual insects buzzing about, but the entrance hole when they are all inside."

His Junkers and Dorniers were so successful against the British that by October of 1941 they claimed more than 100 kills. But on the 13th of that month Hitler ordered Kammhuber's intruder force transferred to the Mediterranean to take on the increasingly troublesome British stronghold on the island of Malta. In any event, Hitler declared, shooting down bombers in faraway England did nothing to improve the morale of the German people: they wanted to see the enemy bombers brought down closer to home. Kammhuber protested in vain.

Yet he still had aces in the hole—night-fighter aces. One was 25-year-old Prince Heinrich of Sayn-Wittgenstein, a Danish-born aristocrat. Unlike most of his comrades, who disdained home-front defense duty, the Prince relished the hide-and-seek life of the night fighter. In order to savor it he had, in fact, given up flying bombers after 150 missions. Intense and high-strung, he was, in the words of one admirer, "as out of place in a bomber squadron as Hitler at a Churchill dinner party." But in a fighter plane the Prince came into his own. "He had an astonishing sixth sense—an intuition that permitted him to see and even to feel where other aircraft were," one of his commanders recalled. "It was like a personal radar system." Whatever his gifts, Prince Heinrich was destined to be credited with a remarkable total of kills of enemy bombers—seven in one night, six in another night and five in another—before his own death in the air in January of 1944.

By late 1941, the RAF's bombers were finding it more and more difficult to get across the Kammhuber Line. The defending Me-110s and Junkers-88s no longer had to rely solely on the searchlights to help them spot the enemy aircraft. They could home in on the incoming foe with the guidance of a powerful ground-based German radar system, the Würzburg. Unlike the earlier Freya system, which could track only the direction of an enemy plane, the Würzburg could also determine its altitude.

With the Würzburg's introduction, Kammhuber set up a new chain of defenses in front of the searchlight barrier. It consisted of overlapping rectangular zones about 20 miles in length and width—roughly the effective range of the Würzburg. The Germans called these zones "boxes."

Each box had its own fighter-interceptor, a Freya radar, two Würzburg radars and a ground-control station. The Freya radar served to give early warning of the approaching enemy aircraft. One Würzburg then plotted the course of the British bomber as it crossed the box. The other set plotted the course of the German interceptor. At ground control, the two courses were displayed on a frosted glass screen. A spot of green light indicated the position of the bomber; a red light showed the position of the interceptor. It was the job of the ground controller, talking by radio to the two-man interceptor crew, to give directions that would bring the two dots so close that the fighter pilot could actually see the bomber.

These new tactics created a hell for the RAF bombers. Until late 1941, British losses had been running at a rate of just 2.3 per cent—mostly attributable to flak, mechanical failure and other noninterceptor causes. But on the night of November 7, 1941, when some 400 RAF bombers set out across the newly reinforced Kammhuber Line en route to targets in Cologne, Berlin and other German cities, they were caught between the enemy fighters and flak, and 37 British planes failed to return. This was nearly double the 5 per cent loss rate deemed acceptable by Bomber Command. And among the bombers that headed for the Ruhr, risking the most formidable sector of the Kammhuber Line, the loss rate was a frightening 21 per cent.

Churchill knew that such losses could not be sustained. This realization, and the photographic evidence that Bomber Command had scattered 40,000 tons of bombs on the German countryside with negligible impact, forced him to a painful decision. On November 11, four days after the costly raid, Churchill imposed a drastic cutback on Bomber Command's activities; it amounted to a virtual ban on the bombing of Germany for the coming winter. Only small bomber forces were to be sent, and then only to the nearest targets and only in the most favorable weather.

In his melancholy order to the air chiefs, Churchill wrote: "It is now the duty of . . . Bomber Command to re-gather their strength for the spring." The man who had unleashed the bombers against Germany 18 months earlier had now reined them in.

HARD TIMES FOR THE RAF

Wellington bombers take off at dusk for a raid on Germany. Fondly nicknamed "Wimpys," Wellingtons carried the main load of the RAF's offensive through 1942.

MEN, PLANES AND AN INVINCIBLE SPIRIT

Ready for a raid on enemy territory, RAF air gunners head for their bombers laden with ammunition belts, logbooks and oxygen helmets.

Britain in the summer of 1940 stood stripped of allies by the German blitzkrieg and facing an enemy that vowed to "eliminate the English motherland." The burden of defense—and later of a token offense—was dropped squarely on the shoulders of an outnumbered and underequipped RAF. Against a potential attack force of some 2,000 German aircraft, the British mustered barely 600 fighter planes. Many RAF men were boys of only 19 or 20, fresh from flight school. But they fought with an insouciant verve that made them a match for their battle-hardened adversaries.

Fighter pilots characterized their deadly encounters with the Luftwaffe as "a rather noisy game of hide and seek." Bomber crews spoke of their nighttime raids over Berlin, Hamburg and Cologne as "visits." One crewman said of the missions that it was "a wonderful thing to have an evening's entertainment provided for you."

RAF Wing Commander Guy Gibson had no illusions concerning his chances for survival: once he skipped a dental appointment because he "didn't see any point in having my teeth fixed when I was likely to die within the next few days." But Gibson was well aware of the dangers of fatalism, and he took his crews on boisterous rounds of the pubs to keep them together and, he said, to "lead them into thinking they were the best: that they cannot die."

The spirit that drove these young fliers captured the imagination of Frank Wootton, an artist who had volunteered for the RAF at the approach of the War. To his dismay, he was put to work making drawings of bombsights and other equipment for use as training aids. But he also found time to paint the fliers' aircraft: to him, the dashing Spitfire fighters, the great grim Lancaster bombers, were as full of heroic personality as the men who flew them.

Wootton eventually was appointed the official RAF artist and given free rein to paint pictures of the planes and their battles. His vivid images, some of which are reproduced on these pages, revealed the beauty of the planes, and paid eloquent tribute to the indomitable RAF fliers who saved Britain in the desperate early years of the War.

An RAF student pilot maneuvers his Tiger Moth biplane into a loop high above the training field. The trainee's flight instructor is seated in the rear cockpit.

Flying high above a plowman on England's coast, a squadron of Defiant fighters heads for the Channel en route to Dunkirk, there to cover the evacuation of

BEHIND THE PILOTS, A "MIGHTY PANORAMA" OF SUPPORTING PLAYERS

A Short Sunderland, one of the Coastal Command's flying boats, flies over the Southampton docks on a patrol.

Destined for bomber duty, a student gunner trains his machine gun on a model Messerschmitt fighter.

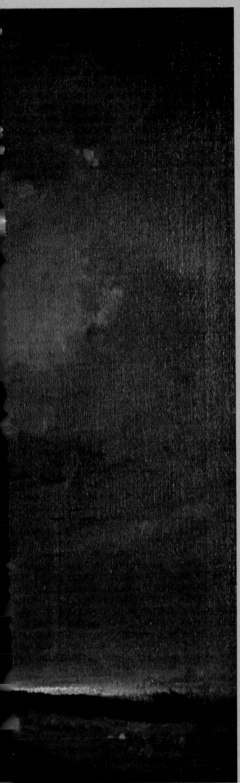

the defeated British and French forces.

Behind the celebrated RAF pilots stood a large contingent of lesser known but no less important personnel. Every pilot was backed by mechanics, ground crews, and Coastal Command reconnaissance and rescue teams. And on bombers each pilot relied on the further support of his crew.

Bomber pilot Leonard Cheshire recalled sensing a still wider indebtedness during a raid over the Ruhr in 1940. He saw the mission as "a mighty panorama" with himself in the spotlight and the whole island of Britain standing in the wings as supporting players. "A vast organization has been created to provide a pilot capable of executing these orders, and equally a whole system of supply and maintenance of aircraft and bombs and guns and petrol and countless other tools . . . has been created to allow one pilot to drop one bomb."

DUELISTS ARMED WITH THE RAPIERS OF THE AIR

Moments from a kill over France, Spitfire pilot Robert Stanford Tuck goes into a dive to fire on an Me-109. The Luftwaffe formation attacking the bombers at

Three weary RAF fighter pilots give an intelligence officer an account of their just-completed mission.

"Pretty and precious looking as a cavalier's jeweled rapier" was an admirer's phrase for the slim Spitfires flown by many of the pilots of RAF Fighter Command. The description was felicitous in more ways than one. Some RAF fighter pilots adhered to the code of the gentlemen swordsmen of an earlier age; rules of honor, fair play and courtesy provided a framework for their duels to the death.

Luftwaffe fighter pilots had a kindred code, as British ace Robert Stanford Tuck discovered when he was shot down and taken prisoner in 1942. His Luftwaffe captors treated him chivalrously, and before he was sent off to prison camp, Tuck was entertained at dinner by a group of pilots commanded by ace Adolf Galland. Over cigarettes and Scotch, the two men chatted amiably in English about the earlier encounter depicted at left, in which both Galland and Tuck had scored victories. So, said Galland, he and Tuck could part company "even Stevens."

lower left was led by ace Adolf Galland.

On patrol high over southern England, Spitfire fighters search the autumn skies for enemy aircraft in 1940.

Ground crewmen feed bombs into the bays of a pair of Hampdens at an RAF airfield at Waddington.

Hidden from searchlights by heavy clouds,

A base commander awaits bombers returning from a raid.

Life in RAF Bomber Command offered little of the continuous headlong excitement of fighter combat. An anonymous tail gunner with a six-man Wellington crew said of his night missions over Germany: "We get shot up, iced and fed up, but for the most part our outings lack the Hollywood element. The highlights of combat come only now and then. At the end of seven and a half hours in the tail turret, one rather sighs for them."

The RAF bomber crewmen concentrated on further developing their skills and on perfecting the disciplined teamwork that was, in itself, a kind of reward for those who served in Bomber Command. "Crew life becomes unendingly intimate," continued the Wellington tail gunner. "Without being sentimental, there is a sense of comradeship about the venture. None of you would probably have chosen each other if crews were made on the picking up principle, but after a bit you would not dream of changing."

Blenheim bombers fly over a German target in 1940. Lightly armed and highly vulnerable to German fighters, Blenheims were gradually phased out of service.

LONG WAITS FOR THE "HIGHLIGHTS OF COMBAT"

Roaring over the Alps, a formation of Lancasters heads for the Italian port of Genoa, whose lightly defended docks and shipping yards were popular targets for

RAF bomber crews. Six such raids on the port city in the autumn of 1942 helped prevent Italian naval forces from opposing the Allied invasion of North Africa.

Soon after he took over RAF Bomber Command in February of 1942, Air Chief Marshal Arthur Harris was hurrying to his headquarters at High Wycombe west of London when he was stopped for speeding. On the front fender of his Bentley convertible was an official sticker exempting him from the speed limit. Seeing the sticker, the policeman gave Harris a bit of polite advice instead of a ticket.

"I hope you will be careful, sir," he cautioned. "You might kill somebody."

"My dear man," Harris replied, "I'm paid to kill people."

The bluntness of this remark said a good deal about Harris. A martinet with strongly held opinions and a tart tongue, he had risen from World War I pilot to group commander to deputy chief of the Air Staff by sheer tenacity of purpose. Now, at 49, he was at the top of Bomber Command and in a position to further his most cherished aim—the relentless bombing of Germany. So single-minded was his dedication to the eventual aerial destruction of the Reich that the press called him "Bomber" Harris. His air crews were later to hit on a different name for him. Partly in admiration of his hard-driving methods and partly in resentment over the high human cost of some of his missions, they came to call him "Butch"—for "The Butcher."

Harris took charge of Bomber Command at a time when it desperately needed his forceful leadership. Its morale was ebbing, its detractors multiplying. Its much-touted ability to find and hit targets in Germany by night had proved more mythical than real, resulting in Churchill's cutback of the air offensive in November of 1941. In the three months since, the bombers' chief assignments—a lot closer to home than Germany, and undertaken by day as well as by night—had ended in another dispiriting failure.

The assignment, carried out under the direction of Harris' predecessor, Air Marshal Sir Richard Peirse, called for the destruction of three German warships sitting just across the English Channel in the harbor of Brest, on France's northwestern coast. Since defeating the French, the Germans had made Brest a major way station for their ships en route to and from the intensifying Battle of the Atlantic. The trio targeted by RAF Bomber Command—the 26,000-ton battle cruisers *Scharnhorst* and *Gneisenau,* and the 10,000-ton cruiser *Prinz Eugen*—had already scored heavily against the British. The *Prinz Eugen* had helped dispatch the mighty

"BOMBER" HARRIS TAKES OVER

battle cruiser *Hood;* the *Scharnhorst* and the *Gneisenau* had sunk the carrier *Glorious* and sent 115,000 tons of merchant shipping to the bottom.

The three warships were in Brest for repairs and refitting, and blasting them as they lay in dry dock proved impossible. After 1,875 sorties by Bomber Command, in which 1,962 tons of bombs were dropped, the targets were still intact. Moreover, the antiaircraft guns that were massed around Brest's dock area and vigorous defensive action by Luftwaffe fighters cost the British 43 bombers. The jubilant Germans saw added cause for satisfaction. Their warships, by serving as what one Luftwaffe commander described as "a sort of flytrap," had diverted the enemy aircraft from what might have been productive missions elsewhere.

The crowning humiliation for Bomber Command came on February 12, 1942. Late the previous evening, the *Scharnhorst,* the *Gneisenau* and the *Prinz Eugen* left Brest to make a dash through the Channel toward Germany. Hitler, in a sudden onset of prudence, wanted the ships near home in order to avoid further risk. Escorted by seven destroyers, some 50 smaller vessels and a fighter cover of 250 planes working in relays, the three ships steamed through the Straits of Dover virtually under the noses of the British—although heavily cloaked in mist and rain.

Bomber Command, belatedly alerted on the afternoon of February 12, sent 242 planes in pursuit. The weather was so bad that only 39 of them found the ships. Then the ceiling was so low that the bombs had to be dropped from as little as 200 feet, and they literally bounced off the armor-plated decks of the ships. The quarry escaped with only minor damage—and that was caused by mines that had been previously sown in the sea.

To the British public, the fact that bombing conditions were almost hopeless that day was no excuse for what was clearly a fiasco. As one blunt critique put it: "The plain truth seemed to be that Bomber Command . . . couldn't even hit a target 250 yards long in broad daylight on its own doorstep." The popular reaction was so furious that Churchill himself, attempting to gauge it, came to the conclusion that it was even worse than the response to a second, more spectacular calamity the same week: the surrender of Britain's Far Eastern bastion, Singapore, to the Japanese. "It was certainly not strange," the Prime Minister wrote, "that public confidence in the Administration and its conduct of the war should have quavered."

The Prime Minister's personal response to the Channel episode was to come out fighting. Two days later he lifted his ban on missions deep into Germany and ordered a full-scale resumption of the bombing offensive. Ten days later Bomber Command had a change of chiefs. Air Marshal Peirse was sent to India to head the RAF force based there, and Bomber Harris took over in his place.

Harris was on the spot, and he knew it. He recalled: "I had to prove, and prove quickly, to the satisfaction of those who mattered, that the bomber force could do its work if it was large enough and if its efforts were not frittered away on objectives other than German industry as a whole."

Beefing up the bomber force was the paramount priority. Harris, who had spent more than half of 1941 in Washington on an RAF supply mission, was dismayed on settling in at Bomber Command to find that its frontline strength was scarcely greater than at the start of the War two and a half years earlier. He had available a daily average of little more than 300 long-range bombers—and only 69 of these were heavy bombers. Though 18 new squadrons had been organized during 1941, some had been sent to support the ground forces fighting the Germans in the North African desert, and the rest had been turned over to RAF Coastal Command to support naval operations against the U-boats in the Atlantic.

More vexing to Harris, the War Office wanted additional bombers for an expected new offensive by the redoubtable chief of Germany's Afrika Korps, Lieut. General Erwin Rommel. The Navy wanted at least eight and a half more squadrons, including two to try to cope with the Japanese now rampaging through British possessions in the Far East.

Still, Harris saw a number of reasons for optimism. Britain's aircraft factories were producing at a faster rate than ever. New types of four-engined heavy bombers—Stirlings, Halifaxes and Lancasters—were coming into service. Bomber Command's sorry record in finding and hitting targets in Germany had spurred the development of new means and methods of aerial attack.

Above all, Harris was heartened by a basic shift in government policy concerning the air war on Germany. So-called precision bombing, the pinpointing of specific targets, was to be replaced by generalized "area bombing." Precision bombing had been hampered to begin with by the government's inability to decide which German factories or rail-heads or shipyards should be attacked; at one point the leadership's vacillation had led one exasperated member of Parliament to offer the Air Ministry a memorandum on priorities prepared by his greengrocer. But even when a firm choice of a target had been made, the RAF's bombers had trouble hitting it; the results were nowhere near as crippling as the economic experts in London had predicted, and Germany's industrial machine kept chugging along.

Britain's own experience at the hands of the Luftwaffe helped clinch the argument for area bombing. The German raid on Coventry in November of 1940, while primarily directed at industrial targets, had devastated some 100 acres of the city; the havoc to workers' housing and to such public services as transportation, water and electricity had apparently delayed the return to war production more than the bombing of the factories themselves.

The possibility that damage to morale might outweigh damage to key factories in the prosecution of the War seemed worth investigating, and subsequent German raids on Birmingham, Hull and other cities prompted a survey of the effects on the inhabitants. The results were then ana-lyzed by none other than Lord Cherwell himself, the man whose scientific judgment Churchill most trusted. Cherwell, a physics professor on leave from Oxford, drew two conclu-sions: that the worst damage to morale came from the loss of one's house—"people seem to mind it more than having their friends or even relatives killed"—and that this finding should be utilized in carrying the war to Germany.

Cherwell bolstered his case with statistics. He figured that for every ton of bombs the Germans had dropped on the cities in the survey, between 100 and 200 people had been made homeless. By this measure, a British bomber, assum-ing it lasted long enough to make 14 sorties, could "de-house" 4,000 to 8,000 Germans. Cherwell noted that much of the German population—22 million people—was con-centrated in 58 cities. He estimated that if these cities were subjected to area bombing over a period of 18 months, the RAF could "de-house" at least a third of the entire German population and thus "break the spirit of the people."

Cherwell's statistics were hotly disputed by others in the scientific establishment—one dissenter pronounced them "at least 600 per cent too high"—and in time both German and British civilians would disprove Cherwell's assumption that the stress of losing one's house was bound to shatter morale. Churchill, however, was smitten by the clarity and certitude of his mentor's analysis. Even before he received Cherwell's finished report in March of 1942, he moved to make area bombing official government policy. In late Feb-ruary, when Air Chief Marshal Harris took over at Bomber Command headquarters at High Wycombe, he found for-mal notification of the policy shift awaiting him.

Harris, who had long opposed precision bombing be-cause it dealt with what he dismissed as mere "panacea" targets, was delighted. The new orders from the Air Ministry authorized him to attack Germany "without restriction," and added: "The primary object of your operations should now be focused on the morale of the enemy civil popula-tion and in particular, of the industrial workers." Translated into practical terms, this meant that in attacking Germany's cities, British bombers would henceforth drop their lethal loads on heavily built-up and densely populated districts without attempting to pinpoint one or another site within the designated area.

Bomber Command scored its first major success under Har-ris less than two weeks after he was chosen to lead it. Ironically, the raid involved precision bombing, and the

Four-engined Stirlings–Britain's first heavy bombers—receive servicing at an RAF bomber station. The big bombers, which made their combat debut in February 1941, had several shortcomings. They could not carry a maximum bombload above 16,500 feet, their bomb bays were unable to hold anything larger than 2,000-pound bombs, and their landing gear had a tendency to collapse. As improved bombers replaced them, Stirlings were increasingly used to tow gliders and transport troops.

target was not even in Germany. On the night of March 3, he dispatched 235 bombers to attack the huge Renault works at Billancourt, near Paris. Instead of automobiles, Renault was now busy turning out tanks and other armor for the Germans, performing a vital service for Hitler's war machine. All but 12 of the raiders hit the target. By one estimate, the Germans lost the output of enough armor and transport to have supplied five motorized divisions, and almost four months were to elapse before Renault could get back to full production.

Though the target was nowhere near Germany, Harris' preferred arena of operations, at this early stage of his stewardship he needed a quick triumph to restore the confidence of his crews, and of the British public, in the mettle of Bomber Command. Renault was easy to reach and far less heavily defended than the Reich's own industrial concentrations. It also made a good choice psychologically—as an object lesson to industrialists in occupied countries.

What gratified Harris most about the Renault attack was the high level of effectiveness his bombers achieved, thanks in large part to two innovations that he had decided to test. One was a way of marking a target so that it would be readily spotted by the incoming bombers and easier for their bombs to hit. The mission was divided into three waves of planes, all carrying as many flares as their bombloads would permit. The first wave, using the most highly trained crews, dropped some of their flares, then their bombs; they then dropped the rest of the flares to windward to serve as beacons for the next wave. The second wave repeated the process for the third wave. The target was thus continuously illuminated for the raid's duration.

The other innovation was also tactical. Instead of sending in his bombers at random during the night, Harris scheduled them to arrive within a one-hour period. The concentration of the attack not only saturated the light antiaircraft defenses around the Renault plant but also overwhelmed the fire-fighting crews attempting to contain the damage.

Five nights after the Renault raid, Harris launched his first attack on Germany itself—and his first attempt at area bombing. He sent 211 planes to attack Essen, the chief city of the Ruhr (map, page 61). By the criteria of the new British policy, Essen was a prime objective. It was so heavily industrialized and built up that—according to the experts in Britain's Ministry of Economic Warfare—a bomb could be dropped on the city at random and still stand "an even chance of hitting some work of man."

Though the attackers were instructed to aim their bombs at the large square in the center of Essen's old town, with no precise targets specified, it was fully expected that extensive damage would befall the gigantic Krupp steelmaking and armaments enterprise, which made its home in Essen. This outcome seemed to be inevitable; Krupp factories sprawled everywhere in the city. But Krupp emerged virtually untouched by the raid of March 8—and by a follow-up raid the next night. The brunt of the attack was borne not by the center of Essen but by its outskirts and neighboring towns.

The trouble lay with one of the two innovations Harris had employed with such success at the Renault works. Sending in the bombers on a tight time schedule proved its worth in breaching the formidable Kammhuber Line that guarded the approaches to the Ruhr; the German interceptors along the line, accustomed to dealing with the enemy bombers on a one-to-one basis, could not cope with their concentrated numbers. But over Essen itself, the Harris plan to have the advance force light the way for the main force went awry. The flares that were dropped to start with burned out before they could serve as guidelines for the incendiary bombs that were dropped next; as a result, many of the incendiaries went astray, and the fires they set were scattered enough to mislead the incoming main force in aiming its own bombs.

A third innovation also proved to be something of a disappointment. This was a radio signaling system known as Gee, and it was primarily intended to guide a bomber to an objective without the need for making visual fixes en route. Synchronized signals from three ground transmitters in England appeared as pulses on a special receiver aboard the aircraft. The navigator measured the time intervals between pulses and related the figures to coordinates that had been previously prepared and printed on a chart of Europe overlaid by the lines of a grid ("Gee" simply stood for "grid"). These calculations determined the location of the plane at a given moment.

Gee got high marks as a navigational guide to Essen but flunked an important secondary task that the British had hoped it would fulfill—as an aid to so-called blind bombing. They had assumed that Gee would eliminate the need for visual fixes not only en route to the objective but also over it, and could thus serve to direct the dropping of bombs without any help from the human eye. It had failed in that mission, dismally.

Harris was bent on offsetting the fiasco at Essen by a clear-cut success elsewhere, soon. The objective he chose was Lübeck, a historic north German port on the Baltic. The city was a tempting target. It served as a supply funnel for German operations in Norway and Russia. Its antiaircraft defenses were not especially strong. And it was bound to burn fast. Lübeck was, in fact, a veritable tinderbox. It dated back to medieval times and was largely built of wood. Harris planned accordingly: about half the 300 tons of bombs his planes were to carry were incendiaries.

On the night of the 28th of March, 234 RAF bombers left for Lübeck. Those in the vanguard had Gee receivers—"goon boxes," the crews now called them. Though the city lay beyond Gee's maximum range, 400 miles, the goon boxes got the lead planes nearly four fifths of the way. Then an easily identifiable landmark, the mouth of the Trave River, provided an excellent visual fix of position.

That night Lübeck won the distinction of becoming the first German city to go up in flames. The raiders were able to swoop as low as 2,000 feet to disgorge their fire bombs. Some 200 acres, about half the city, were totally laid waste.

Lübeck's 12th Century cathedral was destroyed, along with the central power station, factories and warehouses. By the Germans' own count, 15,707 people were—in Cherwell's word—"de-housed."

In Germany the high-level reaction to Lübeck was delayed; the dimensions of the disaster took a while to sink in. That weekend Propaganda Minister Joseph Goebbels noted in his diary that the raid had "thoroughly spoiled" his Sunday at home. An entry a week later was less casual. "I have been shown a newsreel of the destruction," Goebbels wrote. "It is horrible." He speculated about the possible demoralizing effects on the people of Lübeck, then drew some comfort from the traditionally tough fiber of the region's inhabitants. "Thank God it is a North German population," he noted.

In England the men of RAF Bomber Command added a new term to their vocabulary: "to do a Lübeck," which meant "to flatten."

On the day after the success at Lübeck, Harris issued an order that typified his autocratic style of leadership. He forbade wives of the bomber crews to live within 40 miles of the bases at which their husbands were stationed; he wanted no distractions from the job at hand. He was well on his way to giving his men a new sense of purpose, while inspiring a healthy terror of their new chief.

Moreover, Harris was managing to make his presence felt

by remote control. He seldom visited his air bases. The majority of his crews never even saw him. To keep informed about what the men were thinking and saying, he relied on his deputy commander, Air Vice-Marshal Saundby. They were friends of long standing. Two decades earlier in Iraq, Harris, as commander of a bomber squadron, and Saundby, as his senior flight officer, had helped police rebellious tribesmen; together they had worked out an ingenious tactic for aiming a bomb from a prone position rather than over the side from the cockpit. They simply sawed a hole in the wooden floor of an old Vickers Vernon.

When Harris became head of Bomber Command, he invited Saundby to share his Victorian home near headquarters so that they could stay in constant touch. Saundby was so devoted to Harris, and to bombing Germany, that he later refused a promotion to an RAF command of his own.

The two men complemented each other. Harris was hard-bitten and aloof, Saundby gentle and sociable. Saundby often had an afterhours drink with subordinates, talking of matters far removed from the War, including his favorite hobbies—catching fish and catching butterflies. Unworried about appearances, he was sometimes seen in his air vice-marshal's uniform chasing butterflies with a net.

Saundby's twin passions figured in his choice of code names for the bombing targets in Germany. He was torn between fish and butterflies but, as Harris later reported, "there were not enough short names of butterflies and moths to go round and it would obviously be inconvenient to use words like 'Broad-bordered bee hawk.'" Fish won the day; Berlin became Whitebait, and Cologne was code-named Trout.

Harris spent much of his time casting his net of persuasion over "the people who mattered"—newspapermen, politicians and government officials all the way up to Churchill, with whom he met almost weekly. On such occasions, Harris could abandon his usual gruffness and summon up the artistry of a born public-relations man. What he aimed to sell was the concept of strategic air power. In the spring of 1942, he recalled, "I had to regard the operations of the next few months not only as training or trial runs from which, and only from which, we could learn many essential lessons, but also as commercial travelers' samples which I could show to the War Cabinet."

Harris meant "commercial travelers' samples" quite literally. Among them was his *Blue Book*, an album of aerial photographs showing the destruction wrought by the raids on Lübeck and other German cities. Copies of the *Blue Book*, regularly updated, were sent to the Prime Minister and to Buckingham Palace—and to Stalin, Britain's new ally in Moscow—as evidence of Bomber Command's rebirth.

Harris continued his proselytizing afterhours. By the end of the War, he and his attractive young wife, Jill, had entertained an estimated 5,000 visitors at their home. After dinner, the host—wearing a plum-colored velvet smoking

At RAF Bomber Command headquarters 30 miles from London, Air Chief Marshal Arthur Harris pores over his Blue Book—a group of photographs surveying damage caused by RAF bombers—with his second-in-command, Air Vice-Marshal Robert Saundby (on his right), and two aides. The main building of the headquarters complex was a closely guarded underground shelter (right), hidden beneath a grassy hill and heavy layers of concrete.

jacket—would lead guests to his study, which he called his conversion room.

While Harris gave them a blow-by-blow account of a bombing raid, the guests could view aerial photographs of gutted German cities on a stereopticon machine. This device, soon known as "Harris' juke box," displayed the photographs in three dimensions. Many a viewer felt as if he were peering down at the ravaged shells of actual buildings, with the flames still flickering. More often than not, skeptics came away from this sobering experience converted to the gospel according to Bomber Harris.

By the end of April, 1942, Harris had impressive new evidence to offer. Beginning on the night of April 23, his bombers hit another old Baltic port, Rostock, for four nights running. Strategically, Rostock was more important than Lübeck; the Germans' standard combat plane then, the Heinkel-111, was assembled at a plant on the city's outskirts. The attack involved both area and precision bombing. Planes carrying incendiary bombs focused on the heart of the town itself, providing a spectacular flaming marker for planes bearing high-explosive bombs destined for the Heinkel works. Aerial photographs taken the day after the second raid showed the Heinkel plant ablaze, and also included a new kind of scene for Harris to display on his stereopticon: Rostock's railroad station aswarm with black dots—people scrambling to flee the shattered city. By the local Germans' estimate, 100,000 had to be evacuated.

After the last Rostock raid, Harris calculated that Bomber Command's attacks on Germany thus far had resulted in the devastation of a total of 780 acres—approximately equal to the devastation wrought by the Luftwaffe on England in 1940 and 1941. As Harris reckoned it, the attacks on the two Baltic ports "about squared our account with Germany."

Hitler was infuriated by the raids on Rostock and ordered the Luftwaffe to launch a series of reprisal attacks on England. He made no secret of his plan; he proclaimed it in a broadcast not only to the Germans but to British short-wave listeners as well. In return for what he denounced as *Terrorangriffe*—terror attacks—on historic Lübeck and Rostock, he vowed to mete out the same treatment to historic English cities. As the Luftwaffe wiped them out one by one, he informed his audience, he would check off their names in his copy of the famous Baedeker guide to England. A day or so later Hitler expounded on the theme at a luncheon with his propaganda minister, and Goebbels duly recorded the discussion in his diary. The Führer, he wrote, "shares my opinion absolutely that cultural centers, health resorts and civilian centers must be attacked now.... There is no other way of bringing the English to their senses. They belong to a class of human beings with whom you can talk only after you have first knocked out their teeth."

The German reprisals, soon known to the British as "Baedeker raids," went on for two months and visited Hitler's wrath on five cities that, like Lübeck and Rostock, were only lightly defended. Far greater damage was done to tradition than to Britain's war effort. The Luftwaffe's bombs gutted the venerable cathedral town of Exeter and destroyed the Assembly Rooms at Bath, where generations of stylish Britons used to gather after sipping the curative waters of a spa built by the Romans.

But at the end of May, Hitler's attention was forcibly diverted back to his own domain. On the 30th of the month a city of major importance to his war machine, Cologne, was hit by the biggest air attack in the War thus far.

In the weeks before the Cologne raid, Bomber Harris had spent a great deal of time fretting about his failure to do serious damage to cities of the Ruhr and the similarly industrialized cities of the adjacent Rhineland. Again and again in April his bombers flew over Essen, Cologne and Dortmund with little effect. Since the Gee system had failed its test as an aid to blind bombing, finding the aiming point still depended on the bombardier's eye. The constant industrial haze and smoke over the Ruhr and the Rhineland, the glare of searchlights and the maze of factories, railroads and canals made the bombardier's task almost impossible.

The patience of the crews wore thin. At Bomber Command headquarters one day, during the customary morning planning conference, an aide summoned up the nerve to say to Harris: "Excuse me, sir, but I think the boys are getting a little browned off going to Essen every night." Harris snapped back: "So's Essen." But there was a touch of bravado in the retort. Harris knew that nibbling away at Essen, or blasting secondary objectives such as Lübeck and Rostock, was not enough.

He needed something more, a mission against what he

called "a first-class target" that would demonstrate—to the doubters in his own government as well as to the Germans—the fearsome possibilities of an enlarged bomber offensive. "If only we could put on something really big," Harris remarked to Saundby one evening. "One spectacular raid, big enough to wipe out a really important target. Something that would capture the imagination of the public. A thousand aircraft—a thousand bombers over Germany! If only we could do something like that, we might get the support we need."

A thousand bombers—no raid in the brief era of air warfare had come even close to using so prodigious a number. The record thus far was held by the Luftwaffe, which had sent 487 bombers against London on a memorable night in October of 1940. But the British had never yet been able to muster more than 235 bombers for a single mission. And Harris had nowhere near 1,000 planes in his frontline force in May of 1942. As a daily average, he now had at his disposal only 416 serviceable aircraft with crews.

His brainstorming brought no immediate response from Saundby. But the next morning the deputy chief of Bomber Command quietly began making inquiries of various units and putting figures together. In early May Harris raised the subject again. His need to produce a single bold stroke was now urgent: the War Cabinet was weighing a proposal to disperse fully half of the bomber force to the Atlantic, the Middle East and India.

Saundby astonished Harris by reporting that, mathematically at least, a 1,000-plane raid was not beyond the realm of possibility. By committing all of his reserves and by drawing instructors and students from his training units, Harris could double his frontline strength. Then, Saundby continued, if Harris could borrow back 250 or so bombers and crews that had been transferred to RAF Coastal Command for duty in the Atlantic, he would be tantalizingly close to the magic number.

Saundby's assiduous paper work, and his chief's instinct for the main chance, thus produced what the two men informally called the "Thousand Plan." Harris, with his flair for irony, would later give it the official code name Operation Millennium.

While Saundby started begging and borrowing bombers, Harris began to gather political backing for the Thousand Plan. He sought and got an invitation to dinner with the Prime Minister and, on a Sunday evening in mid-May, drove his Bentley to Churchill's weekend retreat, Chequers.

Churchill, his gambling instincts aroused, was immediately charmed by the boldness of the Thousand Plan. It might help relieve the pressure on him from two different fronts—from members of the War Cabinet who were frankly skeptical about the worth of the bombing offensive and from his prickly allies, the Russians, who were demanding a show of more effective action against Germany.

Harris told Churchill that the choice of a target would most likely boil down to either Hamburg or Cologne. Both were easy to identify from the air. Hamburg lay on an estuary leading to the North Sea; Cologne, some 250 miles southwest of Hamburg, was on the winding River Rhine. Cologne had the added advantage of lying within the range of Gee's navigational guidance. The name of Essen came up, and clearly Churchill, like Harris, would have preferred it as the target. But they decided that its location in the still seemingly invulnerable Ruhr made the prospect too chancy.

Then Churchill posed a blunt question. "How many are you going to lose?" he asked. "Say 50 aircraft and crews," Harris replied. "I'll be prepared for the loss of a hundred," Churchill stated. Harris expressed confidence that losses could be kept to no more than 5 per cent because he planned to overwhelm the German defenses with his new saturation tactics: all 1,000 planes would be concentrated over the objective within a period of just 90 minutes.

Harris also intended to overwhelm the German interceptors en route to the target, along the Kammhuber Line. Up to now, his bombers had crossed the line at widely separated points. But on the night of the proposed raid, they would swarm across it in a loose procession—a "bomber stream," Harris called it—of 600 planes an hour. Each 20-mile sector of the line was patrolled by only one German night fighter, and experience had shown that although any one German fighter was much faster than a British bomber, it could engage no more than six an hour. Thus, while it took on individual bombers, the rest would pass through its sector unchallenged.

Churchill was so fascinated with the Thousand Plan that Harris stayed on and explained the details until 3 a.m. He drove home humming an old war tune and enjoying a new sense of buoyancy.

Soon afterward, Harris scheduled Operation *Millennium* for May 27 with either Hamburg or Cologne as the target, depending on the weather. But on May 26 unexpected trouble loomed. Harris was suddenly confronted by a steep drop in the number of planes he had counted on: the subtraction of 250 bombers that Coastal Command had agreed to lend him. Though organizationally a part of the RAF, Coastal Command came under the Navy's operational control, and the Admiralty had decided that the Navy had nothing to gain from helping Harris. If the Thousand Plan failed, as the admirals thought likely, the Navy stood to lose many of the bombers it now had. If the plan succeeded, Harris would have a strong argument for denying the Navy the added bombers it sought for the Battle of the Atlantic.

With just over 24 hours to go, Air Vice-Marshal Saundby set out to plug the gap left by the withdrawal of one fourth of the Thousand Plan force. He dug deeper into Bomber Command's plane reserves; he put together more crews made up of students still in training units, along with their instructors. He was also able to juggle some personnel as a result of a recent change in the composition of the heavy-bomber crews. These bombers no longer carried a second pilot; he had been replaced by a flight engineer. By the morning of May 27, Saundby had scraped up enough planes and men to make a grand total of 940 aircraft and crews.

At that point the weather intervened to delay Operation *Millennium*. For three days in a row, thundery conditions and thick clouds persisted over most of Germany, and three times Harris reluctantly had to order a postponement. Clear skies were even more essential than usual for this colossal mission, to reduce the risk of aerial collisions and to enable the half-trained student crews to find the target.

In fact, the weather delay proved to be a boon for the British. While it lasted, ground crews working for 18 hours at a stretch managed to put into shape nearly 100 bombers that had been regarded as unserviceable. At 9 a.m. on Saturday, May 30, when Harris strode through a grove of beech trees at High Wycombe and down into his underground headquarters for his daily planning conference, his available force of planes exceeded 1,000.

The conference followed the customary ritual. Harris sat at his desk while Saundby and a group of top aides stood clustered around him. From an office across the hall, a stern-faced little Scotsman emerged—chief meteorologist Magnus T. Spence, bearing his weather charts. As he spread them over Harris' desk and began spelling out his predictions, Harris and the others listened in respectful silence.

Spence's report that morning was almost as discouraging as on the three previous days. Thunder clouds still covered much of Germany; Hamburg was blanketed. However, the weather to the south was improving. "There's a fifty-fifty chance," Spence said, "that the cloud in the Cologne area will clear by midnight."

Harris sat staring at the weather charts through his glasses while he considered the forecast's implications. The Thousand Plan had engaged him in the biggest gamble a commander could take. Not only was he committing all his reserves, but by using student crews and the instructors who trained them, he was risking the very future of Bomber Command. The weather was chancy, yet time was running out on the full moon. Another postponement would mean putting off the raid for nearly a month. By then, Bomber Command might be "frittered away," as Harris later put it, to other fronts.

The drama of the decisive moment was described by one of the aides, Group Captain Dudley Saward:

"The C.-in-C. moved at last. Slowly he pulled an American cigarette carton from his pocket, and, flicking the bottom with his thumb, selected the protruding Lucky Strike. He lit the cigarette and then drew from his right breast pocket a short, stocky cigarette holder. Very deliberately he pressed the cigarette into the end of the holder and grasped it firmly between his teeth. He continued to stare at the charts and then slowly his forefinger moved across the continent of Europe and came to rest on a town in Germany. The pressure on his finger bent back the end joint and drove the blood from the top of his finger nail, leaving a half circle of white." Harris turned to Saundby.

"The Thousand Plan tonight."

"His finger," wrote Saward, "was pressing on Cologne."

That afternoon, 53 air stations across England resonated with what one chronicler later called "the dreadful note of preparation." At little-known places such as Binbrook,

The Ruhr region of west-central Germany—a cluster of key industrial cities near the confluence of the Ruhr and Rhine Rivers—was one of the prime targets of the Allied strategic bombing offensive. The British estimated in 1943 that the Ruhr processed more than 60 per cent of Germany's steel and two thirds of the country's high-grade alloyed metals for weapons and aircraft engines. During the next two years, this production was repeatedly reduced by Allied bombing—and restored by the Germans.

Feltwell, Alconbury and Marston Moor, ground crews readied the aircraft and loaded them with bombs ranging from high-explosive 4,000-pounders to four-pound incendiaries. The air crews, in the meantime, tried to snatch a little sleep. There were 1,046 crews in all, an unprecedented air army of some 6,000 men—Englishmen, Scots, Canadians, Australians, New Zealanders, Rhodesians, South Africans, Poles and five Americans. The Americans included a boy from Brooklyn, Charles Honeychurch, and a pair of Texans, Bud Cardinal of Fort Worth and Howard L. Tate Jr. of Dallas, who proclaimed themselves members of the "RTAF"—Royal Texan Air Force.

The crews had known for several days that they were in for a "really big show," but they did not learn until 6 p.m. just how big and where. In the briefing rooms at the 53 stations, the windows were closed, blinds drawn, doors locked. Then, with suitable ceremony, the sheet of paper covering the target map was ripped away to reveal the night's destination. The sight of the name brought an audible surge of relief. Many of the men had been to Cologne before and knew that the city was heavily defended; it was ringed by some 500 antiaircraft batteries and 150 searchlights. But there could have been a much worse mission in store; one rumor was that Harris planned to send the crews on a suicidal low-level daylight mission to Hamburg.

Relief gave way to astonishment when the crews were told that 1,000 aircraft would take part in the raid. At one station the men leaped to their feet cheering, and began to dance about and pound one another on the back.

The main concern expressed at the briefings was one that had bothered Harris from the first. With more than 1,000 planes concentrated over the target in a 90-minute period, the specter of collisions loomed frighteningly large. But Harris' technical experts—whom the crews called "boffins"—had assured him that this danger would be minimal if three different aiming points were designated and if the attack force was divided into three parallel bomber streams over the target.

The briefing officer at one station reported: "The boffins are confident that the risk is negligible. They have assessed the chances at one in a thousand." There was a murmur of skepticism as the audience pondered the likelihood that the congestion caused by all those planes twisting, turning, diving and climbing over the target could result in only one collision. After a time someone piped up: "Have the boffins worked out which two aircraft it will be?"

A gale of laughter broke the tension. The briefing officer then read a special message sent from Harris himself, urging the crews "to strike a blow at the enemy which will resound, not only throughout Germany, but through-

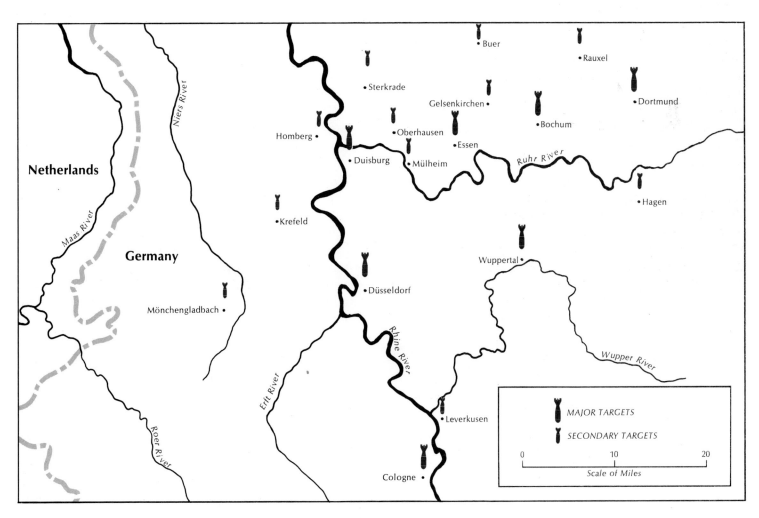

out the world. . . . Let him have it—right on the chin."

When the first bombers rumbled down the flare-lit runways at about 10 p.m., however, Harris was not there to see them off. He was just sitting down to dinner at Chequers with the Prime Minister and selling the merits of his night offensive to Churchill's other guests, a delegation of American brass that included the commanding general of the United States Army Air Forces, Henry H. "Hap" Arnold.

By midnight the planes had taken off. The bomber stream stretched across the North Sea into Holland. It was an awesome procession, some 70 miles long, with the planes flying at various altitudes over a span of about 4,000 feet.

The planes were a mixture of the old and the new. About 70 per cent of the force was made up of the old more-or-less reliables—the twin-engined bombers that had been waging war against Germany for almost three years now and were soon to be replaced. Among them were the ungainly Whitley and the odd-shaped Hampden, whose crews called it the "frying pan." By far the best as well as the most numerous of the old bombers was the fabric-covered Wellington, better known as the "Wimpy," named for the hamburger-loving character in the Popeye cartoons, J. Wellington Wimpy. The Wellington's rugged "basket-weave" construction enabled it to absorb considerable battle damage and keep flying. Some 600 Wellingtons were taking part in the raid.

The remainder of the force consisted of 338 of the newer heavy bombers—the twin-engined Manchester and the four-engined Stirling, Halifax and Lancaster. Of these, the Stirling and the Manchester had already proved so disappointing that they were gradually being phased out of long-range bombing. The Stirling was limited by a ceiling of about 16,000 feet as a result of design specifications drawn up to fit conditions in the late 1930s: its short 99-foot wingspan had been dictated by the 100-foot width of RAF hangar doors in those days.

The twin-engined Manchester was woefully underpowered. That weakness, however, had led to the birth of a powerful bigger brother. The basic Manchester had been redesigned and equipped with four Rolls-Royce Merlin engines, the same power plant used on the agile Spitfire fighter. The new plane had been rechristened the Lancaster; Harris was later to claim that it was "the greatest single factor in winning the war." With a seven-ton load of bombs, the Lancaster could cruise at 210 miles per hour over a range of 1,660 miles. It could climb on two engines and come home on one.

Bringing up the rear of the bomber stream were approximately 75 Lancasters and 130 Halifaxes, the heavy bombers that ranked next to the Lancasters in performance. The job of this last bomber wave was to spend the final 15 minutes of the raid over Cologne delivering the knockout blow with high-explosive 1,000- and 4,000-pounders.

The bomber stream lacked fighter escorts, but an intruder force of 50 planes had been sent ahead to keep the German night fighters busy. The intruders—light bombers from Bomber Command and fighter-bombers from RAF Fighter Command—attacked enemy night-fighter bases in the areas of Holland, Belgium, northern France and western Germany straddling the bomber-stream route to Cologne.

Before too long, however, the bomber stream started to shrink. A few of the planes were pounced on by German fighters, Messerschmitt-110s and Junkers-88s, as they crossed the Kammhuber Line. Many more, especially the patched-up older aircraft, developed mechanical problems or ran into severe icing conditions over the North Sea and were forced to turn back. These so-called boomerangs totaled more than 100.

As the Gee-equipped lead planes approached the German border, less than an hour from Cologne, the predicted break in the weather was nowhere to be seen. Then, suddenly, as they moved toward the target, the clouds broke; the full moon flooded the night with light. The crews of the lead Stirlings and Wellingtons could see the Rhine glistening some 15,000 feet below them. Like a great crooked arrow, the river pointed toward the heart of Cologne.

Among the first planes over the target were a pair of Stirlings piloted by Wing Commander J. C. Macdonald and Squadron Leader R. S. Gilmour. Their aiming point was an area known as the Neumarkt, which was located in the center of Cologne's old city on the left bank of the Rhine. The aiming points of other planes lay a mile to the north and a mile to the south.

Macdonald and Gilmour could see Cologne's celebrated 13th Century cathedral northeast of the Neumarkt. The

During a raid staged on March 8, 1942, British bombs score direct hits on the Matford works, a German-run truck factory in Poissy, France. This attack was followed up by two more in April, reducing the factory's production level from close to 1,000 vehicles per month to a mere trickle.

cathedral was not a target, though some of the student crews from the training units had been ordered to aim at its twin towers. That, so the reasoning went, was bound to ensure the cathedral against damage—and, in fact, the damage proved to be relatively minor.

At 12:47 a.m.—eight minutes ahead of schedule—the two Stirlings released their incendiary bombs to start fires as beacons for the bombers to follow. Below them, the residents of Germany's third-largest city were hurrying to underground shelters, roused from their predawn Sunday sleep by the routine wail of air-raid sirens half an hour earlier. In all, since the War's start, the 800,000 residents of Cologne had endured 106 bombing attacks. But the British took pains to inform them that this one would be worse than the rest. Along with the falling incendiaries, the vanguard planes dropped leaflets warning: "The offensive of the RAF in its new form has begun."

For the first 15 or so minutes of the raid, the new form of offensive was chaotic. The 100 planes of the first wave, carrying incendiaries to mark the way for the next wave, ran into heavy flak and began weaving to avoid being hit. Some pilots—either confused or unable to break their old freelance habit of approaching a target in whatever way they found convenient—ignored briefing orders to follow predetermined paths and made direct bombing runs on their own. Others dropped their bombs, then lingered, circling the city to watch while Cologne began to burn. "There were aircraft everywhere," a crew member recalled. "The sky over Cologne was as busy as Piccadilly Circus."

With the planes converging willy-nilly from every direction, the risk of collision multiplied. A Wellington rose slightly; the Stirling above it dipped. The propellers of the Wellington sheared off the tail of the Stirling. The Wellington blew up; the Stirling plummeted into the flaming city. It was the first of two collisions—only twice the number predicted by Harris' "boffins."

Shortly after 1 a.m., just as the second wave of bombers—the main force—reached Cologne, the German gun batteries suddenly went silent. Searchlights continued to probe the crowded skies, apparently setting the stage for the German night fighters to enter the arena. But because of an administrative mix-up at the local air-defense command, the interceptors remained on the ground. When the Ger-

man batteries finally started firing again, they were overwhelmed by the RAF bombers. Bomber crews later reported that the defenses—plus the few interceptors that did get off the ground—seemed "weak and confused."

Most of the bombers in the main attack force thus encountered little difficulty over Cologne. The exceptions tended to be the underpowered twin-engined Manchesters. The 20-year-old pilot of one Manchester, Flying Officer Leslie Manser, found that he had to fly at about 7,000 feet—less than half the altitude of many of the other bombers—because his engines overheated if he tried to climb. At that height his Manchester found itself alone, a stray that was now a sitting duck for the frustrated German searchlight and gun crews. Caught in a cone of searchlights, Manser held the plane straight and level over the aiming point. Then his navigator, Richard Barnes, who was known as "Bang On" Barnes for his accuracy in getting to a target, reported: "Bombs gone." Almost immediately, the Manchester was rocked by a direct flak hit in the bomb bay.

Manser had to fight to control the plane. To elude the searchlights, he resorted to the classic tactic, "Fly straight down the beam," and went into a steep dive. At 800 feet, he wrestled the control stick back and began climbing into the darkness. But his port engine overheated under the strain and burst into flame.

The five men of Manser's crew, watching the fire spread along the wing toward the fuel tank, were ready to bail out. Manser told them to hold on; he hoped they could somehow make it back home or at least to the English Channel. The fire on the port wing stopped short of the tank, but the starboard engine began to fail. Some time later, when the plane was over Belgium and rapidly losing altitude, Manser ordered the bailout. A crewman named Leslie Baveystock tried to fasten Manser's parachute on him but was thrust away. There was scarcely time left for Baveystock to escape—and none for Manser. Less than 200 feet from the ground, Baveystock jumped. Though his parachute did not open completely, the water in a drainage ditch broke his fall. Some 100 yards beyond the ditch, the Manchester crashed and burned, with Manser still at the controls.

Bang On Barnes was captured by the Germans. Baveystock and the other three members of the crew, with the help of the Belgian underground, eventually made it back to England. Their story of Manser's heroism resulted in his receiving the posthumous award of the Victoria Cross, Britain's highest military honor.

Cologne had been under attack for 75 minutes when the heavy Lancasters and Halifaxes of the third and final wave began their approach. The city was burning with such fury that the crews first saw the crimson glow while flying over the Dutch islands nearly 150 miles away. Leonard Cheshire, piloting a Halifax, thought that it was "the most monstrous sight in all the history of bombing" and later recalled feeling "a slight chill in my heart." Then his thoughts turned to his brother Christopher, a bomber pilot who had been shot down and was now in a German prisoner-of-war camp, and the chill faded.

When the third wave reached Cologne, the aiming points were dense with flames: an area three miles long and two miles wide was solidly ablaze. Many of the newly arrived bombers sought out peripheral targets. At 2:25 a.m., precisely on schedule, the last bombs were dropped and the planes turned for home.

All, that is, but one lone straggler. A Lancaster piloted by Flight Lieutenant George Gilpin had taken off so late that, as it flew high over the North Sea, it met bombers returning from the raid. But Gilpin had been so determined to go on the raid that he had put together a scratch crew, including a navigator to serve as one of his gunners.

Now, though he was aware that his plane would never make it home under the cover of darkness—the 2:25 a.m. deadline for the final bombing had been set for just that reason—Gilpin flew on. Alone over Cologne at 3:10 a.m., his Lancaster released its bombs into a pillar of smoke that rose 15,000 feet above the city. The bombs brought the total dropped by the British to 1,455 tons. When Gilpin's Lancaster finally limped home on three engines, daylight had long since descended on his base at Syerston. His was the 898th plane to bomb the target that night and return home safely.

In Cologne the glare of the burning city outshone even the sun. Some 600 acres lay in flaming ruins. More than 250 factories—including metal and rubber and chemical works, and plants that manufactured machine tools and submarine engines—were either destroyed or badly damaged. The dead numbered 474. More than 45,000 people were homeless, and the roads leading out of Cologne were clogged with refugees. So many people were fleeing the stricken city that local officials fretted about the demoralizing effect on the rest of Germany and made a futile attempt to hush up eyewitness accounts of the horror.

Air Chief Marshal Harris, with one massive stroke, had restored British confidence in strategic bombing and given new hope to the Allies, at a time when they were still in retreat on other fronts. The cost of the Cologne mission was less than either Harris or Churchill had anticipated—40 of 1,046 bombers, or 3.8 per cent. Soon after the raid Harris was knighted. On June 17, 1942, "Sir Bomber" Harris—as the irreverent now called him—wrote Churchill a memo on how to win the War. It began: "Victory, speedy and complete, awaits the side which first employs air power as it should be employed."

But in the weeks following Cologne, Harris could not repeat his success. On June 1, two nights after Operation *Millennium,* he launched another huge strike against Essen. Though he sent forth 956 bombers, a combination of cloudy weather, heavy flak and the lack of easily identifiable landmarks prevented them from attaining good concentration over the Ruhr city. Three weeks later, on the night of June 25, Harris sent 904 bombers against the North Sea port of Bremen, a submarine-building center, with only limited success and the loss of 49 planes.

Meanwhile, less than a month after its ordeal by fire, Cologne was returning to normal, a sign of the remarkable resiliency of Germany's city dwellers. As Harris later conceded: "Not one or two such strokes, but the cumulative effect of hundreds of them, would be needed before the enemy felt the pinch."

Such an offensive could not be sustained by Bomber Command until it grew bigger. By mid-August of 1942, Harris was averaging fewer than 300 planes on major attacks, and he could no longer rely on Gee, which the enemy was beginning to jam.

Harris needed some help in his night offensive, and he thought that he could get it from the Americans, who were now building up a bomber force in England. But the Americans, even though they were extremely impressed by the master stroke against Cologne, had their own ideas about how to bomb Germany out of the War.

ALL-SEEING EYES IN THE SKY

A lone American photoreconnaissance pilot heads for his unarmed, camera-equipped F-5A Lightning, standing ready for a mission over German territory

AIR RECONNAISSANCE COMES OF AGE

Early in the War, the RAF dispatched a series of Blenheim bombers to photograph German naval operations in the North Sea; the lumbering Blenheims were all shot down or driven off before they could complete the job. The failure nettled Sidney Cotton, an intrepid Australian flier who, in the guise of a salesman of aeronautical products, had delighted British officials with his prewar airborne espionage across Germany. Cotton, now a civilian photographic consultant to the RAF, took off in his swift, camera-equipped spy plane *(left)* and returned in hours with the photos.

This flight proved Cotton's then-radical concept of wartime aerial photography: the plane had to be fast enough to evade Luftwaffe fighters, and it should be stripped of guns and radio to make room for extra fuel. The RAF put Cotton in charge of revamping its reconnaissance service and began switching its cameras from Blenheims and Ansons to 392-mile-per-hour Spitfires.

Cotton also led in developing the techniques and personnel needed to exploit high-altitude photography. Announcing that photo interpretation required "the patience of Job and the skill of a good darner of socks," he organized a corps of specialists, including many members of the Women's Auxiliary Air Force. By 1942, photos taken by RAF pilots and analyzed by experts were supplying priceless information on the disposition of enemy defenses, the effectiveness of bombing and the location of camouflaged war plants.

Despite the British successes, the new intelligence tools were adopted slowly by the Americans. Early reconnaissance models of the twin-engined Lightning were no match for Luftwaffe fighters. One U.S. recon unit lost more than a quarter of its pilots in its first three months of active duty.

But by 1943 the Americans were catching up. Pilots who had scorned recon flights as unmanly work were now volunteering for the risky missions. One veteran, Lieut. Colonel Karl Polifka, was judged too old, at 33, to fly low-level missions, so he signed up as a Lieutenant Jones. His daredevil dives to photograph German positions at point-blank range made him the best known recon pilot of the War

Pioneering aerial espionage, Sidney Cotton boards the Lockheed-12A from which he covertly photographed German war preparations in 1939.

An RAF photographer, seated at the open observation port of a Blenheim bomber in 1940, focuses his cumbersome F-24 camera upon a ground target.

Two U.S. fliers (left) are briefed for a night mission while a sergeant carries a flash bomb for taking photos in the dark.

Two ground crewmen adjust the

huge telephoto lenses, to be used on high-altitude flights, are checked by a technician for their power to capture details

aerial cameras in a Lightning's nose. Most Lightnings took three wide-angle cameras for general coverage and two long-lens cameras to zero in on target areas

NEW EQUIPMENT FOR HIGH-ALTITUDE PHOTOS

As reconnaissance pilots flew higher in order to escape German flak, they discovered that the altitude was as formidable an opponent as the gunners below. In the sub-zero temperatures encountered above 30,000 feet, film cracked inside the cameras and lenses frosted over with condensation. Fortunately for the Allies, Sidney Cotton found an answer: he improvised

ducts that sent warm air from the Spitfire's engine blowing across the cameras.

Cotton's crude heating system eventually was replaced by electrically heated camera covers. Later models of reconnaissance planes were able to photograph at even greater altitudes, using 40-, 50- and 60-inch lenses *(left)* that took clear pictures from as high as eight miles up.

The man who was primarily responsible for the high-powered lenses was George W. Goddard, the U.S. chief of photo research. Goddard also extended photore-

connaissance into the hours of darkness by inventing the "flashlight bomb" *(top left)*, a 50-pound cylinder of magnesium whose explosion illuminated a ground area and, at the same time, tripped a photoelectric camera shutter. For fast, lower-level reconnaissance, Goddard helped to develop an ingenious shutterless camera that recorded enemy positions on a continuous strip of film. And to speed film processing, Goddard designed portable field laboratories and a printing machine that churned out 1,000 photos per hour.

On a low-level reconnaissance of the Saar River, U.S. Captain Robert Holbury photographed an uncompleted bridge and German fortifications. His Lightning

LOW-LEVEL FLIGHTS INTO ENEMY GUNFIRE

Photographs of strategic targets, such as the German war plant at top right, were usually taken at flak-free high altitudes. But when ground commanders required detailed tactical reconnaissance of enemy positions, pilots flew risky low-level sorties, which the British called "dicing runs" because they were gambles with death.

On a dicing run shortly before D-Day, U.S. Captain Charles Batson sped at tree-top level along the invasion coast of Normandy. He returned with his engines full of twigs and leaves and with 130 bullet holes in his plane. But photos by Batson and others pinpointed nearly every German gun and landing obstacle in the area, doubtless saving the lives of thousands of troops on D-Day. Dozens of recon pilots, however, made one flight too many and failed to return; Batson was among them.

Photos taken before and after an RAF raid reveal that bombs nearly destroyed a Cologne tire factory

was so badly shot up that it had to be junked.

Preparing for D-Day, a pilot skimming a Normandy beach pinpoints mined antilanding-craft obstacles

SEEING THROUGH THE CAMOUFLAGE

As Allied air forces began their heavy day and night bombing of Germany in 1943, the Germans tried with increasing desperation to hide their vital installations from the prying eyes of reconnaissance planes and the bombers that soon followed them. Enormous camouflage nets were draped over navigational landmarks—such as Berlin's broad boulevard Unter den Linden —to confuse Allied bombardiers. German specialists in camouflage applied paint in ingenious ways to disguise factories and military depots. And in Rumania, carpenters constructed an enormous wood and canvas replica of a refinery, complete with fire-making devices that sent up plumes of oily smoke.

But Allied photo interpreters rose to the challenge. They detected camouflaged installations by studying pictures taken at various times of the day; painted shadows did not move with the sun. A German airfield, camouflaged with painted extensions of the irrigation ditches from a nearby farm, was finally discovered when water in the real ditches froze and produced a telltale reflection in aerial photos.

The very thoroughness of German camouflage artists was sometimes their undoing. At U-boat shipyards in Kiel, camouflage nets were neatly extended as each section of the hull was completed; simply by measuring a lengthening net, Allied experts could predict exactly when the submarine would be launched.

Without waiting for prints, a pilot and an interpreter make a preliminary study of negatives.

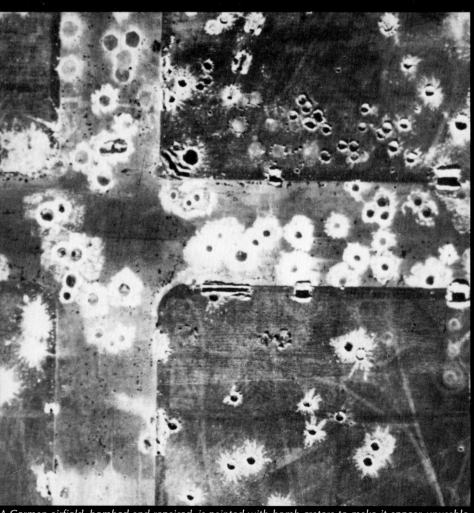

A German airfield, bombed and repaired, is painted with bomb craters to make it appear unusable.

Laborers drafted by the Germans built a wood and canvas replica of Czechoslovakia's Skoda arms works (above and below left) to draw Allied bombers away from the real factory in Pilsen (below right), three miles away. The decoy was close enough to fool Allied airmen on one mission.

THE PUZZLING VIEW FROM MILES UP

Before their unit moved ahead to Europe, inexperienced American photograph analysts made an embarrassing mistake in the North African campaign. In studying a set of photos, they interpreted a suspicious line as a column of German tanks. British mobile forces raced some 60 miles to intercept the tank column, only to find out that it was actually a camel caravan.

The reason for the novices' mistake is unmistakably clear in the 11 aerial views of occupied Europe shown on these pages. Like most recon photos, they were taken at very high altitudes, and ground objects show up as baffling shapes and patterns. Well-seasoned analysts were expected to solve hundreds of such visual riddles every day—and they usually did.

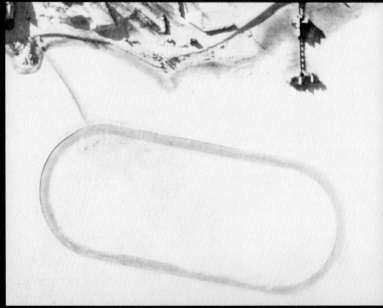

GERMAN DIRECTION-FINDING RADIO MASTS

HERRINGBONE PATTERN OF DRAINAGE DITCHES

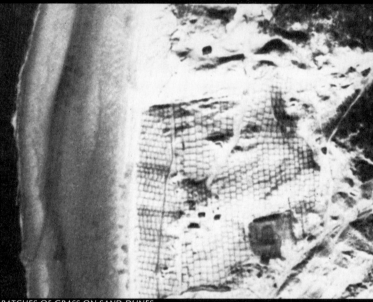

PATCHES OF GRASS ON SAND DUNES

ORCHARD TREETOPS REFLECTING SUNLIGHT

A SNOW-COVERED SKATING RINK

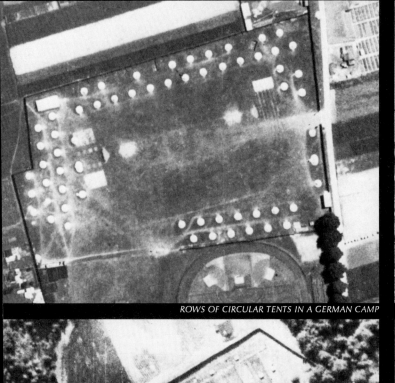

ROWS OF CIRCULAR TENTS IN A GERMAN CAMP

A SUBDIVISION OF THREE-WING HOUSES

HUTS AND PENS OF A FOX FARM

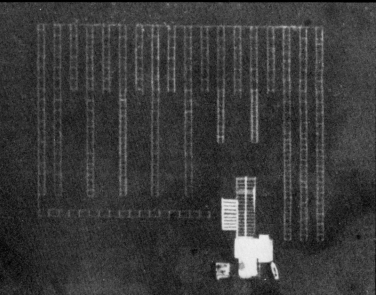

UNDERWATER SHELLFISH-CULTURE BEDS

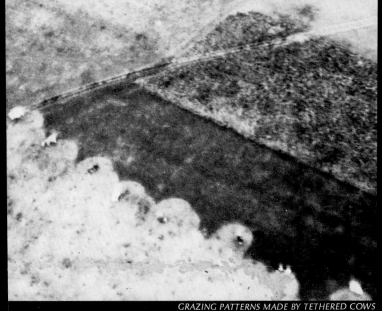

GRAZING PATTERNS MADE BY TETHERED COWS

A NETWORK OF WORLD WAR I TRENCHES

Peering through a stereoscope, a photo interpreter moves two prints until the separate images seem to merge into a single three-dimensional view.

TRANSLATING PICTURES INTO THREE DIMENSIONS

The intelligence gleaned from aerial photos was usually disseminated in the form of written target reports soon after the recon pilot returned. For particularly important operations, expert craftsmen translated the evidence of the photographs into three-dimensional models of the target area.

After studying pairs of photos under a stereoscope *(above)*, interpreters provided the modelmakers with the precise dimensions of objects in the target area. The craftsmen then constructed a scale model that included each natural and man-made feature more than three feet high. Artists painted this miniature landscape, taking care to reproduce the foliage colors of the season.

Bomber crews found the models invaluable for target recognition and analysis of enemy defenses. By walking around the models, they could see, in depth, exactly what their objective would look like on approach from any direction or altitude—information that not even the sharpest aerial photograph could provide.

Built for target study by American bomber crews, a tabletop model matches a

German synthetic-oil refinery in painstaking detail. It includes every bomb crater from previous raids and even shows the different crops in the surrounding fields.

3

The American fliers who began swarming into England in the summer of 1942 brought to the air war a flamboyant style and a controversial bombing strategy. Equally free with their money, their emotions and their opinions, they were the first Americans to inspire the celebrated British lament that "the trouble with the Yanks is they're overpaid, oversexed and over here."

A graphic example of the American style was the way the air crews personalized their big bombers. In contrast to the RAF crews, who gave their planes such staid names as "E for Edward," the Americans came up with suggestive puns like "Ima Vailable" and "Dinah Might"—and with illustrations to match. One visiting U.S. congressman, after inspecting several of these raffish displays on the sides of American planes, advised adding some clothes to the female figures to avoid offending any chance viewers. The proposal was impassively received and promptly forgotten.

The projected strategy of the Americans unsettled the British even more than their style. The newcomers intended to attempt something the RAF believed was just about hopeless—to bomb Germany successfully by day. The RAF had tried daylight bombing periodically since the start of the War and had suffered severe losses; its night attacks had proved more effective and less costly. Air Chief Marshal Harris and his staff at RAF Bomber Command were convinced that if the U.S. joined the RAF's night missions, the War could be shortened by many months. But in their efforts to push this idea, they found themselves up against a stone wall. "War without allies," Air Vice-Marshal John Slessor observed, "is bad enough—with allies it is hell."

The Americans preferred the daylight-bombing strategy for a variety of reasons. They felt that their four-engined bombers—the B-17 Flying Fortress and the B-24 Liberator—were well equipped to stave off attacks by the Luftwaffe's day fighters; they were better armed than the British bombers, normally carrying up to ten .50-caliber machine guns. And installed on board each B-17 and B-24 was the new Norden bombsight, which was said to be so accurate that the bombardier could "drop a bomb in a pickle barrel" from 20,000 feet. The Americans expected that with the help of this remarkable device they could make short work of German airplane factories, synthetic oil plants and other so-called pinpoint targets. In their view, precision bombing

BOMBING ROUND THE CLOCK

had a pronounced advantage over area bombing, the British practice. They believed that precision bombing could cripple Germany faster and more efficiently while causing fewer civilian casualties. Besides, the very notion of precision bombing appealed to the American psyche: it summoned up the old frontier pride in marksmanship.

British planners were cool toward the projected American strategy, and none more so than Harris. The leader of Bomber Command had already heard the case for precision bombing from a number of his own countrymen; once, in a moment of fury, he had suggested that such "panacea mongers" were the tools of a German plot. Though he sometimes employed precision bombing when it suited a particular mission, he regarded it as essentially a futile exercise. The Germans, he argued, could easily repair or otherwise compensate for the damage to a pinpoint target.

Harris also opposed the American plan on a technical basis. He did not share the Yanks' high regard for their Flying Fortresses. Early in 1941, a score of Forts—as they were called—had been sent across the Atlantic for the British to use on daylight missions and, in Harris' words, "got the hell shot out of them." From their performance in action, he had concluded that they were too slow and clumsy. Worse still, they accommodated only about half of the bombload carried by his beloved Lancaster. Harris clearly felt that the Americans could better apply their rising industrial might to turning out Lancasters.

As for the Norden bombsight, Harris pointed out that its only tests thus far had taken place under ideal circumstances: during practice missions in the sunny, cloudless—and flak-less—skies of the U.S. Southwest. The skies over Germany were seldom as benign; thick cloud cover, or the haze and smoke of German industry, could turn the bombsight into a useless toy. Allan Michie, an American war correspondent who interviewed Harris, reported his summing up of the problem in one pithy sentence: "In order to hit a barrel from 20,000 feet, *you must first see the barrel.*"

Behind these specific criticisms lay a basic worry that Harris left unspoken. The British now saw themselves cast in the irksome position of a seasoned veteran confronted by a younger brother who has suddenly acquired new muscle and a know-it-all air to boot. Though they genuinely admired the Americans' talent for organizing and zest for experimenting, they felt that they had a lot to teach the novices from the States.

The Americans, for their part, genuinely admired the RAF's battle record, particularly the 1,000-plane raid on Cologne, but they did not feel that experience guaranteed freedom from error. They believed, for example, that the British had botched the handling of the Flying Fortresses sent over for their use in 1941. While conceding that these planes—an early model known as the B-17C—needed improving, the Americans were annoyed by the British failure to exploit the Fortresses' strong point. Forts were intended to fly in massed formation, a dozen or more together, so that their firepower could be brought to bear collectively against an attacker. RAF Bomber Command had chosen to avoid large formations and had dispatched the Forts instead in twos and threes—with costly results.

The Americans' irritation at this outcome reached all the way to the top. General Arnold, chief of the Army Air Forces—whose nickname "Hap" was short for Happy, his normal disposition—later recalled the Fort episode in blistering terms. The first B-17s, he wrote, "were so badly mishandled by R.A.F. Bomber Command's people that it was obvious it was their place to learn; and they didn't."

Clearly, the Americans did not intend to be treated as younger brothers, or even as junior partners.

Unlike the British, the Americans who believed in air power had been compelled to campaign long and hard before their cause was won. One of their first problems had been to persuade doubters of the basic worth of the airplane. In 1921—three years after the Royal Air Force had been officially accorded equal status with Britain's Army and Navy—the people of San Francisco engaged in a spirited debate as to which traveled faster: a plane or a pigeon. A local newspaper had raised the issue, and the man who finally laid it to rest was Hap Arnold, then a major in the Army's Air Service. Arnold got a coop of carrier pigeons from the Signal Corps, released them at Portland, Oregon, and raced them to San Francisco. The birds made it in 48 hours, Arnold's plane in seven and a half—and his lighthearted stunt earned a handsome publicity dividend for the cause.

Arnold and his friends in the Air Service openly rallied around Billy Mitchell when America's most vocal advocate of air power was court-martialed in 1925. Their show of support did not sit well with General Mitchell's foes among the Army's top brass. Arnold, for one, was exiled from Washington, where he held a post as an information officer, to Fort Riley, Kansas, where he was put in charge of a squadron of rickety observation planes.

Clearly, the argument that the plane had enormous military potential needed more evidence of a solid sort. Such evidence could be amassed only by the development of new aerial devices and techniques and by patient probes of the airplane's capabilities. Much had been achieved along those lines in the early 1920s. The effort was now intensified in an all-out drive "to expand the limits of aeronautical knowledge," as one account described it.

Among the successes of import for the future were several record-breaking feats of long-range and endurance flying. In January of 1929, a trimotor Fokker monoplane named "Question Mark" took to the skies over Southern California and—thanks in part to the recently developed technique of refueling in mid-air—remained aloft for an unprecedented stretch of more than 150 hours. The plane also made history of another kind. The project's leader was

Major Carl "Tooey" Spaatz, the chief pilot Captain Ira C. Eaker. Spaatz, 13 years later, was to be chosen to direct all American air operations over Europe as commander of the U.S. Eighth Air Force; Eaker was to direct the Eighth's bombers in their strikes at German targets from bases in England.

Throughout the 1930s, the champions of air power kept pleading their cause with a largely uncaring government in Washington. They sought greater autonomy within the Army; though the Air Service had been renamed the Air Corps, it was answerable to the Army General Staff and had little authority of its own. More important, the Corps wanted money to train many more pilots and to finance the building of many more planes—especially heavy bombers.

The opposition was multiple: from Army chiefs unwilling to yield any meaningful control to the Corps, from others in the military with a total faith in ground and sea power, from congressmen dead-set against large-scale spending. The economic depression of the 1930s was itself an obstacle. With the drop in federal revenues, every request for appropriations was closely scrutinized; even when it was approved, the funds did not always follow.

The Air Corps also ran into trouble by harping on the need for heavy bombers. Most military thinkers strongly disagreed. They believed that the function of the Corps in a war would be to help the Navy defend America's coasts and to provide support for the Army's ground forces—and that neither task would require heavy bombers. Aircraft of such power suggested independent offensive missions, and these were flatly ruled out by a special fact-finding board set up by the War Department in 1934. Independent air missions, the board concluded, "have little effect upon the issue of battle and none upon the outcome of war." After two years, the Air Corps managed to win approval to order the first of its heavy bombers—the Flying Fortress—but by 1939 it had only 13 on hand and 40 on order.

More than a decade before becoming air war commanders, Captain Ira C. Eaker and Major Carl Spaatz (second and fourth from left) stand with associates alongside their Fokker monoplane "Question Mark," after setting an endurance record of more than six days in the air. The marathon flight, in January 1929, was made possible by a series of 43 mid-air linkups with a Douglas C-1 transport (upper plane, above), which poured fuel into the Fokker through a borrowed fire hose.

The outbreak of war in Europe that September, and the sudden boom in the U.S. aircraft industry as a result of a rush of British and French orders, muted much of the antagonism to air power. But the last vestiges of opposition faded only after the fall of France in June of 1940 attested to the Luftwaffe's might. Later that month Hap Arnold, now chief of the Air Corps, went to Capitol Hill to talk about appropriations. He was assured that any amount he named would be granted. Senator Henry Cabot Lodge Jr. told him: "All you have to do is ask for it."

The Air Corps took full advantage of its blank check. From the 26,000 men and 800 first-line combat planes it had numbered in September of 1939, it expanded to 354,000 men and 2,846 planes just before Pearl Harbor in December of 1941; by then the Corps had been reconstituted as the Army Air Forces. By the spring of 1945, the AAF would reach a peak strength of 2.4 million men and nearly 80,000 planes.

Less than three months after Japan's attack on Pearl Harbor plunged the U.S. into the War, Ira Eaker, now a brigadier general, arrived in England to set up headquarters for the newly formed Eighth Air Force's Bomber Command and to arrange the reception of its first combat units. Luck attended Eaker's own trip to England. Since military aircraft for such uses were still scarce, he and his advance staff of six took a commercial airliner, by way of neutral Portugal, and narrowly escaped an apparent attempt by a German interceptor to shoot down the plane over the Bay of Biscay.

By coincidence, Eaker reached England shortly before Air Chief Marshal Harris took over RAF Bomber Command. That Sunday the two men walked to church together, talking all the while about the hellfire they intended to visit upon Germany, and formed an immediate liking for each other. Like Harris, Eaker had been an early and fervent convert to strategic air power and had never swerved in his belief; he had even put his military career on the line by serving on the defense staff at Billy Mitchell's court-martial. The affinity that Eaker and Harris felt for each other was not only personal but also professional—what a sentimentalist once described as "the bond that makes all airmen one."

Harris invited Eaker to stay at his home until Eaker could get settled. On April 13, Harris' 50th birthday and Eaker's 46th, they held a joint celebration. They also shared a few laughs about the headquarters Eaker had chosen near Harirs' command post at High Wycombe—an imposing country house that had served as an exclusive school for the daughters of what Harris called "the port-drinking classes." On the night the Americans moved in, the duty officer was startled to hear a sudden cacophony of bells. It turned out that each of the bedrooms contained a relic of its recent past as a girls' dormitory—a placard proclaiming, "Ring twice for mistress"—and the new tenants were complying.

Once settled in, Eaker had to deal with a logistical problem of staggering dimensions. Sites for his bomber bases had to be selected and built up to house personnel and planes. Much of the Americans' equipment, including the bombers, had to be ferried by air nearly 3,500 miles across the North Atlantic in the face of fierce weather. The logistical problem was further complicated by the Americans' penchant for clinging to little bits of home. The amused aeronautical correspondent for the London Times reported: "They have actually brought with them their own dustbins—garbage cans, they call them."

Eaker had the wholehearted cooperation of Harris in his gigantic task. Harris smoothed the way for the establishment of the first of some 60 bases that the Eighth Air Force eventually occupied and helped to ease the training headaches of Eaker's embryonic bomber force. Many of Eaker's gunners had never practiced firing from a moving aircraft; some of his new radio operators were still unfamiliar with Morse code. Harris provided facilities where the rookie American crewmen could brush up on their skills.

Harris' growing regard for Eaker was soon echoed in other British quarters. At one point Eaker was introduced at a community gathering in the town of High Wycombe. The audience, including many British soldiers and sailors, no doubt expected the cocksure American of legend, or at least a facsimile of Harris at his most theatrical. Eaker turned out to be a model of soft-spoken tact. "We won't do much talking until we've done more fighting," he told the crowd. "We hope that when we leave, you'll be glad we came."

Though such modesty would later prove appropriate, the results of the earliest U.S. bomber raids exceeded most expectations. The first raid took place on the afternoon of August 17, 1942. A dozen Flying Fortresses took off from their base at Grafton Underwood in eastern England. Protected by four squadrons of RAF Spitfire fighters, they flew 200 miles to the French city of Rouen, northwest of Paris, and dropped 18.5 tons of bombs on railway marshaling yards and repair shops. All the Forts returned safely, though two sustained slight damage from German flak.

By the standards of the RAF, which had been bombing Germany for 27 months with payloads up to 80 times the tonnage dropped on Rouen, the raid was scarcely what the British called a "really big show." But it was a promising beginning. Only after experimental pinpricks against lightly defended nearby targets in France, Holland and Belgium would the American airmen be ready for what they called "the big league"—Germany.

Eaker himself went along on the mission to Rouen because he wanted a close-up look at combat conditions and because, as he later put it, "I don't want any American mothers to think I'd send their boys someplace where I'd be afraid to go myself." His plane was aptly named "Yankee Doodle," and the following day he received a congratulatory telegram from his British counterpart. "Yankee Doodle certainly went to town," Harris had written, "and can stick yet another well-deserved feather in his cap."

Two days after their mission to Rouen, the Americans returned to France to bomb a German fighter base at Abbeville near the Channel coast. The reconnaissance photographs from this raid, and from the one at Rouen, showed such bombing accuracy that even the reticent Eaker could not contain his jubilation. Extrapolating from the results of both raids, he submitted an excessively optimistic report to Eighth Air Force. Eaker predicted that 10 per cent of the bombs dropped would be dead on the aiming point and that fully 90 per cent would be within a one-mile radius of

it. By comparison, the British night offensive was getting only 5 per cent of the bombs within a mile of the aiming point. "It is safe and conservative to say, therefore," Eaker concluded, "that high-level day bombing will be at least ten times as effective for the destruction of definite point targets as night area bombing."

By early October of 1942, "Eaker's amateurs"—as some RAF officers liked to call them—had flown 13 missions against German targets in France, Belgium and Holland. Despite dire British predictions, they had lost only two bombers to German interceptors and flak. Skeptics began to take notice of qualities they had overlooked. An article in London's *Evening Standard,* remarking at the stamina that enabled American crews to operate from such high altitudes as 26,000 feet without passing out, speculated that they were superior physical specimens—the result no doubt of playing baseball. The superspecimen legend grew when a British doctor went up with one American crew to study the effects of high-altitude flying and quickly fainted. Apparently he had improperly fitted the oxygen mask that was required gear under such conditions.

Some of the steam began to go out of the RAF campaign to convert the Americans to the night-bombing strategy. In a private memorandum to Chief of the Air Staff Portal, Air Vice-Marshal Slessor wrote of the Americans: "They are, I think, a bit unwarrantably cock-a-hoop as a result of their limited experience to date. But they are setting about it in a realistic and business-like way. . . . I have a feeling they will do it. . . . They have hung their hats on the day bomber policy and are convinced they can do it."

On October 9 the Americans mounted their most ambitious raid to date, a mission against the steelworks at Lille in

A Yank in the RAF, Eugene "Red" Tobin prepares his Hurricane fighter for takeoff from a British air base in 1941. Tobin was a member of one of three RAF Eagle Squadrons composed entirely of Americans who volunteered to fight before the United States entered the War. The squadrons were responsible for destroying more than 70 German aircraft from February 1941 until they were incorporated into the U.S. Army Air Forces in September of 1942.

northern France. The force of 108 bombers included, for the first time, B-24 Liberators. A friendly rivalry had already developed between the crews of the Liberators and the Flying Fortresses. Liberator crewmen boasted about their plane's 225-mile-per-hour speed—14 miles an hour faster than the Fort's—and its greater bombload capacity. Fort crews touted the B-17's ability to fly at higher altitudes and to withstand greater damage, and scoffed at the Liberator's graceless, boxlike fuselage. The Liberator, they joked, was actually the crate that the Fort was shipped in.

That day over Lille, the crews of neither Liberators nor Forts had much to brag about. Due to mechanical failures and human error, only 69 planes managed to reach the primary target; only nine bombs fell within 500 yards of the aiming point. Moreover, the crews had their first taste of heavy opposition from the Luftwaffe. "Lille was our first real brawl," one navigator later recalled.

Still, the Americans returned to base feeling that they had scored a triumph. Against the loss of three Forts and a Liberator, they claimed no fewer than 56 German fighters shot down. The claims proved to be preposterous. Double-checking by Allied intelligence cut the estimate by almost half, while the Germans' own records put their fighter loss at exactly two. In the confusion of battle, some American gunners had laid claim to the same plane. The German fighter pilots had compounded the chance for error by playing possum—deliberately deceiving the enemy by flipping over their planes and plunging them earthward with smoke pouring from the exhausts (smoke pots were sometimes installed to enhance the illusion).

The inflated claims of the Americans reflected their euphoria at this stage in the air war. Eaker's airmen had been flying under excellent conditions: fighter escort to and from the French coast by British Spitfires and U.S. Lightnings and—before Lille—relatively little show of interest by the Luftwaffe. Now, however, the problems began piling up.

The weather itself became a prime obstacle. Eaker was receiving extremely accurate forecasts of conditions over Europe through Ultra, the remarkable British system for cracking German coded messages, and the reports were mostly bad. The weather over England was no better. For the American airmen, it was a new experience, as an officer said, "to start down the runway in sunshine and before clearing the ground to be in the midst of a downpour."

In the 12 days after the raid on Lille, the weather forced cancellation of 11 U.S. missions, and only 12 were flown all through November and December. Many of the cancellations came after the bombers were airborne—a special blow to morale since abortive missions did not count toward the 25 that were required to complete a tour of duty in England. One American gunner later estimated that he had gone through briefings for 65 missions but had completed only 15; all the rest had been scrubbed.

Another major problem was thrust upon Eaker by the Allied invasion of North Africa in November of 1942. This massive operation not only cost the Eighth Air Force its top-priority claim on new planes and crews but also compelled the transfer of two of its bomber groups from England to support the invaders. Eaker lost nearly 100 of his planes, about a third of his strength. And to prevent U-boat attacks on American and British convoys bound for North Africa, the rest of Eaker's bombers were sent to blast the German submarine bases on France's Atlantic seaboard. The missions proved largely ineffective. The German submarine pens were so massive—the concrete roofs were as much as 12 feet thick—that many of the one-ton U.S. bombs bounced off as harmlessly as marbles on a city pavement.

Moreover, the Luftwaffe's fighters were becoming increasingly aggressive. On November 23, a squadron led by Lieut. Colonel Egon Mayer confronted a number of Flying Fortresses over the submarine base at Saint-Nazaire and dealt them a nasty surprise. Instead of attacking the Forts from the rear—the standard tactic—Mayer and his comrades came at them head on. To make such a frontal assault required nerves of steel; the combined speeds of the bomber and fighter added up to a closing rate of nearly 600 miles per hour, posing the risk of collision. But the Forts were vulnerable up front: the nose lacked a power-operated turret and the hand-maneuvered machine guns mounted there had a limited field of fire. That day, Mayer's head-on tactic cost the Americans four of their 56 Forts. The Germans lost seven of their fighters.

By the end of 1942, the daylight offensive that had begun so hopefully in August was bogging down. Only 27 U.S. missions had been flown in all. The loss rate was only 2 per cent, about half the rate incurred by RAF bombers during the same period—but, as Winston Churchill acidly noted in a memorandum to Chief of the Air Staff Portal on November 2, 1942, the Americans had not yet succeeded in dropping one bomb on Germany. The Prime Minister, who had been dubious about the daylight-bombing strategy from the start, was now so outspokenly critical about what he viewed as its "pitifully small" results that Portal and others in the Air Ministry felt compelled to defend the Eighth Air Force. Too many barbs, they feared, might lead the Americans to pick up their Forts and Liberators and send them off to the Pacific for use in the war with Japan.

The showdown over daylight bombing was soon to come. The arena was not the wintry skies over Europe but balmy Morocco and a compound of luxurious villas outside Casablanca. In mid-January, Churchill and President Roosevelt met there to plan Allied strategy for the year ahead. On Churchill's personal agenda was the issue of daylight bombing: he intended to persuade Roosevelt to scrap the strategy and order the U.S. bombers to join the RAF night missions.

Among the American brass attending the Casablanca conference was Hap Arnold. When the Chief of the Army Air Forces got wind of Churchill's plan, he summoned Eaker from England to try to talk the Prime Minister out of it.

On the morning of January 20, Eaker appeared at Churchill's villa. He was understandably nervous. Not only his bombers were at stake, but his Eighth Air Force as well; a few weeks earlier he had been named commanding general of the Eighth, succeeding General Spaatz, who had been put in charge of the new Allied air force in North Africa.

Eaker had armed himself for the Churchill meeting with a one-page brief he had prepared on the case for daylight bombing. Originally it had run to 23 pages, but Eaker had ruthlessly pruned it. He had a knack for condensing an argument—in addition to his career as an airman, he had studied both law and journalism—and he was also aware of Churchill's distaste for long-winded presentations.

When the Prime Minister appeared, he was wearing an air commodore's uniform. Eaker thought this a good omen. Churchill was known to have different military uniforms for different occasions and might have chosen, instead, to appear in the garb of an admiral or general. The conversation opened with a few amenities in which Churchill noted that

he was half-American by reason of his mother's birth in New York and expressed regret to Eaker over the "tragic loss of so many of your gallant crews." Then he took Eaker's single sheet of paper and began to read. Most of the arguments for daylight bombing were familiar to him, and he mumbled through them without pausing. But one sentence caught his fancy, and he read it aloud with the obvious relish of a veteran phrasemaker:

"By bombing the devils around the clock, we can prevent the German defenses from getting any rest."

Years later Eaker vividly recalled Churchill's reaction to that key sentence. The Prime Minister, he said, "rolled the words off his tongue as though they were tasty morsels."

After some further discussion, in which Eaker assured Churchill that his men would be bombing Germany within a month, the Prime Minister rose and declared: "Young man, you have not convinced me you are right, but you have persuaded me that you should have further opportunity to prove your contention. How fortuitous it would be if we could, as you say, 'bomb the devils round the clock.' "

On the following day the Allied leaders at Casablanca produced a document that formally endorsed round-the-clock bombing—the Americans by day, the British by night. Known as the Casablanca Directive, it listed the top target priorities, including submarine-construction yards and aircraft plants, and defined the purpose of the joint air offensive for the benefit of the men who were to conduct it. "Your primary object," the directive read, "will be the progressive destruction and dislocation of the German military, industrial and economic system, and the undermining of the morale of the German people to a point where their capacity for armed resistance is fatally weakened."

On January 27, precisely a week after Eaker's momentous conversation with Churchill, the bomber crews at the U.S. bases in eastern England were roused before dawn and began the usual premission ritual. First they walked to the latrine huts and shaved: a one- or two-day growth of beard caused their oxygen masks to leak around the edges. Then slogging through the English mud—described in one official report as ranging from "watery slop to a gelatinous mess with all the properties of quick-setting cement"—they went to the mess hall to breakfast. The fact that they were to fly

THE BOMBER TEAM: 10 VERSATILE MEN IN ACTION

Pilot (left) and Copilot

Bombardier/Nose Gunner

Navigator/Nose Gunner

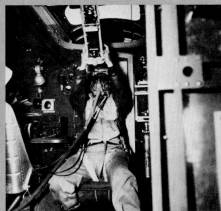

Radio Operator/Gunner

Flight Engineer/Upper-Turret Gunner

Ball-Turret Gunner

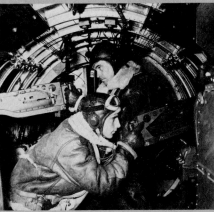

Two Waist Gunners

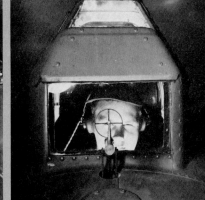

Tail Gunner

The highly trained 10-man crew of a B-17 bomber comprised four commissioned officers—pilot, copilot, navigator and bombardier—and six noncommissioned officers. Each crew member was a specialist but was also trained to perform at least one of the other jobs.

The versatility and teamwork of the crew were best displayed when enemy fighters rose to the attack. The navigator and bombardier manned a pair of nose guns, the flight engineer was assigned to a gun in the upper turret, and the four full-time gunners defended their plane's tail, flanks and underbelly; in some models the radiomen fired as well, through a port in the top of the fuselage. Only the pilot and copilot remained where they were, flying the plane while trying to direct the fire.

this day afforded them at least one luxury: real eggs instead of the customary powdered substitute. Inside the drafty metal Nissen briefing huts on the airfield proper, they struggled, groaning, into their fleece-lined flight suits and gathered together their bulky gear—parachute harness, oxygen mask, escape kit complete with foreign currency in case they were shot down.

So far it had been a normal mission day. In the briefing room, however, they learned that this was to be no ordinary mission. On the big map, the path from home base to target was marked, as usual, by a strand of yarn. But this time the strand did not stop short in France, Belgium or Holland. "Gentlemen," the briefing officer began. Then, with a subtle change in tone that stilled the sleepy murmuring and the idle foot shuffling, he went on: "Gentlemen, the target for today is Germany."

Out of the silent audience came one airman's emphatic response: "Goddam."

The target was Wilhelmshaven, the submarine-building center on the North Sea. It was not, in fact, very far into Germany—only 40 miles from the Dutch border. But none of the previous American raids over occupied territory had involved so long a stretch of time and distance. Getting to Wilhelmshaven and back required a 600-mile flight, most of it without benefit of escort.

The sheer duration of the flight magnified the discomforts, giving the bomber crews a grim preview of what even-longer missions into the Reich would entail. Flying at more than 20,000 feet over France had introduced them to the rigors of cold at high altitudes, but now the cold was protracted; it knifed through layers of clothing to infuse the flesh with a seemingly ineradicable chill. Oxygen masks chafed the cheeks and nose and chin, but they could not be held away from the face for more than 15 or 20 seconds; any longer risked mortal peril.

The need to urinate was another agony, one of the great unmentioned hazards of the air war. Though the planes were supplied with so-called relief tubes, they very rarely worked. The men were compelled to wait many painful hours to use the latrines back at base.

Underlying all the physical torment was a natural human emotion that each man tried to conceal from the others: the fear of dying. As one B-24 copilot later put it: "You don't know what it is to be really scared until you're up in the sky, your fighter cover gone, and you suddenly see an Me-109 coming at you from out of nowhere, with guns blazing. All you can do is listen to your gunners firing back—and pray."

Over Wilhelmshaven that day there was much to be scared about. Of the 91 Fortresses and Liberators that had set out on the mission, only 53 reached the city. More than 100 Luftwaffe fighters swarmed up to meet them. In the savage combat that followed, the Americans claimed seven fighters downed but lost three of their own bombers—a loss rate of more than 5 per cent. Moreover, the cloud cover made accurate bombing difficult; the results of the mission, as one U.S. report described them, were "only fair."

Still, back at base that night the men were in high spirits, jovially arguing at mess about which of their planes had been the first over German soil. But the issue was less than momentous. What mattered was that the Americans had hit Germany at last.

Eaker's amateurs were now in "the big league," and the Germans were impressed. Luftwaffe Lance Corporal Erich Handke, who was aboard one of the twin-engined Me-110s that had taken on the American bombers over Wilhelmshaven, recalled: "The sight put me into a bit of a flap, and

In the company of an armed guard, two student bombardiers (left) head for their plane toting a canvas-covered section of a top-secret Norden bombsight. This section (at top, above) comprised a telescopic sight and a mechanical calculator that computed bomb trajectories, allowing for the plane's speed, altitude and drift. The sight was linked to the plane's automatic pilot; as the bombardier operated the sight, the sight flew the plane.

the others felt the same. We seemed so puny against these four-engined giants."

But the Germans, faced now with defending the homeland against the Americans as well as the British, soon overcame their surprise. When the Eighth Air Force returned to Wilhelmshaven a month later, on February 26, Luftwaffe fighters shot down seven U.S. bombers.

Six American correspondents went along on the mission, the first time that newsmen had been permitted to accompany a U.S. raid over Europe. It was a rugged introduction to what the crewmen had to endure as matter of course—not only the German flak and interceptors but also the intense cold of high-altitude bombing. Frigid air blasted in through the large openings on either side of the fuselage where the waist gunners were stationed. The United Press correspondent, Walter Cronkite, reported that above 20,000 feet he and his colleagues could no longer make notes; the cold actually froze the lead of the pencils. Cronkite summed up the mission as "an assignment to hell—a hell 26,000 feet above the earth."

As aids to survival in this environment, the Eighth Air Force kept devising new equipment and tactics. The crewmen were given new "vests" to protect them from flak. Made of overlapping two-inch-square steel plates on top of heavy canvas, the flak vest proved to be so effective that one bombardier survived unhurt when a 20mm cannon shell exploded only two feet away from his chest. Another innovation that was gradually replacing the crews' leather and fleece-lined clothing was the electric flying suit; it could be plugged in at receptacles inside the bomber.

The new tactics that were worked out had two principal aims: to increase bombing precision and to make the massed bomber formations more invulnerable to Luftwaffe attack. Some of the methods were devised by an irascible, cigar-chomping 36-year-old Ohioan, Colonel Curtis E. Le-May, who commanded the 305th Bombardment Group. LeMay was such a slave driver that his men called him "Iron Ass." In their dispatches home, American correspondents softened the term to "Iron Pants," only to earn LeMay's scornful charge that they feared "offending some delicate old-maid type readers."

LeMay was never to curb his notorious penchant for plain speaking, but in the winter of 1943 he was better known for

two tactical innovations. The first was the flying formation known as the "combat box." In contrast to the loose bomber stream used in the British night missions, the Americans' choice of a daylight strategy had required their planes to be tightly bunched for effective defense against attack. LeMay's combat box further strengthened the defense. It consisted of as many as 21 planes staggered vertically and horizontally in such a way that the bombers' guns provided maximum firepower all around, and especially against head-on attacks. On large raids, three of these boxes were formed into a combat wing, with one box in the lead and the others stacked 1,000 feet above and below it.

LeMay's second innovation, designed to increase bombing accuracy, was to place his most proficient crews in the lead planes of the combat boxes. All the planes in the box dropped their bombs simultaneously—but only at the signal of the lead crew. The result, at least in theory, was a closely packed pattern of hits on the target.

These tactics, combined with new flight-control gadgetry,

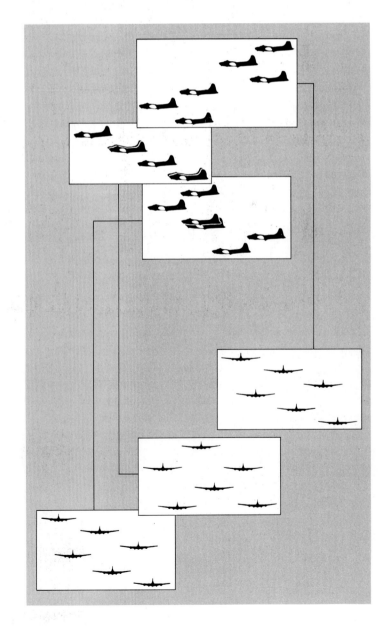

Three squadrons made up of six or seven planes each—here isolated in individual compartments and shown from both the side and front—formed one "combat box," a compact defensive formation devised by Colonel (later General) Curtis E. LeMay to protect unescorted U.S. bomber groups from head-on attacks by Luftwaffe fighters. From the side, the combat box resembled a slanted flying wedge, with the lead squadron in the middle; as seen in the front view, other squadrons were stacked 250 feet to the lead squadron's right and left. This arrangement opened up a clear field of fire for the bombers' forward-firing gunners and enabled them to catch the attacking fighters in coordinated cross fire.

helped the Eighth Air Force achieve its most successful raid to date. The mission, against the submarine-building yards at Vegesack in northwestern Germany, involved an unusually large force of 97 bombers and was carried out on March 18, 1943. The Forts were equipped with the new AFCE—automatic flight control equipment—which provided a link between the bombardier and the aircraft's automatic pilot. This gave the bombardier control of the plane during the crucial bombing run: he flew the plane simply by lining up the cross hairs on his Norden bombsight, which was connected to the automatic pilot. Largely thanks to AFCE, the attackers put 76 per cent of their bombs within 1,000 feet of the aiming point at Vegesack.

Individual acts of heroism also contributed to the mission's success. A Texan, First Lieutenant Jack Mathis, was the bombardier in the 359th Squadron's lead plane. Less than a minute before Mathis was due to release his bombs, flak exploded just outside the nose compartment. The shrapnel nearly severed his right arm and hurled him back nine feet. In great pain, Mathis crawled forward to his bombsight, released the bombs and started to call out over the intercom, "Bombs away." He never finished the familiar phrase; in a few moments he slumped over dead. But he had released his bombs on time and on target, enabling the planes in his box to lay down an effective pattern. Posthumously, Mathis became the first member of the Eighth Air Force to be awarded the Congressional Medal of Honor.

The results at Vegesack—seven U-boats damaged and two thirds of the shipyards destroyed—led Eaker to call a press conference at which he indulged in a rare bit of puffery. Vegesack, he told the assembled reporters, marked "a successful conclusion to long months of experimentation in daytime, high-level precision bombing. After Vegesack comes a new chapter."

Eaker's elation masked some nagging worries. His average daily operational strength in March of 1943 barely exceeded 100 bombers. To replace combat losses, he desperately needed more planes and crews, and he was receiving very few of either. The extent of the manpower shortage was signaled in early April, when Eaker raised from 25 to 30 the number of missions that crews were required to fly to complete a tour of duty. His men now joked that if they didn't survive 25 missions, it wouldn't be so bad—at least they wouldn't have to fly the extra five.

Another of Eaker's problems stemmed from the growing realization that despite the vaunted ability of his bombers to go it alone in the face of enemy attacks, they would fare better with fighter-escort protection. But there were no planes with sufficient range to accompany Eaker's bombers all the way to Germany. The available fighters—the British Spitfire and the American Thunderbolt—had a radius of action of no more than 175 miles, enough to escort the bombers only partway to the target and partway home. The gravity of the problem was underscored in mid-April, when 16 of a mission of 115 Forts were lost in a raid on an aircraft factory in Bremen.

Eaker had to wait for the arrival of new and improved fighters, but meanwhile he could and did demand more bombers. While his crews continued to hit points in Germany, he launched a paper blitz against Washington. He wrote letters, sent cables and asked his RAF allies to bombard Washington with pleas for more bombers. At dinner with Eaker one night, Prime Minister Churchill jocularly proposed they send a joint cable to General Arnold that would say: "We are dining together, smoking your cigars, and waiting for more of your heavy bombers."

Arnold was waging his own battle over airplane priorities on the home front; the Navy was badgering him to divert more bombers to the war in the Pacific as well as to anti-submarine duty in the Atlantic. But Arnold was a skilled political infighter, and 35 years in the Army had taught him that something in writing could be a useful weapon.

Arnold had Eaker and his staff draw up an elaborate proposal, documented with statistics and projections of sweeping results, that would rescue the Eighth Air Force from its current plight. The proposal evolved into the Combined Bomber Offensive Plan. Similar to the preceding Casablanca Directive, it outlined the respective day and night bombing roles of the Americans and the British and listed top-priority targets.

But it also contained some new elements. The Allied bombing was envisioned as specific preparation for the invasion of Western Euorpe, now scheduled for 1944, and—in recognition of the growing effectiveness of the Luftwaffe—aircraft factories rather than U-boat shipyards topped the

Spraying a fountain of light as it detonates at a preset altitude, a target-marking bomb illuminates a French aircraft-engine plant for an RAF night raid. British marker bombs flamed in yellow, red or green, thwarting German efforts to confuse the raiders with hastily lighted decoy fires.

priority list. Most important, the plan pledged the U.S. to enlarge the Eighth Air Force to numerical parity with RAF Bomber Command; Eaker was to receive an additional 944 heavy bombers by July 1, 1943, and nearly double that number by the year's end. The plan was approved by the U.S. Joint Chiefs of Staff on May 4 and formally issued as a joint Anglo-American commitment on June 10 under the portentous title of Pointblank Directive.

By then, the paper war waged by Eaker had already helped ease the strain on the Eighth Air Force. On a single day in mid-May, for example, the number of available combat crews jumped from 100 to 215. New U.S. bases began to dot the English landscape, giving the island the appearance of an enormous aircraft carrier. One Englishman recalled: "The sky was never still."

Eaker was able to step up the size of his attacks on Germany while continuing his missions against targets in the occupied countries. The new momentum of the U.S. offensive gave him a sense of personal triumph, but before long it also brought him a somber reminder of the face of war as seen by the men that were under his command.

In late June the Eighth Air Force launched its Mission No. 69, a raid in two parts. The main force of 191 bombers was dispatched to the U-boat pens at Saint-Nazaire. A diversionary force of 50 bombers was sent to hit a German airfield on the outskirts of Brussels. As was customary when there was a risk of killing friendly civilians, the crews of the diversionary force had been especially cautioned at the premission briefing about hitting anything but the designated target.

The approach to the German airfield took the 50 planes directly over Brussels. It was the safest route, since the Germans seldom wasted flak protecting occupied cities. As the U.S. force passed over the Belgian capital, the bombardiers prepared for their attack by opening bomb-bay doors and checking bombsights. The lead bombardier in one of the three combat groups happened to notice a large rectangular park in the middle of a residential area. He selected it as a simulated aiming point to rehearse the bombing run he would make over the targeted airfield. Suddenly, to his horror, he felt the jolt of bombs being released. Behind him, the other bombardiers in his combat group took the cue and also dropped their loads. The explosions ripped a path

of destruction through the park and the houses alongside.

American bombs had gone astray before, killing civilians sympathetic to the Allied cause, but never had an entire group of bombers dropped its payload in one huge collective error. Two days later the pilots, bombardiers and navigators of the lead crews were summoned to the headquarters of Brigadier General Robert Williams, commander of the 1st Bombardment Wing. The meeting opened with the customary postmission critique of the main raid on Saint-Nazaire. And then came the moment that the men had been awaiting in dread.

The bombardier who had caused the accident over Brussels rose and stepped forward. Colonel Budd Peaslee, who had led the diversionary raid, later remembered him as "a slight blond young man wearing the silver bars of a first lieutenant, hardly out of his teens but with the face and expression of a man twice his age." The room was dead silent as he attempted an explanation. "I don't know how it happened," he concluded. "Whatever the cause, I alone am to blame—the bombs of the entire formation are on my head. . . . I can only say I have regretted the day I was born."

Then General Williams spoke again, his one eye sternly fixed on his audience—he had lost the other eye in a German bombing raid while on a stint as an observer during the Battle of Britain. After noting how often the men had been warned about the possibility of bombing errors, Williams revealed that an investigation of the Brussels incident had been made "through agents in Belgium and other intelligence sources."

He paused, and the men braced for the verdict. "We find these results are not so bad as had at first been feared," Williams said. "As a matter of fact we are informed that the German occupation command considered the park area and the better-class adjoining residences an excellent locale for the billeting of troops. The entire circumference of the park was used for this purpose. We are informed there were 1,200 casualties among these forces and only a few Belgians were injured or killed. Across the Channel this accident is

being called a remarkable exhibition of American precision bombing. Such are the fortunes of war, gentlemen. This meeting and the incident are now closed."

The fortunes of war were also looking up for RAF Bomber Command. Like the Eighth Air Force, it had spent most of the past winter in frustrating attacks on the virtually bombproof U-boat bases along France's coast. But by March 1943, Air Chief Marshal Harris, taking advantage of a build-up of planes and new technological devices, turned his attention back to what Bomber Command considered its main job: "to render the German industrial population homeless, spiritless and as far as possible, dead."

On the night of March 5, a force of 367 RAF planes roared in over Bomber Command's toughest and most resistant target, Essen. The Ruhr city, ringed by guns and shielded by perpetual haze, had thus far defied Harris' best efforts to make a dent in it; in 1942 alone he had lost a total of 201 bombers there. Now, however, the British possessed new ways and means of getting at Essen.

The attack was led by the Pathfinder Force, an elite group of Bomber Command's most proficient crews. In the vanguard were eight Mosquitoes. The Mosquito was to prove to be the most versatile plane built during the War, serving variously as a bomber, fighter and photoreconnaissance plane. It could exceed 400 miles per hour in level flight—faster than most fighters—climb above 30,000 feet and carry a two-ton bomb. And it required only a two-man crew.

But the most remarkable fact about the Mosquito was that it was largely made of wood. This not only allowed the British to build parts of it in woodworking shops—easing the burden on the country's metal supplies—but it also enabled the Mosquito to elude detection by enemy radar.

In the raid on Essen, the Mosquitoes carried their own variety of radar, a target-finding device known as Oboe because it transmitted a continuous note that sounded a lot like the wood-wind instrument. Oboe depended upon pulse signals transmitted from two ground stations in Eng-

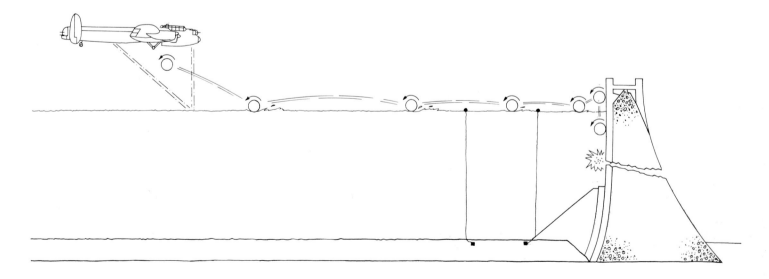

land. Signals from one station, code-named Mouse, kept the bomber on course. Signals from the Cat station told the bombardier precisely when his plane had reached the predetermined point for releasing the bombs.

On cue from Oboe, the Mosquitoes dropped special target-marking flares over the center of Essen. These target markers exploded at 3,000 feet, sending out a spray of brilliantly colored lights—yellow followed by red—that ignited like Roman candles and showered to earth in great pools of fire. In the wake of the Mosquitoes came 22 heavy bombers, also part of the Pathfinder Force, which supplemented the red indicators with a barrage of green markers. When the main bomber force arrived moments later, a giant Christmas-like display of red and green festooned the target, lighting the way for the RAF's deadly gifts.

More than 600 acres of Essen were either destroyed or badly damaged that night, and four more RAF raids were to come. The Krupp steelmaking complex was left in such ruins that after the head of the family, Gustav Krupp von Bohlen und Halbach, viewed the wreckage, he suffered a stroke from which he never recovered.

Essen was only the start of a sustained RAF campaign against the Ruhr. The operation was to exact a high price from the attackers: 872 bombers carrying more than 5,000 crewmen failed to return. During the next four months, more than two thirds of Bomber Command's missions concentrated on the area, and the centers of several cities were burned out. To a British pilot, looking down upon the flaming Ruhr one spring night, "the clouds were like cottonwool soaked in blood."

Cities were not the sole targets during the Battle of the Ruhr. The most memorable mission of the RAF offensive was one that Harris himself strongly opposed; it was executed only after he had been overruled by his superiors on the Air Staff. More than ever intent on area bombing, he resented going back to pinpointing specific objectives.

But the Air Ministry's planners sharply disagreed with Harris in the case of the projected mission—a raid on three of the big Ruhr dams that supplied the valley's water and hydroelectric power. By knocking them out, the argument went, the RAF's bombers could not only flood the valley but also paralyze Germany's entire armaments industry. This assessment was later to be confirmed by the Reich's own production czar, Albert Speer. Had the mission entirely succeeded, Speer said, it would have had the same effect as removing the ignition from a motor—rendering it useless.

The dams—the Möhne, the Eder and the Sorpe—were enormous piles of concrete, masonry and earth, some 150 feet high and nearly as thick at the base, and they were virtually impervious to conventional bombs. But early in the War a British aeronautical engineer named Barnes Wallis had come forward with an ingenious design for a dam-busting bomb. It was a barrel-shaped cylinder, five feet long and four feet in diameter. Weighing nearly five tons, it was designed to be slung crosswise in a special cradle beneath a Lancaster bomber. A belt-drive motor attached to the cradle would impart a rapid backspin to the bomb just before it was released at a low altitude. The backspin would make the bomb skip across the surface of the water. When it hit the dam, the backspin would force it down to a depth of 30 feet, where its pressure-sensitive fuse would go off. The explosion, magnified by water pressure, would function like a small man-made earthquake and breach the dam.

In mid-March, shortly after the first successful strike at Essen, a squadron of 147 men, hand-picked for the dam mission, began training for low-level flight without knowing their ultimate target. The new squadron's chief, Wing Commander Guy Gibson, was at 24 already a legend in the RAF. Once rejected by the peacetime RAF because his "legs were too short," Gibson had since flown 173 missions in both bombers and fighters.

The requirements for the projected mission far exceeded any in Gibson's experience. To elude radar detection, the squadron would have to fly all the way to the targets at altitudes under 1,500 feet. Then, over each dam, they would have to swoop down in their big Lancasters to a precisely fixed bomb-release point—exactly 60 feet above the water and 425 yards from the dam—while flying at a speed of 220 miles per hour. A crude bombsight, fashioned from a peephole, a piece of plywood and two nails, was devised to aid the task of the bomb aimer; he would line up the two nails with a pair of towers at either end of each dam. A more difficult problem involved finding a device that would tell the crews when they had come down to 60 feet. This was finally solved with the help of simple trigonometry. Spot-

The RAF's ingenious "bouncing bombs," which breached two of the hydroelectric dams near Germany's Ruhr industrial region, were released by Lancaster bombers with a rapid backspin to send them skipping over antitorpedo nets (vertical lines in diagram) and caroming downward after hitting the top of the dam wall. As the bomb reached a depth of 30 feet, a hydrostatic fuse triggered the five-ton explosive charge, whose force was concentrated upon the dams by the pressure of the surrounding water.

lights were rigged under the Lancaster, fore and aft, and fixed at just the proper angles. When these two lights intersected on the surface of the water, the plane was at 60 feet.

After eight weeks of training, the squadron was deemed ready to go. On the night of May 16, 1943, with the moon full and the reservoirs behind the dams reported at levels about four feet below the top, the squadron's 19 Lancasters took off in three waves. The first wave of nine, led by Gibson, headed for the Möhne. After several misses and the loss of one plane to flak, the attackers scored three direct hits. A breach about 100 yards wide opened in the dam, and a wall of water rushed through and poured down the valley. Gibson's wave then flew south and breached the Eder Dam. Circling overhead, Gibson watched the onrushing water "extinguish all the lights in the neighborhood as though a great black shadow had been drawn across the earth."

The second and third waves of the squadron had less success. Only one of the five Lancasters in the second wave got through to the target, the Sorpe Dam. The plane was piloted by an American, Flight Lieutenant Joseph McCarthy of Brooklyn, who had enlisted in the RAF before the Americans entered the War and had chosen to stay with Bomber Command. McCarthy's bomb fell on the dam itself instead of on the water. That hit, as well as another by a plane of the third wave, damaged the Sorpe but failed to breach it.

With two of the three dams breached and the third damaged, the squadron had achieved a feat for which the participants later received 34 decorations, including the Victoria Cross for Gibson. But flak and accidents had cost Bomber Command eight of the 19 Lancasters and 56 of its most highly trained men. Nor was the effect on the German war machine anything near what the strategists in London had envisioned. Though both the Möhne and the Eder reservoirs were virtually emptied and the flooding extended up to a distance of 16 miles, the damage was repaired within three months. Experts summoned by Speer from all over Germany dried out the soaked electrical installations at the Möhne Dam's pumping stations and, where necessary, replaced useless motors with others peremptorily removed from factories outside the Ruhr.

The mission's most important result for the Allied cause was one the British strategists had not foreseen. Some 7,000 workers, Germans as well as foreign conscripts, had to be temporarily pulled back to the Ruhr from Hitler's Atlantic Wall, the fortifications he was having built along the French coast in anticipation of an Allied invasion.

For Harris, the dam busters' failure to cause a collapse of production in the Ruhr was a signal to press on with his own area-bombing strategy. In July he shifted his sights from the Battle of the Ruhr northeast to the enemy's biggest port and second-largest city, Hamburg. What Harris intended for its 1.5 million residents was reflected in the code name he chose—Operation *Gomorrah,* after the Biblical city destroyed by fire and brimstone because of its wickedness.

Gomorrah was planned to extend over 10 days, and, for the first time, round-the-clock bombing was to be directed against a single objective. While the Americans hit Hamburg by day, the RAF would punish it by night. By now the number of heavy bombers available to the Americans on a daily basis had risen to more than 300—still less than half of the RAF force, but building steadily.

The night phase of *Gomorrah* hinged on two new devices in Britain's arsenal of electronic gadgets. One device was

Rescue workers pick their way through the smoking ruins of the city of Hamburg, devastated by six major Allied raids in late July and early August of 1943. In addition to taking a death toll of about 50,000 citizens, the 165,000 incendiary and high-explosive bombs dropped on the city sent one million refugees pouring into outlying areas. "Appalling details of the great fires were recounted," wrote a Luftwaffe officer. "In every large town people said, 'What happened to Hamburg yesterday can happen to us tomorrow.' "

known as H2S—a play on the phrase "home sweet home." H2S was a radar-scanning system that gave bomber crews a rough television-like image of the ground below. The device had been tried previously with mixed results; Oboe, the target-finding system used against Essen, had proved more accurate. But Hamburg lay beyond Oboe's 270-mile range. Moreover, the city's location on the Elbe River made H2S particularly suitable because the clear definition between land and water gave a sharper image on the screen.

Bomber Command's other new device, Window, was aimed at fooling the Luftwaffe's defensive radar network. Window was based on a phenomenon first noticed in 1937 by a British research scientist, R. V. Jones. A strip of aluminum foil drifting through the air produces a blip on a radar screen; about 2,000 of them—each a foot long and half an inch wide—produce a blip very similar to that of a British heavy bomber.

The notion was so simple that up until now the British had declined to employ it, fearing that the Luftwaffe would quickly copy it and use it to fool British radar in attacks on England. The Germans had, in fact, developed a Window of their own but had not employed it for the same reason—fear of its use against their own homeland.

Churchill himself made the decision to "open the Window," as he put it, against Hamburg. Several considerations helped persuade him. One was the development in Britain of a new variety of radar that could "see" through the strips, thus rendering Britain's home defenses immune to their possible use by the Germans. Another consideration was the growing effectiveness of Germany's air defenses, which were now employing airborne as well as ground-based radar. Any countering device seemed worth the try.

Bolstered by Window and H2S, the campaign against Hamburg opened on the night of July 24, 1943. Around midnight, the RAF bomber stream began crossing the enemy coast, dropping bundles of aluminum foil—92 million strips in all. The stream was made up of 740 bombers, but on the German radar screens there appeared to be many times that number. To one astonished German radar controller, the British seemed to be "reproducing themselves."

By jamming the Germans' radar sets, Window virtually paralyzed Hamburg's air defenses. Led by H2S-equipped Pathfinders, the British bombed with impunity, dropping a payload of nearly 3,000 tons and losing just 12 planes to the befuddled defenses.

The following day, while the RAF crews were sleeping back at their bases, 68 Flying Fortresses attacked Hamburg's shipyards and submarine-building yards. The next day, 53 Fortresses returned to hit the city's Neuhoff power plant.

About 24 hours of relative quiet followed. But the fires were still burning so brightly when 722 RAF bombers returned on the night of July 27 that they scarcely needed their lead Pathfinders to mark the target. The previous raids had burst water mains and disrupted the well-organized civil defense system of Hamburg, including its fire-fighting capacity. The old fires now merged with new fires ignited by RAF incendiary bombs. As the air heated, it rose and cool air rushed in to take its place. This process, repeated in hundreds of places in Hamburg that night, created furious winds of up to 150 miles per hour, the force of a hurricane or tornado. The result was the War's first fire storm—"a fire typhoon such as was never before witnessed," reported the Hamburg police chief, "against which every human resistance was quite useless."

The fire storm uprooted trees and flung cars into superheated air. Temperatures reached 1,800° F. and the searing winds set the asphalt streets ablaze. They swept across bomb shelters, suffocating those who had sought refuge there, then incinerating their bodies.

The British bombers came again in force on July 29 and again on August 2. Only then could the survivors add up the cost of Hamburg's nine-day ordeal: 10 square miles ravaged, nearly half of the city's buildings destroyed or damaged, an estimated 50,000 dead. The death toll was roughly equal to that suffered by England during all of the German bombing raids of the War. In Germany, Hamburg's ordeal would henceforth be known as Die Katastrophe.

While Hamburg was burning, the Americans were distracting the enemy with missions elsewhere. They penetrated deep into Germany to an aircraft plant only 90 miles from Berlin and flew their longest mission, a 1,900-mile round trip, to demolish harbor installations at the Germans' naval base at Trondheim in occupied Norway.

By "bombing the devils around the clock," the Americans and the British were keeping the enemy defenders from getting any rest.

ANATOMY OF A MISSION

Speeding toward a target in occupied France, U.S. Eighth Air Force bombers and their faraway fighter escorts lace the sky with snow-white vapor trails.

A LONG ORDEAL FOR A BRIEF BOMB RUN

By the winter of 1943-1944, the strategic bombing missions of the U.S. Eighth Air Force were nearing their ultimate form. Tactics, teamwork and equipment had been greatly improved, and the percentage of plane losses was being cut by the potent long-range P-51 Mustang and other fighters equipped with drop tanks that permitted them to escort bombers deep into Germany. Yet for all these hard-won gains, the essential character of a mission had changed very little since the first American aircrews set out to prove that daylight bombing was just as safe as the RAF's night raids, and even more effective.

A mission was still a protracted ordeal. Many airmen spent five to 10 miserable hours jammed into a cramped duty station and weighted down with about 60 pounds of gear. Besides a parachute, they wore steel-reinforced vests to protect them from flak splinters, a bulky flight suit to keep them warm in the frigid upper altitudes, and oxygen masks that felt, said a B-24 copilot, "like a clammy hand clutching the lower part of your face." In this regalia even the simplest tasks required concentrated effort.

Discomfort was accompanied by grinding tedium. Every few minutes the navigator calculated and logged the plane's position. Hour after hour, the radio operator listened to static in his earphones, and the pilot and copilot struggled to hold the plane close—but not too close—to the bombers around it. Interminably, the gunners scanned the skies for Luftwaffe fighters, trying to stay awake and alert.

More than anything else, a mission was hard, complicated work—and not just for the aircrews. For a routine raid, many tens of thousands of men—headquarters planners, operations officers, mechanics and specialized personnel—toiled for hundreds of thousands of man-hours to put several hundred B-17s and B-24s over a German target for about five minutes each. But a successful bomb run made all the travail worthwhile, and an airman could say with satisfaction, as one did after a raid on the port of Emden: "When those Germans start putting those fires out they won't have enough water left to make a good pot of tea."

At the end of an arduous mission over Germany, an exhausted, unshaven bomber pilot completes his official flight report back at home base.

Getting ready for takeoff, the crewmen of a B-24 Liberator bundle up in their flight suits—vital protection against temperatures of 40° below zero at 25,000 feet.

THE MEN ON THE GROUND WHO KEPT THE PLANES IN THE AIR

Contending with Britain's wintertime mud, maintenance men wrestle a replacement tire for a bomber along a narrow boardwalk leading from a storage building.

The order for a mission usually reached the headquarters of the various bomber groups late in the day preceding the raid, and it always set off intense activity along the hardstands—the paved areas in which the planes were parked. A corps of specialists assigned to each squadron hurried to complete any servicing or repairs of the bombers' sheet metal, oxygen equipment, instruments, guns and propellers. But most of the work on each bomber was the responsibility of two or three permanently assigned mechanics. The plane was their pride and joy; they boasted of the number of missions it had flown and suffered—and sometimes wept—when it failed to return.

Toiling all night if need be, the mechanics swarmed over their plane, testing the controls, inspecting the brakes and landing gear, checking tires for burns and rubber-lined fuel tanks for leaks. Most important, they tuned and retuned the plane's four engines, listening intently for any sound of trouble. Replacements of flak-damaged or overtaxed, worn-out engines were common. In one year, the mechanics in the 398th Bomb Group changed 140-odd engines on the squadron's bombers.

Mechanics replace a B-17's four engines. They often salvaged sound parts from discarded engines and used them to rebuild others.

LOADING THE PLANES: A DELICATE BALANCE OF FUEL AND BOMBS

A fueling team fills up a gas-guzzling B-17. Fully loaded, a Fortress burned 400 gallons an hour climbing to cruising altitude, 200 an hour en route to the target.

Cradled in a hoist, a 500-pound bomb swings toward the bomb bay above. Bombs sometimes broke loose and crushed a crewman's feet.

Early on the morning of a mission, fueling teams and ordnance men rolled out to the paved hardstands in their trucks to top off the gas tanks and load the planes with bombs and ammunition. The exact weight of fuel and bombs had been specified by mission planners, whose calculations took into account many factors—the distance to target, the expected wind speed and the planned cruising altitude. Typically, fuel made up more than half the total load. Both the B-17s and the B-24s consumed gas ravenously and required nearly 2,800 gallons, or about nine tons, for a mission deep into Germany.

No matter how carefully the load was apportioned, unforeseeable circumstances might cause emergencies. The allocation of gasoline assumed a return flight without bombs, with the lightened planes getting appreciably better mileage. However, unexpected bad weather sometimes forced the bomber formation to turn back short of the target. In such cases, the mission commander faced a Hobson's choice: to head for his preselected alternate target, choose a target of opportunity or simply order his pilots to jettison their bombs. A few German towns devoid of military targets were hit by bombers forced to drop their payloads out of self-preservation.

At the "time-tick" in the briefing room, airmen synchronize their watches to the official time announced by an operations officer.

In an orderly procession, B-24 Liberators taxi down the runway—"just like a gaggle of geese going to a pond," remarked one navigator.

P-47s on escort duty pass over a base whose bombers have left one B-17 behind. The speedy fighters gave the bombers a head start.

OUT OF THE BRIEFING ROOM AND INTO THE SKY

Early on mission day, usually before daybreak, runners roused the aircrews. The airmen dressed quickly, downed as much breakfast as their jittery stomachs could take and headed for the briefing room. When all the airmen were present or accounted for, the operations officers locked the doors and drew open the curtains that concealed the mission map and the length of yarn that stretched across its surface from England to the target in Germany.

In careful detail, the officers described the weather outlook, the target, the proper approach to it, the kind of flak and fighter opposition to expect. Reports of stiff German defenses were often greeted by whistles, groans, nervous laughter and wisecracks. The ritual of synchronizing watches brought the session to a close. Navigators usually had a special briefing afterward.

Then the men climbed into their planes with all their gear. Pilots and copilots ran through the long preflight check list. The bombers got into line on the taxiways and then, 30 seconds apart, thundered down the runways and struggled into the air. When every plane was in position, and squadrons, groups and wings had joined forces, the formation headed for its rendezvous with the fighter escorts.

PUTTING THE PAYLOAD ON THE TARGET

Flying in the standard combat-box formation, Flying Fortresses of the 401st Bomb Group wing their way above the clouds toward a target in western Germany.

On most missions, the bomber formation managed to meet its fighter escorts over France with clockwork precision. But many of the fighters reached the outer limits of their operating range and dropped out as the bombers were crossing the border into Germany; then only the long-range fighters were left to protect the formation from Luftwaffe Messerschmitts and Focke-Wulfs that rose to pick off their lumbering prey.

As the bombers approached the ground defenses around the target area, the enemy fighters would veer away to give a clear field of fire to the antiaircraft batteries. Amid bursting flak, the formation wheeled around the IP (the initial point in the bomb run). The pilot of the lead plane turned on the automatic pilot, which controlled the attitude and direction of the plane.

After opening the bomb bays, the bombardier made minor level corrections by turning two knobs on his Norden bombsight, one controlling lateral movement, the other regulating attitude. The bombsight was connected with the autopilot; hence, during the bomb run the bombardier flew the plane. The bombs were released automatically at a preset interval. This was the cue for bombardiers in the other planes to release their bombs. The pilots then resumed control. The formations flew to a prearranged rally point, then turned for home.

B-24s drop their high-explosive payload on German installations. A large formation could release up to 100 tons of bombs a minute.

Waiting for the bombers' return, ground crewmen and a fire fighter wearing an asbestos suit stand beside a fire truck, prepared to spring into action in case of a crash landing.

A tight formation of bombers usually loosened up as returning pilots sighted the English Channel. Everyone was edgy, weary, eager to land. The Channel was, declared one airman, "the shortest stretch of water in the world when you're going out —the longest when you're coming back!"

As the planes approached their bases, crews aboard bombers carrying wounded men shot off red flares, signaling that they must land first, and ambulances—"meat wagons"—rushed out to greet them. After medics removed the wounded, the rest of the crew members piled out. Invariably, some men celebrated their safe return: a few would run their fingers through the grass or kiss the ground, and those who had just finished their last mission before being rotated cheered and jumped for joy. Then, as the airmen tramped off to their debriefing session, the sheet-metal workers started to measure the damaged aircraft for patches, and an engineering officer made a count of the bombers that were still combatworthy.

Signaling from a jeep and the checkered trailer of their mobile control station, air-traffic controllers direct bombers to a safe landing.

THE HOMECOMING: EXULTATION AND MOURNING

*Wounded in the leg by flak, a pilot is helped
from his bomber by medics at base. His
crew gave him first aid en route from Germany.*

A pilot demonstrates an attacking fighter's maneuvers for two interrogation officers (right). His crew, waiting at the rear for their turn to report, were free to add details to his account.

Gathering in the debriefing rooms for interrogation after a mission, crews milled about, smoked and consumed hot chocolate, gray coffee and Spam sandwiches. They were also offered a shot of whiskey to help them unwind. If the mission had been an easy one, the airmen's talk was loud and animated. After a "rugged deal," they barely talked at all; everyone glanced about furtively to see who had made it back and listened for the sound of crippled bombers limping home.

Intelligence officers interrogated every aircrew as a group. Each man in turn reported the mission as he had seen it from his post. The interrogators reconciled discrepancies and ran through a check list of questions, probing for information about the enemy's response. Did the Luftwaffe employ any new tactic or send up fighters with an unfamiliar unit insignia? Was the flak heavier or lighter than expected?

After interrogation, the intelligence officers rushed their Flash Report—the raw facts of the raid in tabulated form—to the headquarters staff for analysis. Later, when aerial photos of the strike had been developed, they were taken by small plane to be air-dropped at headquarters. The headquarters staff began at once to study the results, looking for clues uncovered in this mission to help in planning the next one.

Safely back at the base, a pilot and copilot stand on a wing of their Flying Fortress and survey the heavy

damage it suffered during a costly raid on an aircraft assembly plant near Brunswick, Germany, in January of 1944. Sixty bombers did not return from the run.

INNUMERABLE WAYS TO DIE IN A PLANE

Every combat airman flew in the face of constant danger, knowing all too well that he might not come back from his next mission. The most obvious perils—food for troubled thought in the agonizing waits between sorties—were enemy fighter planes and antiaircraft fire. But fliers were killed in innumerable other ways. They died in crashes caused by fog and unexpected storms, by errors in judgment or just plain carelessness, and by "gremlins"—inexplicable mechanical bugs, such as clogged fuel lines and malfunctioning controls, which kept cropping up in spite of meticulous maintenance. On one occasion, the wind played a part in an American disaster. During a B-17 raid on Merseburg in November 1944, steady head winds slowed the bombers and helped German gunners shoot down or cripple 56 Flying Fortresses.

Another hazard was purely psychological. As Allied airmen watched their friends perish, they grew ever more anxious about their own chances of surviving the 25 or more missions needed to become eligible for relief from combat duty. In the second half of 1943 almost a third of U.S. bomber crew members failed to complete their quota of missions. The mounting strain on the survivors' nerves impaired their efficiency, contributing to still more casualties.

The life expectancy of German fliers was even shakier. Because the Luftwaffe never adopted a rotation policy, veteran pilots and crewmen had to serve until they were killed or incapacitated by wounds or combat fatigue. Superstitious Germans and Allies alike felt that their luck would run out at some preordained moment, no matter what they did—a notion that undoubtedly led some fliers to get themselves killed in reckless stunts or pointless heroics.

There was a ready antidote to the fliers' forebodings: the knowledge that many airmen survived mishaps that should have proved fatal. American gunner James Raley plummeted 19,000 feet in the severed tail section of his B-17 and landed safely in a tree. Perhaps most encouraging was the charmed life of Luftwaffe ace Georg Peter Eder. He was shot down 17 times but kept flying until the end of the War.

Allied airmen, all of them survivors of crash landings in France, wait at an emergency airstrip for a plane ride back to their bases in England.

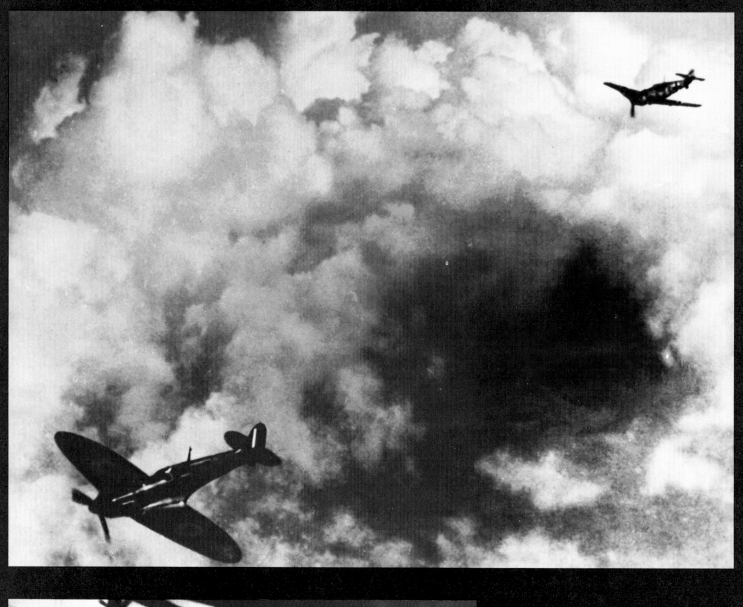

DEADLY DUELS ALOFT

"One of the most unnerving things I have ever witnessed was a group of B-24s being annihilated by German fighters," wrote American copilot Jim Fletcher. "They were way out ahead of us and we could see bombers being picked off. Every so often one would get hit and explode. Seeing it like that had far more impact; you had time to think what might soon be happening to you."

Dizzyingly swift and agile, the enemy fighter planes made many bomber crewmen feel as helpless as swimmers pursued by sharks. British navigator William Anderson, whose bomber was the target of a Luftwaffe fighter over the Ruhr Valley in 1942, later acknowledged, "Then I knew fear. Somewhere outside there was someone crouching behind guns circling round to come in again and kill me. . . . In that brief moment when I watched a pattern of holes appearing in the fuselage beside me I discovered that I was a coward, hopelessly and horribly afraid of fighters."

Furthermore, said Anderson, fighter pilots used "a lot of nasty tricks. A very old one was to turn on their lights. Then, while the bomber crew was watching, another fighter would sneak quietly in from the other side." Anderson also reported that the fighters "liked to sneak up from below and take the bombers' belly with cannon shells." As the shells pierced a bomber's skin they could gouge out holes big enough for a man to fall through.

U.S. pilot Charles W. Paine cited other deadly fighter tactics. "When they peeled off to attack they came in so close together that by the time one ship had shot us up and banked away, the next in line had his lights on us." A second maneuver, said Paine, was to pretend to concentrate on one of the other ships "and then at a ninety-degree turn swing around and let us of us." Paine, too, came under direct fire from Luftwaffe fighters, and he was hard put to describe the harrowing experience. "It was," he said, "like driving the belly of a child's wagon . . . that was being rolled down a steep hill."

Trailing smoke from a damaged engine, a B-24 flies through flak over Vienna. The plane, on a mission in October 1944, managed to get back to its base in Italy.

THE GAUNTLET
OF ENEMY FLAK

Some of the airmen were fascinated by antiaircraft attacks. "Light flak is a pretty sight," recalled British pilot Guy Gibson, "chasing towards you—green, white, red

—rather like a waterfall upside down. But if they hit you, there is a rending of metal and then the tinkling crash of smaller pieces. Larger shells of heavy flak detonate in a predetermined area," continued Gibson, who called them "fat, black, harmless-looking puffs." But he added,

wasn't kidding myself. More than once I've seen a single burst of flak with its throbbing orange heart suddenly explode with a vicious crash right in the midst of the ... formation, and then no more plane—nothing but a few small pieces. And sometimes planes came back with more than fifty flak holes.

A B-26 Marauder, taking its death plunge, loses an engine from a flaming wing. Minutes later, it crashed.

Nearly disintegrated by a German fighter's fire, the wreckage of a B-24 Liberator plunges toward the earth in northern Germany.

CASUALTIES CLAIMED BY CARELESSNESS

One of the problems of formation flying, U.S. General Curtis E. LeMay wrote, "was that a whole bunch of lunkhead wouldn't be on the ball, and we would have mid-air collisions." Unfortunately, mid-air collisions were only one variety of aerial disaster caused by negligence or by simple mistakes that should have been avoided. All too frequently, fighter pilots and gunners on bombers shot down planes in their own formation. Pilots who neglected to check their instruments or to follow instructions from ground control splattered themselves and their planes all across the landscape. And airmen on both sides of the conflict miscalculated their positions or mistook landmarks with calamitous consequences: they strafed or bombed their own troops.

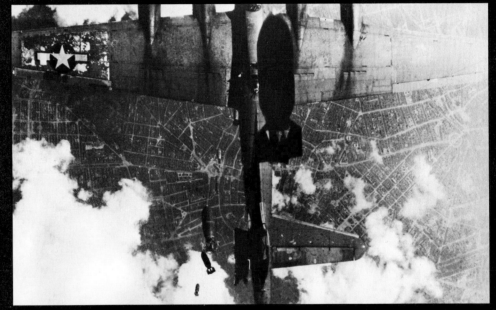

To prevent such blunders, American bomber crews were expected to concentrate at all times on standard routine procedures in the air. Standard routine, the flight instructors repeated, was the only way to get you there and back. If you learned to follow orders, to do what others, ordered, and to do them well, you had a good chance of coming home. Quick thinking individualists didn't last long in the bomber business.

The standard routine also caused a lifetime of nightmares and damage to the minds of many men. As the air war grew in intensity throughout the years 1943 and 1944, with each offense and every mission, by the end of the war, thousands of bomber boys were dead.

...ten expensive aircraft will never fly again

...with their ten expensive crews who took so long to train

Damaged by German antiaircraft fire, a P-38 crash-lands in France. Some pilots managed to nurse crippled planes back to bases several hundred miles away.

TAKING OFF OVERLOADED, COMING IN ON A PRAYER

The first and last minutes of a bomber's mission were frequently the most dangerous times of all. B-17s roared down the runway laden with gasoline and bombs that often weighed thousands of pounds more than the plane was designed to carry, and the engines had to labor at maximum power to get an overburdened plane aloft

before it ran out of runway. "Even in broad daylight with perfect weather," wrote an American squadron leader, "I would be nervous with this load."

Returning home without any bombs, the crewmen had a different set of dangers to worry about. One was their dwindling fuel supply: more than a few pilots ran out of gas and were forced to ditch in the sea or improvise a dead-stick landing in some farmer's field. Or the airmen might have to face the life-or-death challenge of landing

a badly damaged plane. When pilot Everett Blakely's flak-ravaged Fortress touched down on a British airfield, the brakes failed and the plane could not be steered. "At 100 mph we plowed down that vacant airport toward a huge tree," Blakely said later. "And no power on earth could stop us. The tree crashed us between No. 2 engine and the pilot's compartment. That was lucky because another three inches to the right and it would have crushed the pilot and co-pilot."

A B-24 stands on its nose, catapulted into this grotesque position by inadvertent braking during takeoff. Six crew members were killed in the accident.

A wrecked RAF fighter is carried away to a metal collection dump in Germany. It was one of the 33,770 aircraft lost by Britain and the United States in Europe.

4

Hitler's reaction to the catastrophe at Hamburg disturbed even his most devoted lieutenants. Though they were aware of his aversion to viewing the results of Allied air raids—he always ordered the shades drawn when his train passed through bombed-out areas—they felt that the special ferocity of the attack on Hamburg had earned its people the right to a personal visit by the Führer. But repeated pleas from the city's gauleiter for such a visit went unheeded. So did his request that Hitler at least receive and commend some of the harried rescue crews.

Minister of Armaments Albert Speer fared no better when he decided to warn Hitler of the ominous implications of the Hamburg attack. The scale of the devastation, Speer later admitted, "put the fear of God in me." On August 1, 1943, while Hamburg was still under siege, he managed a meeting with the Führer and bluntly predicted that a series of such attacks on six more major cities would bring Germany's war production to a total halt. Hitler waved the warning aside. "You'll straighten all that out again," he said.

Luftwaffe chief Göring did not share Hitler's detached attitude toward the catastrophe, though his initial response was typically insensitive: instead of visiting Hamburg himself, he sent the gauleiter a telegram expressing routine condolences to the people of the city. Prudently, the gauleiter decided not to publish the text of the message, and even a high-ranking Luftwaffe officer later admitted that it "would have created a riot."

Göring's second reaction to the catastrophe was more constructive. As the man ultimately responsible for Germany's air-defense system, he could scarcely deceive himself about its failure at Hamburg. The city's ordeal was still going on when he called an urgent conference of the Luftwaffe's high command to consider ways of ensuring that no such humiliation would ever recur.

The meeting took place at the so-called Wolf's Lair at Rastenburg in East Prussia—the fortress-like headquarters, deep in a pine forest, from which Hitler was supervising Germany's latest military moves. Göring's decision to convene his staff at Rastenburg struck them as a hopeful sign in itself. For months, the Reich Marshal had been sitting out the war at his palatial retreat near Berlin, growing ever fatter and indulging once again in his old addiction to morphine and its derivatives. He had passed much of his time admir-

THE LUFTWAFFE FIGHTS BACK

ing the Rembrandts and Goyas he had plundered from occupied Europe or playing with his jewel collection—"like a little boy with his marbles," one visitor reported.

But the Hamburg debacle roused Göring from his torpor, and at Rastenburg he displayed flashes of the same vigor and spirit that had marked his build-up of the Luftwaffe in the 1930s. No longer inclined to denounce reports of its failings as craven lies, he was now ready to accept a realistic appraisal by the men who knew the Luftwaffe best: what had once been the world's most powerful and up-to-date air force was lagging behind its Allied counterparts in new technology. Moreover, it was being stretched dangerously thin—not only by Hitler's strategy of involvement on many fronts but also by the necessity of defending Germany itself against round-the-clock bombing attacks.

To remedy the situation, strong measures would have to be taken. Fighter production would have to be boosted to more than 1,000 a month—twice the previous year's rate. The defense of the homeland would have to be given top priority. This, in turn, would require diverting planes and seasoned pilots from the support of ground units fighting on the Russian and Mediterranean fronts. Göring's deputy, Field Marshal Erhard Milch, put it baldly: "The soldier on the battlefield will just have to dig a hole, crawl into it and wait until the attack is over. What the home front is suffering now cannot be suffered very much longer."

Lieut. General Adolf Galland, who as chief of the fighter arm of the Luftwaffe had been pressing for such action for months, was cheered by the atmosphere of unity at the conference. He was one of the few men present with a firsthand knowledge of modern aerial combat; a fighter pilot during the Battle of Britain in 1940 and 1941, he had scored 94 kills and won acclaim as one of Germany's boldest aces. In his more recent role as an administrator, he had come to detest the maneuvering that usually went on at high-level meetings, and he was relieved by its absence at Rastenburg. "It was as though under the impact of the Hamburg catastrophe everyone had put aside either personal or departmental ambitions," Galland recalled later.

When the sessions ended, Göring declared that all that remained for him to do was to go to the Führer's bunker and get approval of the measures the Luftwaffe proposed. He returned looking shattered; without a word, he walked past his waiting staff into his office. After a while Galland and another officer were told to go in. They found Göring with his head buried in his arms, mumbling incoherently.

"We stood there for some time in embarrassment." Galland remembered. "At last Göring pulled himself together and said we were witnessing his deepest moments of despair. The Führer had lost faith in him. All the suggestions from which he had expected a radical change in the situation of the war in the air had been rejected. The Führer had announced that the Luftwaffe had disappointed him too often. A changeover from offensive to defensive in the air against the west was out of the question. He would give the Luftwaffe a last chance to rehabilitate itself. This could be done by a resumption of air attacks against England, but this time on a bigger scale. Now as before, the motto was still: Attack. Terror could only be smashed by counterterror."

Up against what Galland called "an invincible barrier—the Führer's orders," the Luftwaffe set about complying with Hitler's demand for a renewed assault on England. But the task of assembling the bomber force of new Junkers-188s and Heinkel-177s would take months, and meanwhile the immediate threat of more Allied raids had to be faced. Barred from making the changes they had urged at Rastenburg, the Luftwaffe's leaders had to rely on their existing air-defense setup. But they were under no restraints against improving and refining the fighters' tactics and trying some new combat tricks, and on this they rested their hopes.

By mid-August, within three weeks of Hitler's rebuff of Göring, three massive U.S. raids on targets crucial to the German war machine gave the Luftwaffe's leaders reason to believe that they might stem the Allied air tide. The first raid took place on August 1, the day Speer warned Hitler that continuing Allied attacks could halt the Reich's war production. The Americans' choice of a target was the oil fields of Ploesti, in Germany's satellite, Rumania. Ploesti was, in Churchill's phrase, "the taproot of German might." From its refineries flowed a third of the Reich's petroleum needs.

Ploesti, located in the southeastern corner of Rumania, was too far to reach from England. Instead, the mission was launched from bases across the Mediterranean in Libya. Two groups of Liberators from the U.S. Ninth Air Force, which had received its baptism of fire while helping the RAF beat back Rommel's Afrika Korps in 1942, joined with three groups on loan from the Eighth Air Force to deal what was expected to be a decisive blow at Hitler's oil supply.

The plan called for the bombers to fly in radio silence and—in order to elude the enemy's radar—at minimum altitude. Since the German ground defenses were concentrated south of the oil fields, the planes were to cross Rumania to a point northwest of Ploesti, veer back to the target, drop their bombs and then return to North Africa. But just about everything went wrong for the raiders. The Luftwaffe's early-warning network destroyed the essential element of surprise by intercepting the routine American radio transmissions at the time of the planes' takeoff. Over Rumania, the command bomber of the first group turned too soon, misleading another group, and both groups approached Ploesti from the heavily defended south.

Thanks to their early-warning network, the defenders were ready and waiting. Flying in at virtually treetop level, the Americans ran into a solid wall of flak. The antiaircraft crews were able to zero in on them simply by visual sighting. German gunners fired from hidden positions in haystacks, church steeples and even a gun-mounted train that pursued the bombers by rail. German interceptors pounced from above, braving their own flak. Then, as the attackers turned for home, the interceptors overtook them, hanging on "like snails on a log," according to one account.

Of the 177 Liberators on the mission, 53 were shot down; 55 returned to Libya so badly damaged that many were fit only for salvage. Nor did the raid seriously impair Ploesti's oil production. Though an estimated 40 per cent of its capacity was knocked out, Ploesti had sufficient reserve facilities to keep pouring out its monthly quotas for the Luftwaffe and other sectors of the German military.

On August 17, the Americans turned their attention back to Germany itself, and to two targets whose destruction would have crippled the enemy's war effort almost as effectively as a shortage of oil. The first objective was Regensburg, where a Messerschmitt plant was turning out nearly 30 per cent of the Luftwaffe's single-engined fighters. The second objective was Schweinfurt, site of factories that accounted for half of Germany's production of ball bearings; the tiny steel balls, essential to keeping precision machinery free of fric-

tion, were required by the Luftwaffe alone in quantities of several thousand per plane.

Regensburg and Schweinfurt represented the Americans' biggest challenge thus far. Both cities lay deep in southeastern Germany, farther from the U.S. bases in England than any Eighth Air Force planes had yet penetrated. The range of their fighter protection—British Spitfires and American Thunderbolts—extended only as far as Aachen, just inside Germany's border with Belgium and Holland. The attacking bombers would have to go it alone the rest of the way, across vast stretches of hostile and unfamiliar air space.

For the Luftwaffe, the Americans' double strike provided a major test of its new resolve. Alerted by long-range Freya radar, its first interceptors were aloft a few minutes after 146 Flying Fortresses, bound for Regensburg, began to cross the English coast at 9:35 a.m. The German fighters—the vanguard of 300 that were to defend the homeland that day—bided their time while the armada crossed Holland and headed for the German border. As the last of the enemy escorts peeled off and turned back, the Germans moved in. Long before Regensburg, a furious battle was on.

Never before had the U.S. bombers faced such an array of aerial firepower—cannon and machine-gun shells, mortar rockets, even bombs. Single-engined Focke-Wulf 190s and Messerschmitt-109s blazed away with 30mm heavy cannon that fired at the rate of 10 rounds per second. Me-110s—the slower, twin-engined aircraft normally used only at night—cruised just beyond the range of the Fortress gunners and lobbed time-fused rockets. These missiles, adapted from the Germans' infantry mortar, were fired from as many as four tubes slung under the wings of the fighters. They were four feet long, weighed 248 pounds and exploded with the power of a small artillery shell. Meanwhile, other German fighters flew above the Forts to give them a dose of their own medicine: 500-pound bombs, carried under the fuselage, fused to explode in the middle of a bomber formation.

The Germans' game was to break up the bomber formations, each consisting of three tiers of tightly stacked combat boxes of as many as 21 bombers per box. Along with the unprecedented firepower, the Me-109s and FW-190s unveiled new tactical twists and refinements the Americans had never encountered in previous raids on Germany. Some innovations had been tested in mock battles with Forts that had crash-landed in occupied Europe; the Germans had patched up the bombers to make them airworthy again and then turned them over to a special training unit called the Traveling Circus. The Circus toured the Luftwaffe's interceptor bases, allowing fighter pilots to practice maneuvers against the Forts and even to fly them. More than once the Germans had infiltrated a few of the patched-up planes into U.S. bomber formations to determine their speed and course and even to open fire on the unsuspecting crewmen.

The Americans bound for Regensburg found that the adversary had honed his skills well. Many of the fighter attacks came en masse, with six or so interceptors boring in wing to wing on a combat box. Other fighters sped along parallel with the bombers, then raced ahead and turned to meet them—queuing up "like a bread line," one U.S. navigator said. Still other fighters concentrated on the so-called coffin corner of each bomber formation—the corner occupied by the combat box that was stacked below and slightly behind the other two boxes in the three-tier formation. The Germans quickly broke up the coffin corner occupied by the U.S. 100th Bomb Group, then set upon the stragglers, as one account put it, "like wolves on wounded deer."

It took the U.S. bombers 90 minutes to cover the 300 miles from the German border to Regensburg, and they were hounded all the way. From interceptor bases that lined the attack corridor on either side, the Luftwaffe's fighters rose in relays. When one unit exhausted its fuel and ammunition, it landed and a fresh unit from the next base took off.

The carnage suffered by the raiders would have been even worse but for a move the Germans had not anticipated. After the badly mauled formations dropped their bombs on the Messerschmitt factory, they turned south across the Alps on a preplanned route to U.S. bases in Algeria. This enabled the Americans to elude the refueled and rearmed Luftwaffe fighters awaiting the bombers' return along the expected route to England.

The second phase of the U.S. mission that day, the attack on Schweinfurt, was to have started only 10 minutes after the first wave of bombers left for Regensburg—a plan designed to overtax and confuse the Luftwaffe. But a sudden heavy fog that descended on England delayed the takeoff for Schweinfurt by more than three hours.

When the 230 Fortresses of the second armada reached the German border, the full fury of some 300 Luftwaffe fighters was again unleashed. This time the Germans were able to hammer at the Americans not only all the way to the target but back to the border, pulling off only after the Thunderbolt escorts came to the aid of the Forts.

During the battle, an Me-109 ace named Hans Langer slipped up from below and joined a box of Fortresses, flying along between two bombers so closely that he could see the startled faces of the American waist gunners on either side of him. Neither gunner fired, for fear of hitting the other Fort. Langer, who just weeks before had been decorated by Hitler himself for shooting down 45 Allied planes, opened fire on the Fort directly ahead of him. The wing exploded and the crippled bomber flipped over and collided with another Fort. The impact flung Langer's own plane out of the formation, but he managed to land safely.

Despite the punishment they took, both the Regensburg and Schweinfurt raiders managed to inflict substantial damage on their targets. At Regensburg, every important building of the Messerschmitt complex was hit by incendiary or high-explosive bombs. At Schweinfurt, the production of

Luftwaffe chief Hermann Göring (center) adds to the smiles in an informal portrait of the Luftwaffe staff at an unidentified country retreat. But beneath the apparent camaraderie lay constant dissension and intrigue that led General Staff chief Hans Jeschonnek (fourth from right) to commit suicide in August 1943.

ball bearings plummeted by 38 per cent. But the price exacted by the Luftwaffe made many of the Americans wonder whether the bombing results were worth it. Against German losses of 25 fighters, 60 of the U.S. bombers were shot down and 47 others were so badly damaged that they had to be scrapped. For the total of 376 Fortresses sent into action that day, the loss rate was more than 15 per cent. One alarmed American noted that a week of such operations would wipe out the Eighth Air Force.

For the RAF's night missions, the Luftwaffe had other innovations in store. One stemmed from the Hamburg experience. The Germans now knew that they could no longer trust radar to help them find incoming enemy bombers in the dark; the RAF's dropping of Window—the strips of metal foil that appeared on radar screens as blips—had thoroughly confused the ground controllers and sent the Luftwaffe's fighters off on fruitless sweeps through their stations along the Kammhuber Line on Germany's western approaches. To eliminate this waste of time and effort, the Germans decided on a new defensive plan that posed a high risk, but seemed worth the gamble. The plan called for circumventing Window by waiting until an attack on a city was already under way—at which point an alert by area ground control would send the pilots speeding directly there. In the glare of searchlights—and burning buildings—they would have no trouble spotting and engaging the enemy. Moreover, the illumination would allow the Luftwaffe to use day fighters as well as night interceptors.

The new plan required a special sort of airman—one who would rely on his own judgment, ingenuity and daring rather than on conventional ideas of combat. To find such men the Luftwaffe's high command turned to 30-year-old Major Hans-Joachim "Hajo" Herrmann, a veteran of 300 bombing missions against England and Malta. Herrmann was famous in the Luftwaffe as a tireless promoter of inventive ideas; one of his more imaginative proposals had envisioned an aerial attack on the United States by huge flying boats that would take on fuel and bombs from U-boats stationed off America's East Coast. Herrmann's latest concept called for putting together a special group of Luftwaffe fighter pilots who would, in effect, act as freelancers in battling the British. Herrmann code-named his group *Wilde*

Sau—Wild Boars. One Luftwaffe general characterized the men as "a motley collection, loosely organized and rather like guerrilla bands in their attitude to authority."

About a dozen Wild Boars, flying FW-190s and Me-109s, had been sent into action as an experiment during an RAF raid on Cologne in late July, with some success. The experiment was expanded on the night of August 17. Hours after the last American planes had landed in England from the afternoon's raid on Schweinfurt, the British were poised for an attack of their own. The RAF's target that night was Peenemünde, site of a top-secret German research station on a small island in the Baltic Sea. The veil over activities there had been pierced by British intelligence agents. At Peenemünde, Hitler's scientists were perfecting and test-firing two pilotless projectiles—"vengeance weapons" that the Führer planned to unleash against England in the wake of the renewed bomber assault: the V-1, a jet-powered flying bomb, and the V-2, a liquid-fueled rocket.

Thanks to an intercepted RAF radio message, the German night-fighter chief, General Kammhuber, knew that the British were coming that night, though not where. From his headquarters in Holland, he put on alert the largest force of night fighters yet assembled—more than 200 pilots, including many who had flown against the Americans earlier that day and who were exhausted but exhilarated. Among them were 55 Wild Boars, primed to put their own tactics to use.

The British, too, had a trick up their sleeve. To divert the Germans from the real target, eight Mosquito bombers flew to Berlin and dropped flares that ordinarily would have signaled a major attack. In the meantime, at night-fighter headquarters in Holland, communications cables connecting General Kammhuber with the rest of his ground-control network inexplicably went out of commission—possibly the work of two British undercover agents.

Kammhuber was cut off from the battle, and his ground controllers, fooled by the decoy raid on Berlin, dispatched the German fighters to the capital. When they roared in, the ground units manning the antiaircraft batteries assumed that the main force of RAF bombers had arrived. They opened up, firing some 11,000 rounds at their own planes.

As the outraged German pilots dodged the flak, some of them spotted the yellow glow of target-marking bombs over Peenemünde, 100 miles to the north. They radioed the

A low-flying B-24 Liberator skims a cluster of towering smokestacks during an attack in August of 1943 on Astra Romana, the largest of 11 refineries operated by the Germans in Rumania's Ploesti oil fields. Even though Astra Romana's main facilities were heavily damaged and two nearby refineries were knocked out, the results were disappointing. Astra Romana possessed an enormous reserve capacity, and the refinery soon outstripped its preraid production by approximately 33 per cent.

Berlin ground controller, asking permission to go on to Peenemünde; unaware of the target's top-secret importance, he ordered them to remain over the capital. As the planes continued to circle, they began to run out of fuel—the single-engined planes of the Boars had virtually none left—and landing became imperative. At one field, about 100 fighters came down almost simultaneously; in the resulting jam, 30 crashed, so littering the runways that take-offs were impossible.

But some of the more experienced pilots who had re-fueled at other fields ignored the ground controller's orders and sped north. Not all of them were Herrmann's Wild Boars, but all were now following the basic Wild Boar dictum that authority was to be flouted when circumstances warranted. In all, 30 fighters got to Peenemünde in time to intercept the final wave of the 597 RAF planes on the mission. They bagged 29 of the 40 bombers lost by the British—a hint of what they might have achieved with an earlier start. But the British dropped a total of 2,000 tons of bombs, killing several of Germany's leading scientists and setting back the V-1 and V-2 programs by four to six weeks.

The Wild Boars got another chance at the foe less than a week later, on the night of the 23rd of August. This time Berlin was the RAF's true target, and the Luftwaffe's ground controllers were not fooled. Nearly an hour before the 727 British bombers reached the capital, German fighters were

133

heading for the city from bases throughout Western Europe.

The Berlin sky was lighted up like a stage. Along with the usual searchlights, Herrmann had arranged for extra lighting effects—incandescent rockets sent up by the gun batteries. Combined with the glare of the British target-marking flares, the illumination supplied by the Germans turned night into day. Berliners scurrying for shelter found the spectacle bizarre. They had gone through three years of strict blackouts during which it had been a punishable offense even to light a cigarette in the open. Now it was possible to read in the street. From their vantage points high in the sky, the Luftwaffe fighter pilots could look down and see the silhouettes of the RAF bombers moving across the illuminated clouds "like flies on a tablecloth," as Field Marshal Milch jubilantly described it. Between them, the fighters and the ground batteries downed 56 of the raiders. An additional 67 RAF planes fell to the newly confident night defenses when Bomber Command returned to Berlin in force twice more within a fortnight.

Göring was so pleased that he promoted Hajo Herrmann to lieutenant colonel and ordered him to triple the strength of the Wild Boar units. Herrmann had no trouble recruiting. His units quickly attracted scores of free-spirited airmen, among them a number of fliers with black marks on their records who hoped to redeem themselves.

The Luftwaffe's new successes, trumpeted by the German press and radio, served as a national tonic. Popular morale had remained remarkably steady in spite of the earlier Allied onslaughts; now it stiffened even more. The embattled Berliners gave full play to the sarcastic humor for which they had long been noted. One wag tacked a sign on a gutted warehouse announcing that it was now "open day and night." Watching the piles of bomb rubble grow more and more mountainous, people told one another: "A Third World War and Berlin's in the Alps!" Instead of saying the usual goodbyes, friends parted with the wry admonition to make sure "you're left over"—from the next Allied raid.

Any feelings of despondency beneath the humor were kept private. "The Nazi regime was not prepared to tolerate any depression," wrote Hans Rumpf, who, as the wartime inspector general of fire prevention, was in a special position to assess civilian reactions to the Allied bombings. Fear of being punished for defeatist talk was, in fact, one of several reasons for the Germans' impressive display of backbone. Rumpf cited additional reasons. Some people, he noted, simply became too numbed emotionally to feel any fright at the bombings. In others, a deep-seated urge to "live dangerously" came to the fore. Still others took refuge in religion, accepting their sufferings as "acts of God."

By and large, however, people just adapted to the ordeal—as they would have done to recurrent earthquakes or floods—and went on as best they could. Many Germans, indeed, resisted efforts to evacuate them from their devastated cities, or found ways to return. Less than a year after the catastrophe at Hamburg, when four fifths of the city still lay in ruins, 900,000 citizens—almost two thirds of the normal population—were back there again.

Germany's war production proved to be as resilient as the people. The bombs that destroyed the structure of a factory did not necessarily wreck all of its machines and machine tools, and assembly lines could operate without benefit of a roof overhead. Moreover, Germany had an asset of incalculable value in a conscript force of some six million laborers who could be moved at will—sometimes by the hundreds of thousands—to speed the repair of damaged installations. This immense reservoir of manpower, composed largely of prisoners of war and workers forcibly recruited in occupied lands, made it possible for German industrialists to rack up a startling record for 1943. Throughout the year, despite the enemy's intensified air offensive, German factories—unlike their Allied counterparts—remained on a single daily shift and had no need to hire women.

In a curious way, the Allied bombings gave the Reich's industrialists a new sense of freedom, a release from hectoring by the Nazis' economic bureaucrats and from the reams of paper work they ordinarily demanded. Preoccupied by having to wage war at home as well as abroad, the regime loosened some of its hold on the industrial sector, leaving the practical-minded men who ran it more and more to their own devices—and to their skills at improvising. In this they had the full blessing of one of the few men around Hitler who took a long and objective view of Germany's situation: Minister of Armaments Speer.

With Speer's approval, priorities for critical raw materials and essential machine parts were quickly reassigned, when necessary, from one plant to another. Factories were dispersed; some were relocated in Germany's satellite countries to the southeast; new factories were built underground to produce airplane engines. Despite Hitler's disenchantment with the Luftwaffe's fighter arm, the monthly output of fighter planes rose from less than 700 in December of 1943 to a new high of more than 2,000 by April of 1944.

Aside from their own stepped-up efforts, the Germans profited from a mistake in Allied strategy, as later attested by Speer. His country's war machine would have come apart much earlier, he reported, had the Allies been more persistent in their attacks on key targets. He cited Schweinfurt as a case in point. By failing to follow up immediately on the raid of August 17, 1943, the Americans provided the Germans with a vital breather. While the factories at Schweinfurt were being repaired, the gap in the production of ball bearings was filled by other factories in Germany as well as in Switzerland and Sweden, and the simpler slide bearings were also used as a substitute.

The Americans did not return to Schweinfurt for almost two months. In the interim, the Eighth Air Force had largely confined its missions to targets in France, the Low Countries and Germany's western fringes. These targets were near enough so that the bombers could receive fighter protection all the way there and back to England. But Schweinfurt was still uppermost in the minds of the U.S. strategists, and on the morning of October 14 they sent the bombers back there for a second showdown.

There were 291 Flying Fortresses in the armada—61 more than on the first raid. But the Germans, too, were better prepared. Some 300 newly installed antiaircraft batteries of 88mm guns stood ready around Schweinfurt. Along the air corridor from Aachen east to the target, more than 300 interceptors waited. Each pilot was under Göring's orders to fly at least three separate sorties against the Americans, landing and refueling between one and the next.

Added to the Me-109s, Me-110s, FW-190s and Ju-88s that the Luftwaffe had used in the earlier raid, there were speedy new twin-engined Me-410s, Stuka dive bombers, and even four-engined bombers—H-177s and FW-200s—which flew just out of the firing range of the Americans to report on the progress of the battle. It seemed, said one Fortress crewman, that "the whole goddamned Luftwaffe is out today."

Once again, the U.S. bombers had to fly through a seemingly unceasing hail of machine-gun fire, cannon shells and rockets. The intensity of the onslaught was later measured in the reports of American crewmen who survived: in a single minute, they counted at least 40 attacks by the German fighters on just three of the bomber groups.

Colonel Budd Peaslee, one of the American commanders on the mission, later described the feeling of utter helplessness that overcame the bomber crews as their cumbersome craft seemed to crawl across the skies toward Schweinfurt: "I think of the Middle Ages. I see myself strolling across an open plain with a group of friends. Suddenly we are beset by many scoundrels on horseback. They come from every direction, shooting their arrows. We defend ourselves as best we can with slings and swords, and crouch behind our leather shields. We cannot run, we cannot dodge, we cannot hide—the plain has no growth, no rocks, no holes. And it seems endless. There is no way out—then, or now."

The battle went on for more than three hours and was to be one of the most savage aerial encounters of the entire War. The results reflected the carnage: the Luftwaffe lost 38 fighters, the Americans 60 bombers. But despite the decimation of the U.S. planes, General Eaker initially described the raid as a great success for the Eighth Air Force. His report to Washington rated the Luftwaffe's virtuoso performance "as the last final struggle of a monster in his death throes," adding: "There is not the slightest question but that we now have our teeth in the Hun Air Force's neck."

Eaker's misplaced optimism was based in part on the claims by his crews that 186 German fighters had been shot down and in part on photographs showing heavy damage at Schweinfurt. The fact is that though the damage disrupted production for six weeks, no German plane or tank failed to be built for the lack of ball bearings.

Eaker soon had sober second thoughts about the outcome at Schweinfurt; he called a halt to big raids deep into Germany. The bombers would not return there until they could be escorted all the way to their target and back by fighters—American rather than German.

With the Americans temporarily sidelined, the Luftwaffe could focus on the British and the night war. More than ever, during the closing months of 1943, night fighting became a battle of wits and electronic wizardry. Göring was openly envious of Britain's advanced technology. "They have the geniuses and we have the nincompoops," he said. "After this war's over I'm going to buy myself a British radio set." The RAF's continuing use of Window to confound German radar was a particular source of frustration for the Reich Marshal. In search of a technical solution to the problem, he funded a nationwide competition with prizes of up to 162,500 reichsmarks—the equivalent of $65,000—but none of the submitted schemes proved feasible.

Further improvements in tactics appeared to offer a better bet than technology, and so the Luftwaffe's planners embraced an idea that had come from their own midst—put forward by Colonel Viktor von Lossberg, an ex-bomber pilot serving on the general staff of the night-fighter force. The Lossberg plan called for a more effective use of the conventional twin-engined interceptors that guarded Germany's western approaches. These planes were to operate under the code name of *Zahme Sau*—Tame Boars—to set them apart from the Wild Boars; but they, too, were to employ more freedom of action. Instead of being confined to patrolling fixed zones along the Kammhuber Line, they were now to rove far afield in seeking out the foe.

Like the Wild Boars, the Tame Boars took off at an alert from ground control. But rather than speeding to a city already under RAF attack, they aimed to get into the British bomber stream en route to the target. To do so, they moved from one radio beacon to another—there were 21 in all dotted through the western approaches—to get ground control's running commentary on the probable location of the enemy bombers. Ironically, the controllers were able to use the Window device to advantage in determining the likely area—by watching for the biggest concentration of blips on their radar screens. They would direct the Tame Boars to the area indicated, and the interceptors would begin their own visual search for the enemy, then close in.

There were five ground control centers in all, one for each Luftwaffe air division assigned to the defense of the homeland. The centers were underground, in bunkers so elaborately outfitted that one German described them as "battle opera houses." An enormous wall map of frosted glass showed Europe. Opposite the map, in amphitheater-like rows, sat dozens of young women Luftwaffe auxiliaries, wearing headsets and listening for word on the whereabouts of the enemy bombers. The reports came from a vast network of monitoring posts: ground observers, radar stations and new electronic devices that could track the radar impulses emitted by the British navigational aid, H2S. With each report on a bomber's location, the auxiliary would train the beam of a small spotlight at the appropriate point on the frosted-glass map. This function gave the women their special name, *Leuchtspucker*—light spitters.

The ground controller, from his seat up in the balcony, watched the points of light scuttling about the map and then dispatched the Tame Boars accordingly. Sometimes he found himself directing as many as 200 fighters. He was only as good as the information that he received, but the best controllers also employed intuition and educated guesswork to predict the target accurately and to get the Tame Boars to the right radio beacons. The controllers were aware of how much rode on their decisions. A correct assessment could bring the entire night-fighter force to bear on the RAF bomber stream. A wrong one could send the Tame Boars roaming through the skies without firing a shot.

The British did their utmost to fox the ground controllers. They installed powerful radio transmitters in England and aboard Lancaster bombers over Germany and jammed the ground controllers' running commentaries to the Tame Boars with electronic noises. Then they began broadcasting their own bogus running commentaries, using fake ground controllers who could speak German. Further to confuse the Tame Boars, the British broadcast phony weather reports; once they even got the German fighters to land prematurely by predicting the onset of a heavy fog.

Since the British were employing men as their fake controllers, the Germans countered by using a woman controller. But shortly after she began her commentary, the British went on the air with a woman who spoke flawless German. And when Luftwaffe ground control resorted to a musical code to identify the evening bombers' probable target—a waltz meant Munich, jazz signified Berlin—the British retaliated with a barrage of ringing bells, band music and phonograph records blaring Hitler's strident speeches.

On the night of November 18, 1943, the British launched the campaign they called the Battle of Berlin. It lasted for four and a half months, through the end of March of 1944, and included 35 major raids that used an average of more than 500 bombers a night. Nineteen of the raids were directed against various cities scattered around the Reich in an attempt to keep the German air defenses from ganging up. But 16 missions concentrated on Berlin itself—the greatest assault yet mounted against a single target.

Air Chief Marshal Harris was bent upon repeating the kind of devastation that had been heaped upon Hamburg the previous summer. Berlin, as the seat of Nazi power, attracted him much as Schweinfurt's ball-bearing factories had drawn the Americans. On November 3, the leader of Bomber Command wrote Prime Minister Churchill: "We can wreck Berlin from end to end if the U.S. Army Air Forces will come in on it. It will cost between us 400 and 500 aircraft. It will cost Germany the war."

The Americans, still recovering from their heavy losses at Schweinfurt, could not go along with the Harris plan. Nor would they have chosen to in any case. By now, they were under orders to concentrate their efforts on knocking out the Luftwaffe in preparation for the invasion of Europe. This was the officially affirmed aim of the British as well, but Harris clung to the belief that he could somehow bomb Germany out of the War without an invasion. With Prime Minister Churchill's enthusiastic approval, Harris plunged ahead with the Battle of Berlin.

Though Harris vowed to keep hammering away at Berlin "until the heart of Nazi Germany ceases to beat," the capital proved to be an extraordinarily difficult target. Because much of it was built of brick and stone, and because its broad streets served as natural firebreaks, it was harder to burn than the older city of Hamburg. It was too far from England for the RAF bombers to make use of the Oboe target-finding device, and too sprawling to provide clear-cut images on their H2S viewing screens. The Luftwaffe had made the target-finding task even tougher by constructing decoy targets out in the countryside, including a full-sized, plywood-and-cardboard replica of Berlin measuring nine miles in diameter.

Moreover, the new night-defense system proved increasingly efficient, racking up some of the Luftwaffe's best scores of the War: 55 attacking bombers were downed over Magdeburg on January 21, 1944, another 43 over Berlin on January 28, and 78 over Leipzig on February 19. On such nights, it was not unusual for several German pilots to shoot down four or five bombers apiece in a couple of hours. The Luftwaffe's recordkeepers had a relatively liberal system of awarding "kills," and some of the night aces, like the German day aces, were piling up kill totals that would ultimately far surpass those of the top American and British fighter pilots. At least in part, the high scores of the Germans were attributable to the Luftwaffe's practice of not rotating its pilots. The men were kept flying until they were killed or seriously injured.

The Luftwaffe's night fighters accounted for about two thirds of the bombers shot down during the Battle of Berlin, and antiaircraft batteries accounted for the rest. Up to now, some of the Luftwaffe's top brass had questioned the worth of these ground units. By one estimate, shooting down a single enemy bomber required an average of 3,343 88mm shells at a cost of 267,440 reichsmarks—about $107,000. It was also argued that the system tied down guns that could have been put to profitable use on the Russian front, since they had proved to be deadly against tanks. Ironically, the

The deadly flak met by Allied bombers came in many forms and sizes, from 22-pound explosive shells that could be hurled six miles high or more by 88mm batteries (far left) to the 37mm and 20mm tracer shells seen greeting RAF night bombers over an unidentified German city at near left. The smaller guns, which had effective ranges of about one mile, were aimed visually with the help of the tracer trails. In most cases, 88mm guns were brought to bear on their distant targets by radar.

personnel of the antiaircraft units in the Battle of Berlin included Russian prisoners of war, as well as German women, old men and teen-age boys. This fact led one jocular battery commander to address his unit as "Ladies and gentlemen, fellow workers, schoolboys and comrades."

Despite the debate over the worth of the ground batteries, the Luftwaffe had managed over the past year to increase the number of guns by more than a third, including many 128mm's with a much higher reach and greater radius of burst. This weaponry was concentrated in *Grossbatterien,* huge groupings of up to 40 guns each that hurled rectangular patterns of shellbursts known as box barrages. Ordinarily, the British bomber stream was carefully routed around the heaviest concentrations of flak. But on the night of March 24, when the RAF planes visited Berlin for the 16th time in little over four months, unusually fierce winds drove them into the thick of the shellfire. The result was the best score of the War for the antiaircraft guns. They accounted for at least 50 of the 72 bombers shot down that night.

For the British, this ill-fated mission marked the final attempt on Berlin during the long winter campaign. Harris had failed to fulfill his vow to wreck the city. But the last big battle of the campaign was still to be fought. On the night of March 30, Harris dispatched 795 bombers to Nuremberg in southeast Germany.

Nuremberg was relatively unimportant from a strategic standpoint. It was not a major industrial center. It was, however, a celebrated symbol of Nazi power—long associated with the grandiose party rallies held there. But after choosing it as a target, Harris let down his guard on the night of the raid. Instead of routing his bombers on a zigzag course to confuse the German ground controllers, he sent them virtually straight in. And though he anticipated some cloud cover to shroud the bomber stream, the skies proved so clear that the ground controllers could scarcely believe their good fortune.

By 11 p.m. the Germans' early-warning network had detected two separate streams of bombers approaching the coast of Europe. One was a force of 50 old Halifaxes, intended by the British as a decoy. These planes were cruising over the North Sea and dropping the metal-foil strips of Window to jam the German radar. The Nuremberg-bound force, 795 planes, was crossing the English Channel toward Belgium.

By tracking emissions from the H2S radar aboard the bombers, the German ground controllers correctly guessed which bomber stream was bigger, and immediately ordered the Tame Boars to assemble over a radio beacon code-named Ida, about 50 miles east of Aachen.

It turned out to be a fortuitous move for the Luftwaffe. The bomber stream was entering Germany through an area that was known to the British as the Cologne Gap—a 20-mile-wide corridor that would make it possible for the raiders to pass between the big flak concentrations at the southern edge of the Ruhr Valley and a smaller one farther south. Ida was 15 miles to the north of the Cologne Gap.

The lead elements of the bomber stream entered Germany at midnight and threaded their way safely through the Cologne Gap. But the planes in the middle of the bomber stream ran into winds of up to 90 miles per hour and drifted north into the orbiting assemblage of Tame Boars.

Many of the German planes were newly equipped with two devices that the Luftwaffe had managed to keep secret from the British. One was a new variety of airborne radar, Lichtenstein SN-2, which operated on a wave length that made it impervious to jamming by the deceptive strips of metal foil; it could detect a bomber at a range of up to four miles. The Germans had been so anxious to prevent SN-2 from falling into the hands of the British that when an Me-110 equipped with the device landed in Switzerland by mistake, they persuaded the Swiss to blow it up. The Swiss price was a squadron of brand-new single-engined fighters.

The Luftwaffe's other new device consisted of a pair of 20mm cannon mounted on top of the Me-110 in such a way that they could fire upward from beneath a British bomber. Because the cannon slanted slightly forward, this innovation was known as *schräge Musik*—literally, "slanting music," but idiomatically translated as "jazz music."

Jazz Music had evolved from a series of accidents in which night fighters, while flying in their traditional *von unten hinten* position of attack—from under and behind the bomber—had shot down their own comrades. Ordered to fly directly underneath their quarry to obtain positive identification before firing, the night fighters had discovered that the British bomber crews could not see them. On the few previous occasions when Jazz Music had been tried, the RAF crews did not, in fact, know what had hit them. Nearby crews, seeing a bomber suddenly explode, had refused to believe the evidence of their eyes and had assumed that the Germans were trying to scare them with a bizarre flak shell that simulated the flash of a bomber exploding.

As the Tame Boars employed their new devices against the Nuremberg-bound bombers, they also received some assistance from nature. The moon, although it was not full, was unusually bright that night, and the temperature was so cold that the steam pouring out of the bombers' exhausts condensed, leaving brilliant phosphorescent trails to follow. One British airman had the impression of "being on a well-lit main road and being shot at from unlit side streets."

The odds against the bombers were stacked so high that many of the raiders suspected a betrayal; they were convinced that the details of the raid had somehow been revealed to the Luftwaffe in advance. In the first hour after midnight, bombers went down at the rate of one per minute, marking part of the 300-mile route from the German border to Nuremberg with their blazing wrecks.

And when the British finally reached the target after flying so vulnerably through clear, moonlit skies, they found clouds nearly two miles thick obscuring Nuremberg. Many of their bombs fell in open country. Some fell as distant as 55 miles from Nuremberg—on Schweinfurt, the Americans' ball-bearing target that Harris had insisted was too small for his planes to find at night.

By the time the bombers turned for home, a number of Luftwaffe aces had boosted their personal kill scores. First Lieutenant Helmut Schulte destroyed four Lancasters with just 56 shells from his upward-firing Jazz Music. Near Nuremberg, he framed a fifth Lancaster in his sights only to find the Jazz Music jammed. Schulte switched to his conventional forward-firing cannon, but the Lancaster, piloted by Warrant Officer Howard Hemming, went into a weaving corkscrew maneuver and the shells passed harmlessly over the bomber's wings.

Schulte pursued the Lancaster for about five minutes, jockeying for the *von unten hinten* position. Every time he fired, however, Hemming expertly corkscrewed his bomber and eluded the shells. Sometime past 1:30 a.m., after Schulte had been aloft more than two hours, the German decided to let the Englishman off the hook. "He had been through as much as I had," Schulte recalled years later. "We had both been to Nuremberg that night—so I decided that was enough." Hemming thus made it safely back to England, but 95 of the 795 British bombers did not. The Germans lost no more than 10 fighters. It was Bomber Command's worst night of the War—and the Luftwaffe's best.

In all, the Battle of Berlin cost the British 1,047 bombers, more than their total frontline strength on any given night. Like the American strategists after Schweinfurt, Harris at last knew that the bomber alone was not enough. He, too, needed fighter escorts to fend off the resurgent Luftwaffe. Only eight months after its humiliation at Hamburg, it now ruled the night skies over the Reich.

In an underground Luftwaffe fighter control center, women aides (far left) receive telephoned reports of approaching Allied bomber forces and project the planes' positions onto the rear of a translucent map with beams of light. Other aides, silhouetted behind the screen (left), plot the bombers' course, and liaison officers in front of the map radio the formations' latest positions to Luftwaffe fighters. Photographs were made of the map every five minutes for later study of fighter tactics.

THE LUFTWAFFE'S ELITE

Major Josef Priller, the head of a Luftwaffe fighter wing in France, is helped into his BMW in 1943. Priller shot down 101 Allied planes, including 11 bombers.

GERMANY'S FAVORITES BECOME SCAPEGOATS

As the spearhead for Hitler's blitzkrieg in 1939 and 1940, the Luftwaffe fighter command was an elite force that could do no wrong. The pilots fought with gallantry and devastating skill, racking up hundreds of kills. They were idolized and rewarded with French wines, Russian furs, Balkan tobacco, beautiful women and, of course, Iron Crosses. Luftwaffe commander Hermann Göring set aside scarce transport planes to take the fliers home on leaves, and he spent more than one million reichmarks (about $250,000) to set up a mountain resort solely for the distinguished Richthofen squadrons. Hitler's headquarters staff boasted, "The Luftwaffe can do anything."

But the Luftwaffe's days of glory abruptly gave way to years of crisis. The first crucial reverse came as early as 1940, when the Luftwaffe failed to knock out the RAF in the Battle of Britain. At that point, wrote ace Adolf Galland, the myth of Luftwaffe invincibility "had been exploded." Galland and other Luftwaffe realists foresaw an inexorable war of attrition: the Allies, endowed with more manpower and production facilities, would send hordes of bombers to wear down the Luftwaffe fighters. Field Marshal Erhard Milch later warned that "the enemy knows that he must wipe out our fighters. Once he has done that, he will be able to play football with the German people."

Month after critical month, Hitler took no emergency measures to beef up the fighter command. He believed the steady stream of reports he received from self-serving production personnel, who misled him with scrambled and hopelessly overoptimistic figures on aircraft output, which did increase sporadically, but not nearly enough. According to Milch, Hitler was convinced that "he had done too much for the fighters." The Führer seemed determined to punish the hard-pressed pilots for their failure to put an end to the Allied bombing raids.

True to Galland's forebodings, the odds against the fighter pilots mounted steadily. They battled on courageously, but by 1944 they were in the same desperate plight that their RAF counterparts had been in just four years before.

Fighter commander Adolf Galland signs his autograph on an admirer's back. In 1942, at the age of 30, he became Germany's youngest general.

German fighter pilots take a well-earned break between sorties. When the air war turned against Germany, Hitler accused the fighter command of laziness.

REDOUBLED EFFORTS TO STEM THE ALLIED TIDE

"That was a lot of fun," said a diehard Luftwaffe fighter pilot after returning from a mission late in the War. "Why don't we refuel and go again?" The fact is that by then back-to-back missions had become a sheer necessity. Göring ordered that every pilot refuel at least three times before being allowed to quit a battle. Some men flew more than five sorties in a single day. Many pilots chalked up 500 missions and more than 1,000 combat hours—far more than their adversaries.

Fighter commander Galland, who continued to fly combat missions in addition to his administrative duties, gave his comrades due credit for an "aggressive spirit, joy of action, and the passion of the hunter." But the price of gallantry kept rising until it was higher than the Luftwaffe could afford. Galland said, "Each incursion of the enemy is costing us about fifty aircrew." With few exceptions, he said, "our aces fought until they were killed."

Hard-working ground crewmen of a Richthofen fighter squadron rearm and service a Focke-Wulf 190.

Admiring airmen greet ace Günther Rall, landing after a sortie. Rall was grounded by a back injury in a 1941 crash, but returned to combat nine months later.

144

An exultant pilot indicates his victory as he springs from his cockpit.

A fighter pilot relives a maneuver he used to down an enemy plane.

Putting the finishing touches on his latest victory, a Luftwaffe pilot painstakingly paints the tail of his Messerschmitt fighter with a stripe denoting a kill.

Modified to attack tanks, a Junkers-87 dive bomber carries a pair of 37mm cannon under its wings.

A belly gas tank added to an Me-109 extended

Me-109s raid England on a two-hour fuel supply. On one sortie, 12 109s ran out of gas and had to ditch.

GETTING MORE OUT OF LESS

"Fighters, fighters, fighters, that's what we need!" railed Ernst Udet, Luftwaffe production chief, in 1941. But his output remained pitifully small—fewer than 1,400 single-engined fighters in six months—and he soon committed suicide in despair.

Though Udet's successor, Erhard Milch,

146

its range by about 170 miles and also increased its fighting time. Fighters equipped with these tanks frequently lurked aloft to get the jump on bombers.

upped production to more than 9,600 in 1943, the combat odds failed to improve. By 1944, the Luftwaffe was shooting down a bomber for every fighter it lost—a remarkable record, except for the fact that the Allies were outproducing the Reich in airplanes by more than 2 to 1. The problem was compounded by the woeful inadequacy of repair facilities: fully one third of the Luftwaffe's single-engined fighters were out of action in September of 1943.

Hitler had contributed to the shortage of planes by placing the Luftwaffe in fifth place on his priority list for urgently needed metals. Incredibly, the fighter force was allowed to suffer for the lack of aluminum, which was being used to build termite-proof barracks for the postwar occupation of Germany's tropical colonies.

To make do with what they had, the Luftwaffe commanders jury-rigged fighters with extra armament, bombs, spare gaso-

line tanks and whatever else could extend their utility. But pilots complained that the added load detracted from the planes' speed and maneuverability, and increased the casualty rate. The truth was inescapable—there were simply not enough fighters to go around. When Milch later was asked what the Luftwaffe's biggest mistake had been, he delivered the answer with bitter vehemence: "One hundred and forty thousand unbuilt fighter aircraft!"

Luftwaffe recruits watch attack techniques demonstrated with models. The wires attached to the enemy B-24 showed fields of fire that pilots had to avoid.

Fledgling pilots prepare to test-fire an Me-109's guns at a combat base. They completed their studies there because of the shortage of training facilities.

BELATED REACTIONS TO THE MANPOWER PINCH

"The only raw material that cannot be restored in the foreseeable future is human blood," cautioned Field Marshal Milch in 1943. By then, the cumulative effect of fighter-pilot losses was overtaking a training system with far too little depth. Germany had entered the War with only one school for fighter pilots, and the Luftwaffe at first replaced the casualties by faster, sketchier training. General Galland noted that the student pilots suffered "immense casualties during training, which were only justifiable because of the extraordinary state of emergency."

In a belated effort to make amends, the Luftwaffe opened 10 new schools in 1944. But the youths who graduated were so poorly prepared for combat that the main contribution they made was to the list of casualties. Said Galland, "Between January and April 1944, our day fighter arm lost more than 1,000 pilots."

Freeing men for combat, women staff a Luftwaffe fighter control station in occupied France in 1944.

A day fighter gets ready for a night mission. Skimpy training for blind flying at night and in bad weather contributed to the Luftwaffe's alarming loss rate.

Once the terror of the skies, an FW-190 lies hidden in a forest in France.

THE FIGHTER COMMAND IN BATTERED DISARRAY

In 1944, all of the Luftwaffe's losses and shortages came home to roost. The fighter pilots were opposed by vastly superior numbers—8 to 1 in some aerial battles that spring and summer—and they also faced a worsening fuel shortage. The Allies had turned their attention to Germany's crucial gasoline refineries, and production of aviation fuel plunged from nearly 200,000 tons in May to a mere trickle of 7,000 tons by October. The fighter pilots "retired to the forests," Galland said, camouflaging their planes to escape Allied attacks.

Incredibly, the German fighters would be able to mount a major counteroffensive. But in general, bitter recriminations were now the only things still flying. Hitler bellowed at Göring, "Your Luftwaffe isn't worth a damn!" Predicted production chief Milch, "We shall be forced to our knees before the coming year is out."

Luftwaffe crewmen cautiously push a lone Focke-Wulf fighter onto an airfield

in France in 1944. At the time of the Allied invasion, Galland later wrote, "the danger of being detected and destroyed by the enemy was ever present."

5

At the age of 31, Adolf Galland was one of the youngest of the Luftwaffe's generals, and one of the shrewdest. Despite his fighter pilots' successes on the home front in the second half of 1943 and early 1944, he harbored no illusions that their winning streak would continue. And he knew when the turning point would come: when Allied bombers began to appear deep inside Germany with a protective shield of fighter escorts.

Galland kept worrying about this eventuality and watching for signs that it impended. One day in late September of 1943 his forebodings were confirmed by an incident at Aachen. This ancient city, just inside Germany's western border, marked the point beyond which Allied fighters did not ordinarily venture. Once they had accompanied their bombers to the German border, they would turn back, unable to go farther into Germany because of the limited amount of fuel they could carry without impairing their speed and maneuverability. On that September day, several of the escorts—American P-47 Thunderbolts—were shot down and proved to be equipped with auxiliary fuel tanks that would have taken them beyond their usual range.

As it happened, Galland soon had the chance to convey these tidings directly to Hitler. Summoned to discuss what could be done to prevent the Americans' daylight raids, he reiterated his standard plea for more fighters, but he raised his estimate of the number that would be needed. Thwarting the enemy attacks, Galland estimated, would require a Luftwaffe fighter force three or four times the size of the U.S. bomber force. Even this numerical superiority would be insufficient, Galland added pointedly, if the Americans increased their fighter escorts and sent them ever deeper inside Germany.

Hitler, who had listened without demur to Galland's proposal for an expanded fighter force, bristled at the suggestion that the U.S. escorts could extend their penetration of the Reich. Saying he had Göring's own assurance that such a possibility was completely out of the question, he curtly dismissed Galland.

Later that day, Galland paid what he thought would be no more than a routine call on his Luftwaffe boss; Göring was about to leave on his special train for a hunting trip at a forest preserve in East Prussia, and Galland went to bid him goodbye. What ensued instead was a scene so tense that

SUPREMACY IN THE SKY

Minister of Armaments Speer, who happened to be present, never forgot it.

Göring, he recalled, was clearly out of sorts. Galland, self-assured as usual, stood at ease, his general's cap slightly askew, and the ever-present long black cigar clamped between his teeth; in his days as a fighter ace, he had even installed a special holder in the cockpit of his Me-109 so he could park an unlighted cigar while flying on oxygen.

Göring got right to the point. "What's the idea of telling the Führer that American fighters have penetrated into the territory of the Reich?" he snapped.

"Herr Reichsmarschall," Galland coolly answered, "they will soon be flying even deeper."

"That's nonsense, Galland. What gives you such fantasies? That's pure bluff!"

"Those are the facts," replied the young general. "You might go and check it yourself, sir; the downed planes are there at Aachen."

Göring then lamely suggested that the planes had actually been shot down west of the German border and "could have glided quite a distance farther" before they crashed. Galland insisted that the planes were over Aachen at the time they were shot down.

Finally, Göring erupted: "I herewith give you an official order that they weren't there! Do you understand? The American fighters were not there!"

As the Reich Marshal stalked off, Galland smiled cynically and called after him: "Orders are orders, sir!"

By early 1944 Galland no longer needed to argue his case. More and more, the American bombers that appeared in the daylight skies over Germany flew in the company of "Little Friends"—their radio terminology for Allied escort fighters. To the Luftwaffe pilots, the newcomers were soon known as Indianer, in reference to the savage warriors of the American Wild West.

The feisty Little Friends, all single-seaters, came in a variety of shapes and sizes. The biggest, the P-38 Lightning, had two engines mounted on twin fuselages. The single-engined P-47 Thunderbolt had a blunt nose and a stubby body. The single-engined P-51 Mustang was the smallest and trimmest of the three; one early model weighed only 8,800 pounds, less than half the weight of the Lightning.

The Mustang was to prove to be the bombers' most reliable friend and the best all-around fighter plane of the War. Its development was due not to the Americans but to the British. Built to their order by a U.S. plane manufacturer in 1941, the Mustang was at first largely ignored by American air strategists. The early models lacked power at high altitudes, and the British had to relegate the plane to a tactical role in low-level support of infantry.

But in 1942 they fitted the Mustang with a bigger engine, the Rolls-Royce Merlin, which also powered their Spitfires. Flight tests demonstrated that the new model Mustang, the P-51B, could achieve what had been regarded as a technical impossibility: the performance of a fighter coupled with the long range of a bomber. It had a big fuel capacity plus an economical engine that burned only about half the gasoline of other U.S. fighters' engines. It could reach a top speed of 440 miles per hour at 30,000 feet. In all, the tests suggested that the Mustang could outspeed, outclimb and outdive any fighter the Luftwaffe had in service.

Despite the Mustang's exciting potential, the Americans were still reluctant to mass-produce the plane for their own use; they believed that its liquid-cooled engine was far more susceptible to damage by enemy gunfire than the radial air-cooled engine of the Thunderbolt. In any case, some U.S. strategists were not yet convinced of the need for long-range fighters; they continued to cling to the belief that their big bomber formations could defend themselves over Germany.

This faith was shaken by the disastrous losses incurred in the U.S. raids on Regensburg and Schweinfurt in August of 1943. Production of the Mustang was stepped up, and by late November the first few dozen were at Eighth Air Force bases in England, ready for action along with the Thunderbolts and Lightnings that had previously seen escort duty as far as the German border.

Like the Mustang, these older planes were now outfitted with auxiliary fuel tanks. The tanks were at first slung under the fuselage; later they were placed under the wings. Once the fuel in them was exhausted, the pilot could jettison them; relieved of the added weight, he could achieve greater speed and maneuverability in combat. But while in use, the drop tanks gave the Little Friends "extra legs," as Army Air Forces Chief Arnold put it. The Mustang had the longest legs of all: with a 108-gallon tank under each wing, the P-51B and later models would eventually be able to fly all the way to Poland and back to England, a 1,700-mile round trip.

While the fighter force was being expanded and improved, increasing numbers of Flying Fortresses and Liberators were also arriving from the States, along with the crews to man them. By the end of December 1943, the Eighth Air Force was prepared to mount missions of as many as 720 bombers—almost twice the capability it had at the time of the second raid on Schweinfurt only 10 weeks earlier. In addition, it was to have help in the renewed bombing offensive from the U.S. Fifteenth Air Force, now established in the Foggia area in southeast Italy, in the wake of Allied ground advances up the Italian peninsula.

The Fifteenth was a much smaller force than the Eighth, and in need of training and seasoning. But its role in the bomber offensive was critical. From its bases in Italy, the Fifteenth could strike at enemy targets far beyond the reach of the Eighth, hitting at Germany itself through the Reich's southern approaches and at German-held bastions in the Balkans and Greece. Moreover, the flying weather around the Mediterranean was generally better than in northern Europe—though many a Fifteenth pilot, watching his plane ice over as he crossed the Alps into Germany or Austria, would soon argue otherwise.

Before long, the Fifteenth was to shake off its initial assessment as a "pretty disorganized mob." The critique was General Eaker's, who—to his own surprise—was now running the Allied air war in the Mediterranean. Eaker, who had headed the Eighth through its blooding in 1943, had been reassigned so that the original commander of the Eighth, General Spaatz, could return to England from North Africa to oversee all U.S. air operations in Europe. Spaatz was the choice of the newly designated Supreme Commander of the Allied Expeditionary Force, General Dwight D. Eisenhower. The air general had served under Eisenhower in the invasion of North Africa; as Ike moved to England in January of 1944 to prepare for the invasion of the European continent, he wanted Spaatz with him again. Spaatz brought with him a new commander for the Eighth, Lieut. General James H. Doolittle. As a lieutenant colonel, Jimmy Doolittle had lifted the spirits of the American public by a daring carrier-based bombing raid on Tokyo in April of 1942; more recently, he had commanded the U.S. Twelfth Air Force in the Mediterranean.

Eaker was bitterly disappointed at his transfer. He wanted to finish the job he had begun over Germany, and in an emotional appeal to his boss in Washington, General Arnold, declared that it was "heartbreaking to leave just before the climax."

Eaker was somewhat mollified after a stopover in Casablanca en route to his new headquarters in Italy. He had received a message asking that he pay a call on a mysterious "Colonel Holt"—who turned out to be Winston Churchill. Traveling incognito, Churchill was in Casablanca recovering from pneumonia. He received Eaker at the same villa where,

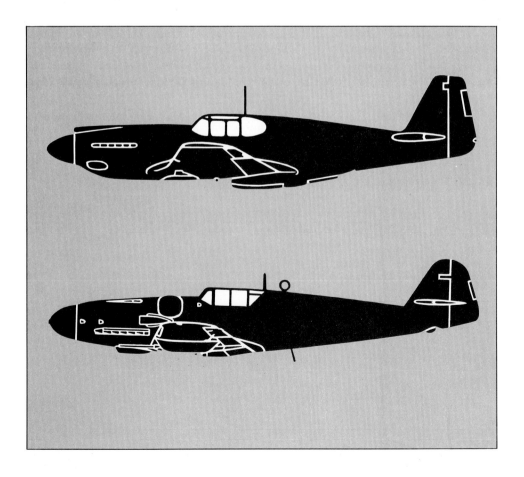

Profile silhouettes of the Messerschmitt-109 (bottom) and the P-51 Mustang (top) reveal the planes' confusing degree of similarity in size and contour. On a number of occasions—many of which understandably were never reported—the resemblance prompted bomber gunners or fighter pilots to shoot down friendly planes that suddenly flashed into view.

just one year earlier, the American general had sold the Prime Minister on round-the-clock bombing. "Your representations to me at that time have been more than verified," Churchill said. "Around-the-clock bombing is now achieving the results you predicted."

The goal of the American air build-up was summed up by General Arnold in a New Year's message for 1944 to his new commanders in Europe. "This is a MUST," he wrote. "Destroy the Enemy Air Force wherever you find them, in the air, on the ground and in the factories."

The goal was essentially the same as the one set forth in the Pointblank Directive in June of 1943. But its realization was now more crucial than ever. As long as Messerschmitts and Focke-Wulfs swarmed the skies over Europe, the projected Allied invasion of France was likely to entail a prohibitive cost in human lives. The date tentatively set for the landings was May 1, 1944, and the time available for removing the threat posed by the Luftwaffe was, in fact, even less. January and February could not be counted on for flying; in midwinter, Europe's weather made most missions chancy. A day without heavy cloud cover was exceptional, a rare opportunity to be watched for and seized.

On January 11, 1944, the Eighth Air Force had a report of clear skies over north-central Germany and quickly went ahead with a mission of special import: this was to be the first large-scale American raid with fighter protection deep into the Reich. The targets, in three cities clustered about 90 miles west of Berlin, figured as high priorities in the Luftwaffe's operations. Most of its FW-190s were produced at a factory in Oschersleben. A plant at Halberstadt was believed to be building wings for Ju-88s. Me-110 parts were made and the planes assembled at three plants in and around Brunswick.

The U.S. strike force consisted of 663 Fortresses and Liberators, divided into three formations. Their fighter escort was made up of 11 groups of Thunderbolts, two groups of Lightnings and a single group of Mustangs—the only one available, numbering 49 planes. Bombers and escorts were to rendezvous over the Dutch coast. The Lightnings and Thunderbolts were to accompany the bombers to within 70 miles of the target and meet them about 100 miles from it on the way back to the coast. Only the Mustangs, with their more extended radius of action, were to stay with the bombers all the way to the target, provide support there and escort them back.

The weather was so bad over England that the mission had trouble taking off and assembling. Conditions en route proved to be even worse, and rapidly deteriorating. The overcast became so thick that a decision was made to recall all planes that had not yet penetrated far into Germany; about two thirds of the bombers turned back, and so did many of the Lightnings and Thunderbolts.

For the planes that flew on, the Luftwaffe provided a reception as tumultuous as the one that had greeted the American raiders at Schweinfurt. The German interceptors were not only out in force but also newly equipped with drop tanks. The extra fuel allowed them to bide their time aloft until the shorter-range enemy escorts had peeled off, then swoop in on unprotected Fortresses and Liberators. A total of 60 U.S. bombers went down—a loss equal to that suffered over Schweinfurt in October.

The raiders managed to inflict heavy damage on the Focke-Wulf factory at Oschersleben, where half of their bombs fell within 1,000 feet of the aiming point, and on one of the three targets near Brunswick, where three quarters of the bombs found their mark. But the brightest spot in the day's picture was the Mustangs' performance. Split into two sections to cover the operations at Oschersleben and Halberstadt, the 49 Mustangs proved more than a match for the Luftwaffe's interceptors. The Mustangs suffered no losses and destroyed an estimated 15 enemy planes.

At one point, some of the Mustang pilots looked down and saw Me-110s and Me-109s below the bombers, "climbing," one pilot recalled, "like a swarm of bees." A voice came over the radio: "Go down and get the bastards!" The fighter pilots swooped to the attack; in the ensuing combat, the eager Mustang rookies shot down nine German interceptors without a loss. But in their headlong dive they had left their bombers unprotected.

As this thought occurred to Major James Howard, the Mustangs' leader, he pulled his plane up short and climbed back. Unlike most of his men, Howard was a veteran of air war—a former Navy pilot who had fought in China with the Flying Tigers against the Japanese before going to Europe.

When Howard reached the bombers, they were under

assault by some 30 German fighters. Ordinarily, an escort pilot was supposed to engage in combat only if his wingman was protecting his rear. Howard took on the entire enemy force alone.

His first victim was a relatively easy target, a slower-moving twin-engined Me-110. "I went down after him," Howard recalled, "gave him several squirts and watched him crash. He stood out very clearly, silhouetted against the snow that covered the ground." Next was a much-faster single-engined FW-190, "cruising along beneath me. He pulled up into the sun when he saw me. I gave him a squirt and I almost ran into his canopy when he threw it off to get out. He bailed out." In short order, Howard attacked four other fighters. During one of these encounters, three of his four .50-caliber machine guns jammed, but he kept hammering away with the fourth.

The entire episode was over so quickly that Howard was not sure how many German fighters he had gunned down. When he returned to England, dangerously low on fuel, he claimed two planes destroyed and brushed aside his performance with a flippant "I seen my duty and I done it."

But the bomber crews who had witnessed Howard's feat —"the greatest exhibition I have ever seen," declared the bomber-formation leader, Major Allison Brooks—claimed four to six kills for him; in the end, he was credited with four. For his solo battle with the Luftwaffe, Howard was awarded the Congressional Medal of Honor, one of the few fighter pilots to win it for aerial combat over Europe.

The Mustang still had a few bugs. As Howard had found, its guns tended to jam during high-speed maneuvers when the force of gravity caused the ammunition belts to clog. This problem was solved on later models by the addition of small auxiliary motors that kept the belts moving.

A second problem was posed by the fact that in silhouette the Mustang closely resembled the Luftwaffe's Me-109. Recognition posters were distributed at the bases in England, and as an added precaution the Mustangs were painted with a yellow band around the chord of the wing. But these measures did not always work. On a number of occasions during the winter of 1944, Mustangs were mistaken for Me-109s and jumped by other American fighters. Another case of mistaken identity might have proved fatal to Mustang pilot Jack T. Bradley. Flying escort over Germany, he lost sight of his squadron mates and radioed a request for their location. Following instructions, he caught up with a formation and settled into his normal slot. After cruising along for several minutes, he glanced casually out the side window and discovered that he was flying in a formation of Messerschmitt-109s. Almost simultaneously, the Me-109s recognized Bradley's plane and started to go after him. Bradley dropped his auxiliary fuel tanks in order to gain speed, then dived out of the formation, leaving his unwanted companions behind.

In spite of the minor problems, American pilots yearned to fly Mustangs and complained that there were not enough of them available. But by the middle of February of 1944, more Mustangs had arrived from the States. In addition, the performance of the Thunderbolt was upgraded. Its range was lengthened by rigging two drop tanks under the wings instead of one under the fuselage. And its climbing speed was increased by a new water-injection system that boosted the engine's horsepower.

Buoyed by their growing fighter and bomber strength, the

General Dwight D. Eisenhower pins the Distinguished Service Cross on American ace Captain Don Gentile at a ceremony in Debden, England, in 1944. At right is Gentile's commanding officer, Colonel Don Blakeslee of the high-scoring 4th Fighter Group.

Americans began preparing for their biggest blow thus far at Germany's aircraft factories, specifically those turning out fighter planes or fighter components. The operation, code-named *Argument,* called for a series of coordinated attacks by the Eighth Air Force from England and the Fifteenth Air Force from Italy, though with the Eighth carrying the main load. But a succession of clear days was required, and the usual forbidding winter weather of the Continent compelled repeated postponements. Finally, on February 19, the meteorologists forecast a break in the skies over Europe. Early on the morning of February 20, when England itself was blanketed by clouds and snow, General Spaatz sent word from his intertheater headquarters at Teddington outside London: "Let 'em go."

That morning the Eighth hurled virtually its entire operational strength against a dozen targets in central Germany and western Poland. For the first time, more than 1,000 U.S. bombers took part. Nearly as many fighters—Mustangs, Thunderbolts, Lightnings and British Spitfires—accompanied them at various stages of their journey. The fighters, clustered in flights of four about 200 yards apart, were positioned like four outstretched fingers of a hand—an arrangement originally devised by the Luftwaffe to guard against enemy attack from all directions.

In a typical deployment of a fighter group, two flights flew "top cover," about 3,000 feet above each bomber formation, while others flew on either side of it. Others flew in front, some up to 10 miles ahead of the formation so as to intercept the Luftwaffe fighters before they could get close to the bombers. To maintain station as they patrolled, the escorts had to keep weaving; otherwise, they would have far outstripped the slower bombers.

The U.S. commanders were braced for the loss of as many as 200 of their bombers on the first day of Operation *Argument.* But the protection afforded by the escort planes, combined with an unexpected show of timidity by the Luftwaffe, paid off. Although 21 bombers went down, the loss rate was only about 2 per cent.

Five more days of massive U.S. raids followed. During "Big Week," as the Americans came to call it, some 3,800 sorties were flown over the targets, 3,300 by the Eighth Air Force and 500 by the Fifteenth, and about 10,000 tons of bombs were dropped—a tonnage roughly equal to that dropped by the Eighth throughout its entire first year of operation. In all, 226 U.S. bombers and 28 fighters were lost.

Big Week destroyed or damaged more than half of the plant facilities of the German aircraft industry. At Leipzig, center of a third of all Me-109 production, 350 combat-ready fighters were demolished, along with hundreds of others that were only half finished on the assembly lines. Heavy damage was done at Gotha, where most of the twin-engined Me-110s were built, and to the Ju-88 factories located at Aschersleben and Bernburg.

The planners of Big Week concluded that the German aircraft industry had been dealt a crippling blow; they were wrong. The shock of the saturation bombing galvanized the Germans into an urgent program of plant dispersal and reconstruction. Fighter aircraft production, up to now the jealously guarded preserve of Reich Marshal Göring, was placed under a special agency in the efficient hands of Minister of Armaments Speer. At his direction, huge quantities of vital machine tools were salvaged from the wrecked plants; roughhewn shelters, hidden in wooded areas, were speedily built to house airframe and final-assembly operations; the legions of conscript labor were set to work anew. By May, fighter output was to total more than 2,200—a new monthly high.

As it turned out, more damage was done to the Luftwaffe in the sky than on the ground. Aerial combat with the U.S. escort fighters and bombers during Big Week cost the Germans 225 of their airmen dead or missing and 141 wounded. Though the Americans, too, suffered grievous losses—some 2,600 killed, missing or seriously wounded—the German losses were proportionately far higher. They represented fully a tenth of the personnel that was available to man the Luftwaffe's interceptors.

In the wake of Big Week the Luftwaffe's commanders became increasingly cautious. Though their resources were still formidable, they began conscious efforts to conserve, backing away from full-scale confrontations with the U.S. bombers and choosing where and when they would send up interceptors in strength.

The Americans took the opposite tack, seeking out rather than avoiding concentrations of enemy interceptors. The Little Friends were encouraged to break away from their escort stations and force the Luftwaffe to do battle. As a German fighter pilot later put it: "No longer was it a case of their bombers having to run the gauntlet of our fighters, but of our having to run the gauntlet of both their bombers and their fighters."

The hope of luring the reluctant Luftwaffe into combat helped dictate the Americans' choice of their next big target—Berlin. Though by now the British were beginning to incur almost unbearably heavy losses in their own four-month-long assault on Berlin by night, the Americans felt confident that they could do much better. They were certain that the German day fighters would rise up in swarms to defend their capital and that the Mustangs and Thunderbolts—now equipped with larger wing tanks enabling them to make the 1,200-mile round trip—could best the Luftwaffe over the heart of Hitler's domain.

The first American attempt on Berlin, made on March 4, had more psychological than practical value. Overcast skies forced the recall of all the 502 bombers that set out, except for 30 bombers that failed to get the radioed message. Escorted by about 20 Mustangs, they scattered their payloads on a suburb of Berlin and turned for home without encountering as much opposition as they had expected. Göring himself saw the Mustangs flying over the capital and could no longer refuse to believe that American fighters were penetrating deep into the Third Reich. "I knew the jig was up," he later admitted.

The Mustangs' leader on this mission was Colonel Don Blakeslee, commander of the 4th Fighter Group. Blakeslee was 27, a square-jawed six-footer from Ohio who—said one of his staff officers—"appeared to be made of cast iron laced together with steel cables." Like some of his pilots, Blakeslee had served earlier with the RAF, flying Spitfires in one of the Eagle Squadrons, which were made up of American volunteers. He was nearing the end of a three-year tour of duty, during which he piled up more than 1,000 hours in combat and flew more missions than any U.S. fighter pilot in Europe. To avoid being rotated home after 200 to 300 combat hours, as most fighter pilots were, he had practiced the simple stratagem of doctoring his logbooks.

Above all, Blakeslee was a superb combat leader. "He was everywhere in the battle," wrote his unit's historian, "twisting and climbing, bellowing and blaspheming, warning and exhorting. His ability to keep things taped in a fight with 40 or 50 planes skidding and turning at 400 miles an hour was a source of wonder."

That first day over Berlin, Blakeslee jumped an Me-109 only to find that his guns had jammed. Swearing loudly, he overtook the German plane, flew alongside and waved in mock courtesy. The German waggled his wings in bewildered acknowledgment, then slipped away.

Two days later Blakeslee again led the Mustangs to Berlin. On this mission there were so many Little Friends—more than 800—that they outnumbered the bombers. They flew in relays across Western Europe. Groups of Thunderbolts and Lightnings flew cover as far as they could, and the Mustangs took the bombers all the way into the target.

Still, there were gaps in the fighter protection, and these were exploited by the largest force of German interceptors the Americans had tangled with since Big Week. One group of interceptors went directly for the bombers while another group engaged their Thunderbolt protectors. The resulting battle raged for 45 minutes along the route to Berlin. Fortunately for the escorts, many of the German fighters were of the slow twin-engined variety more often used for night fighting. These cumbersome planes were so easily outperformed by the Little Friends that the American pilots considered them "meat on the table." The Luftwaffe soon stopped sending them up during daylight hours.

Statistically, the day's combat was a standoff: 80 American aircraft—69 bombers and 11 fighters—went down, many of them to flak. The U.S. pilots claimed 82 German kills. But the Americans now had a seemingly limitless reserve of bombers and fighters to draw on. The Luftwaffe's losses, by contrast, totaled a fifth of the force it sent up that day. When the Americans returned to Berlin on March 8, there were fewer enemy planes to greet them.

This third strike proved to be a particularly memorable one for two of Blakeslee's best pilots: Captain Don Gentile, another Ohioan, and his wingman, Lieutenant John Godfrey, a Rhode Islander. By nature Gentile was low key, Godfrey devil-may-care; but in action their teamwork was faultless. As Gentile and Godfrey rendezvoused with the Fortresses over Berlin, they ran into a swarm of perhaps 20 Me-109s that were attacking one of the bomber formations.

TOP ACES OF THE AIR WAR

Germany

Great Britain

United States

"Johnny, cover me," Gentile called over the radio. "I'm diving on the Jerry at three o'clock."

"Right behind you, Don," said Godfrey. He followed Gentile down, watched as he closed in on the Me-109, then looked up, down and around and reported: "Go to it, Don, your tail is cleared."

With Godfrey keeping watch, Gentile pulled the trigger on his control stick and blew his quarry apart. Then, taking turns at providing cover for each other, the pair went after more Germans. Climbing, banking, diving, pushing their Mustangs to the limit, each man shot down two Me-109s and shared one more kill.

The day's work was not yet done. On the way home, Gentile and Godfrey spotted an American straggler, a Fortress flying alone with one of its engines out. Godfrey, who by now was completely out of ammunition, called to Gentile: "There's a Big Friend that needs company, Don. How's your ammunition?"

Gentile was running low, but they decided to fly the weaving escort pattern over the Fort to bluff away any German interceptors that might show up. They moved in close, approaching carefully; as Godfrey later explained, Fortresses "had a bad habit of shooting at anything that came in their range." But the bomber crew was so elated to have friendly company that as Godfrey came near he could see, in the open waist gunner's positions, "first one man and then another throwing kisses at me."

He and Gentile kept the stricken Big Friend company until the lonely three-plane formation reached safety over the English Channel. Then the two Mustangs raced for home. Godfrey paused only to buzz a hospital where his girl friend worked as a nurse. Later, back at base, he bought drinks for the house—with money borrowed from Gentile.

The U.S. raids on Berlin proved conclusively that the Americans had gained the upper hand in the skies over Germany. When 669 bombers returned to Berlin on March 22, German fighters downed only one or two of the dozen attackers that were lost: flak and accident accounted for the others. U.S. bombers, with the help of their Little Friends, could now attack targets anywhere in Germany with decreasing peril.

As the Luftwaffe threat lessened, the Americans' lust for action and glory increased. To many fighter pilots aerial combat became, in Don Blakeslee's words, "a grand sport." The prospect of outdueling an enemy interceptor, and of running up one's personal total of victories, compensated for such unappealing aspects of the job as sitting strapped in a tiny cockpit for as long as seven hours.

A fighter pilot's score was a subject of intense interest and sometimes bitter contention. Obtaining confirmation of a kill was a relatively straightforward matter: a kill had to be witnessed by another pilot or by bomber crewmen, or it had to be documented by the movie cameras in the wings of the fighters that were activated every time the guns were fired. But some pilots resorted to trickery to fatten their scores. A pilot seeing a squadron mate about to shoot down an enemy plane might yell "break!"—the radio warning to pull away from an onrushing enemy attack from the rear— so that he could move in and grab the kill for himself. Another source of dissension was the current policy of recognizing victories for enemy planes destroyed on the ground as well as in the air.

Rivalry for kills was keenest at the group level—most notably between the Mustangs of Don Blakeslee's 4th Fighter Group and the Thunderbolts of the 56th Group, commanded by Colonel Hubert Zemke of Missoula, Montana. Like Blakeslee, Zemke was a gifted aerial tactician and an inspiring leader who instilled in his men what he called "an inner urge to do combat." Zemke's aggressive tactics in combat won his group the nickname of "Wolfpack." On days off, the Wolfpack's Thunderbolts and the 4th's Mustangs could often be seen in mock dogfights over England. Over Germany the rival groups engaged in what the 4th Group's chronicler described as "a sort of Hun-killing tournament that sparked and stimulated the aggressiveness of all the other outfits."

During March of 1944, Zemke's Wolfpack led the tournament by almost 3 to 2 in total planes destroyed. The group included a pilot who was soon to become a leading American ace in Europe, Major Robert S. Johnson. An Oklahoman who had unaccountably failed gunnery school during flight training, Johnson shot down four German planes on March 15 alone, raising his total kill score to 22.

In April, Blakeslee's Mustangs surged ahead of the Wolfpack, scoring 31 kills in just one day. Early in May, Johnson scored his 26th kill, surpassing Captain Eddie Rickenbacker's World War I record of 25—the highest previous score for any American ace. But in the end, victory in the tournament was to go to Blakeslee's Mustangs, though by the narrowest of margins. Their total of 1,016 German aircraft destroyed was 10 more than the Wolfpack's score.

Bent on adding to the destruction, the Eighth Air Force decided on a calculated campaign to go after the Luftwaffe fighters on the ground. If they did not come up, the reasoning went, the Americans would go down and get them. Beginning early in April, armadas of 600 or more U.S. fighters flew strafing missions against airfields in France and Germany. These forays proved extremely successful. On some days U.S. claims of enemy planes destroyed on the ground climbed over the 100 mark.

But skimming over an airfield at more than 400 miles per hour posed its own great dangers. During April three times as many American fighters were lost to flak and accident on strafing missions as in aerial combat. A number of American aces who had survived dozens of battles in the air went down while attacking parked Messerschmitts and Focke-Wulfs. One of the aces was Lieut. Colonel Francis S. Gabreski of the 56th Group, who finally topped all U.S. pilots in Europe with 28 aerial victories. In July Gabreski flew so low on a strafing run in Germany that the propeller of his Thunderbolt hit the ground. He pulled up the plane, but the engine began to fail. Gabreski belly-landed in a nearby wheat field and got out, unhurt, as the plane burst into flames. He was captured and taken to a prison camp. There he was soon reunited with the Wolfpack's commander, Colonel Zemke, who was forced to bail out over Germany during an air battle, and with one of their old dueling rivals from the 4th Group, Lieutenant Godfrey, who also fell victim to the dangers of low-level strafing.

At the end of April 1944, General Galland sent his superiors in the Luftwaffe's high command a despairing memoran-

Enjoying a smoke after seven hours of escort duty, a P-51 pilot displays the briefing-session instructions he wrote on the back of his hand for ready reference aloft. The notations gave the times for starting engines, taking off, setting course and rendezvousing with the bombers, as well as the compass heading to follow as the planes left the target and turned for home.

dum. "The time has come," the fighter chief wrote, "when our force is within sight of collapse."

What had led Galland to this grim conclusion was not a dwindling supply of planes but a shortage of pilots. The Germans, in fact, were now producing more planes than ever before; as a result of the emergency program instituted after Big Week in February, relocating or rebuilding plants and imposing a 72-hour week on laborers, they were, said one Luftwaffe officer, "virtually drowning in aircraft." But planes were useless without pilots.

Galland's memorandum noted that the Luftwaffe's losses during the past four months had not only included more than 1,000 aircraft—day fighters—but also some of "our best officers." One of them—shot down by a Thunderbolt on March 2—was Colonel Mayer, the 26-year-old commander of the elite Richthofen fighter unit. Mayer had been flying combat since December of 1939 and had pioneered the use of the deadly head-on attacks against U.S. bombers in 1943. In more than four years of action, he had been credited with 102 aerial victories, including 25 bombers.

Such men, Galland knew, were irreplaceable; in fact, there were not enough trained pilots of any kind. The Luftwaffe's flight schools were beset by difficulties. They lacked good teachers; the best pilots stayed in the front line until they were killed or disabled. The schools also lacked enough fuel to give trainees adequate air time. Rookies were being sent to operational units with only 112 hours of flight time, well under half that of American trainees.

The implications of Galland's memorandum were clear: when the Allied forces launched their invasion, the Luftwaffe would need a near miracle to do its job against the invaders. It would have to exploit its newly expanded air fleet with a diminishing number of seasoned pilots.

In England, meanwhile, the planners of Operation *Overlord*—the invasion—were debating how best to use Allied air power in the weeks remaining before D-Day. A ticklish matter of national pride had to be resolved first. Eisenhower insisted that overall control of the bombers—British as well as American—should reside with him as Supreme Commander. The RAF, reluctant to yield up the independence of its Bomber Command even temporarily, opposed the idea and was firmly backed by Churchill. But according to Eisen-

hower's aide, Captain Harry C. Butcher, Ike threatened to "go home," and the Prime Minister quickly caved in. Eisenhower took over direction of both the U.S. and British bombers, though in using the aircraft he actually relied heavily on his British deputy supreme commander, Air Chief Marshal Sir Arthur Tedder.

The issue of how to employ the bombers most effectively stirred far more contention, and this time the split was not along national lines. The chiefs of the U.S. and British bomber forces, General Spaatz and Air Chief Marshal Harris, were in thorough agreement: they felt they could best contribute to *Overlord* by continuing their air offensives against the German homeland—the British by night against the cities, the Americans by day against key industries. In particular, Spaatz wanted to deploy the bulk of the American bombers against Germany's oil-producing facilities. This offensive, he believed, would deny vital fuel to the German ground forces fighting the Allied invaders. Moreover, Spaatz was certain that oil installations would be heavily defended by the Luftwaffe, giving his escort fighters the opportunity to shoot down many enemy interceptors and to extend Allied superiority in the air.

Spaatz and Harris were opposed in the debate by advocates of what was called the Transportation Plan. The plan envisioned using the U.S. and British bombers to cripple the main German lines of communication in northwest Europe. Rather than just temporarily interdicting roads, bridges and rail lines, the bombers would carry out a systematic attack aimed at totally disrupting German traffic. The principal targets were to be some 80 railway marshaling yards and repair centers in Belgium and northern France. Their destruction, proponents argued, would create "a railway desert" around the intended Allied beachheads in Normandy, sealing off the Germans from supplies and reinforcements.

The man who originated the Transportation Plan was an imaginative 39-year-old British scientist named Solly Zuckerman, then a civilian adviser to *Overlord*'s air planners. He had solid credentials as an air strategist. When it was deemed vital to seize the heavily fortified Mediterranean island of Pantelleria before the invasion of Sicily in 1943, Zuckerman's calculations about such seemingly arcane matters as the density of bomb strikes needed to silence gun batteries had helped make it possible to win the island's surrender simply by bombing. But Zuckerman had his detractors. Air Chief Marshal Harris could not resist harping on Zuckerman's academic background: he had been a zoologist specializing in monkeys. The chief, one of Harris' aides said, "felt that Zuckerman did not necessarily qualify as a competent authority on air strategy by virtue of his exceptional knowledge of the sexual behavior of anthropoid apes." (Later, after Zuckerman had been elevated to the peerage as Lord Zuckerman, he acknowledged the incongruity by titling his memoirs *From Apes to Warlords*.)

To the consternation of Harris and Spaatz, the Transportation Plan gained backing at the highest levels. Deputy Supreme Commander Tedder, formerly the Allied air commander in the Mediterranean, had seen Zuckerman's ideas bear fruit. Tedder, once described by a superior as "a practical thinker" with "a great gift for getting his priorities right," was able to look beyond the prevailing dogmas of strategic

bombing. He wanted the most direct help he could get from the bombers in making Normandy safe for invasion. So did his boss; Eisenhower approved the Transportation Plan.

Even then, the plan faced opposition from a formidable adversary. Prime Minister Churchill came down on the side of Harris and Spaatz, attacking the alternative proposal ostensibly for humanitarian reasons. The raids on the rail yards, Churchill argued, would result in the "cold-blooded butchering" of civilians who were living nearby.

Churchill probably had less lofty reasons for the stance he took. Worn and edgy after more than four years as Britain's war leader, he was increasingly concerned with the political future, and killing Frenchmen in bombing raids was not likely to improve Anglo-French relations after the War. At one point, Eisenhower had to remind Churchill that only the previous year he had endorsed full-scale bombing of German U-boat facilities in French ports without expressing undue concern for civilians. Finally, Churchill gave up his opposition to the Transportation Plan—but only after President Roosevelt refused his appeal to intervene.

Though Harris and Spaatz were unhappy about the plan's adoption, not all of their air crews agreed. For British fliers, the attacks on railways and repair shops turned out to be a welcome respite from the costly raids on Berlin, Nuremberg and other German cities. Moreover, the focus on smaller targets proved that Bomber Command was capable of far more accuracy at night than Harris had thought possible.

Much of this accuracy was attributable to a new way of marking and illuminating the target. In past raids a "master bomber" would circle the target during an attack, assessing the accuracy of the marking and broadcasting advice to the other bomber crews. The new tactic called for the master bomber, flying a Mosquito, to swoop earthward, sight the target visually and drop the markers himself.

The change in technique was pioneered by Squadron 617, the elite "dam busters" who had breached the Ruhr dams in the spring of 1943. The squadron was now under the command of Leonard Cheshire, at 25 the youngest group captain in the RAF. In his role as master bomber, Cheshire liked to swoop down to 700 feet, then race along over the streets of the target area, dropping his marker bombs. The accuracy of the low-level marking by the diving dam busters was demonstrated by a Lancaster attack on the rail yards at

On the morning of a combat mission, pilots of the all-black 332nd Fighter Group receive a briefing at their base near Ramitelli, Italy. Arriving in Italy in early 1944, the pilots of the 332nd flew P-47s until the middle of the year, when they were transferred from the Twelfth to the Fifteenth Air Force and reequipped with P-51 Mustangs. Within two weeks of switching over to the new planes, they scored more than a dozen kills. The 332nd was later awarded a Distinguished Unit Citation for defending bombers during a 1,600-mile round-trip raid against a Berlin tank factory— the longest mission ever flown by the Fifteenth Air Force.

Juvisy-sur-Orge, 11 miles south of Paris. Aiming at the master bombers' marks, the Lancasters dropped 1,000 bombs in such tight clusters that many craters overlapped.

The American bombers were permitted to vary their missions in France with occasional returns to Germany—thanks to the stubborn belief of General Spaatz that the real key to Allied victory in Europe lay in destroying Germany's oil installations. Eisenhower approved of a limited offensive against the installations whenever Eighth Air Force bombers could be spared from the campaign against the railways.

Spaatz, however, had another source he could tap without any hampering restraints: the Italian-based Fifteenth Air Force, which was not involved in the Transportation Plan. In the month or so since February's Big Week—the joint venture to Germany with the Eighth Air Force—the Fifteenth had mounted a score of missions ranging from the German submarine base at Toulon to the rail yards of Budapest and Bucharest and including repeated forays over enemy strongholds in Italy itself. The men of the Fifteenth were ready to take on the series of 20 missions—all to the same place—that would represent their most memorable contribution to the Allied cause.

The target was Ploesti, where Africa-based bombers of the Ninth Air Force and others on loan from the Eighth had met with disaster in August of 1943. The fields and refineries of the sprawling Rumanian oil center, once again operating at full tilt, were still Germany's biggest supplier of fuel. On April 5, the Fifteenth was dispatched to hit Ploesti's rail yards, where the oil was loaded for shipment to Germany. Enough of the U.S. bombs fell on the refinery district to cause substantial havoc. The success of the attack spurred others; the Fifteenth continued visiting Ploesti until mid-August, pounding it to a virtual standstill. The Fifteenth's own cost was high: 223 of its planes were lost.

Spaatz meanwhile was pressing his oil campaign in Germany itself as well. Beginning in May he sent planes of the Eighth Air Force, whenever they could be diverted from their primary tasks under the Transportation Plan, to bomb synthetic-fuel plants in the Reich. Spaatz was to be proved right in his insistence on the vulnerability of German oil, though the effects of the U.S. attacks were not fully evident until several months after D-Day.

Altogether, the Allied strategic and tactical air forces, including the medium bombers and fighter-bombers of the American tactical Ninth Air Force, newly based in England, flew some 200,000 sorties in direct support of the impending invasion. They severed France's railway lines at numerous points, destroyed 1,500 locomotives and cut all 24 bridges over the Seine between Paris and the sea. By the beginning of June, rail traffic in France was near chaos.

In addition to smashing the targets designated by the Transportation Plan, the American and British bombers and fighters destroyed 36 airfields, 41 radar installations and 45 gun batteries in the area. All of the raids were carefully calculated to mislead the Germans about the site of the Allied landings: for every target that was bombed in the Normandy area, two were attacked elsewhere.

A separate air campaign concentrated on German launching sites along France's west coast. These were the pads from which Hitler intended to fling his V-1 flying bombs against England. Destruction of the V-1 sites—whose existence had been shown by aerial reconnaissance photos as early as May 1943—was considered so crucial by the Allies that the Americans constructed full-scale replicas of them in Florida to perfect their low-level bombing techniques.

In all, in the six months before D-Day the Allies flew 25,150 sorties against the V-1 sites, knocking out 83 of them. Operation *Crossbow*, as the campaign was called, forced the Germans to abandon the sites and construct prefabricated launch pads. These pads could be assembled quickly and were small enough to be housed in ordinary farm or factory buildings, thus effectively concealing them from Allied aircraft. But the change-over delayed Hitler's plans for sending his *Vergeltungswaffe*—vengeance weapons—against England, and the Allies were ashore on the beaches of Normandy a week before the V-1s began flying.

On D-Day itself—June 6, 1944—the Allied air forces put on a show that overshadowed all that had gone before in the skies over Europe. During the 24 hours of D-Day, more than 8,000 bombers and fighters—the smaller planes had their wings and fuselages painted with bold stripes for quick identification—flew nearly 14,700 individual sorties. The planes pounded coastal gun batteries, dropped airborne troops and towed glider-borne men into battle, flew protective cover for the seaborne invasion convoys, strafed German troop positions and patrolled over the Normandy beaches. They also completed the job of interdicting roads and railways. Their destructive work was so thorough that the German 2nd SS Panzer Division took 17 days to travel 450 miles from southern France to the fighting front, and many of the German troop reserves had to make their way to Normandy on foot.

The strangest Allied air mission on D-Day called for neither bombing nor strafing but for elaborate subterfuge. Long before dawn, two RAF bomber units—the Stirlings and Halifaxes of Squadron 218 and the Lancasters of dam-busting Squadron 617 under Leonard Cheshire—headed across the Channel toward the Pas-de-Calais area on the northwest coast of France. Their purpose was to lead the Germans to believe that the Allied invasion force would land there instead of on the beaches at Normandy, some 150 miles to the southwest.

The scheme—the brainchild of British radar scientist Robert Cockburn—called for flooding German radar screens in the Pas-de-Calais area with bogus blips that indicated the advance of two huge armadas, one of aircraft and the other of ships. Though most of the German radar stations in the area had been knocked out by Allied planes before D-Day, some had been deliberately left untouched for the purposes of this deception.

To carry it out, Cockburn's team of mathematical wizards had worked out an incredibly complex series of calculations calling for the two RAF squadrons to fly a pattern of rectangular orbits each about eight miles long and two miles wide, moving one mile closer to the French coast as they completed each orbit. In the meantime, they dropped the metal-foil strips of Window at the rate of 12 bundles every minute. The wizards had even figured out the size of the strips needed to enhance the impression of the immensity of the invading air armada; the longest were nearly six feet long.

Below the RAF bombers, the "fleet" they were supposedly covering—18 small launches—churned along toward the Pas-de-Calais playing their own part in the deception. Each launch carried at least one 29-foot-long balloon with a radar reflector built into it. This device picked up the pulses of enemy radar, amplified them and sent them back, producing an echo equivalent to that of a 10,000-ton ship.

Cockburn's scheme, which had been rehearsed successfully with captured German radar in Scotland's Firth of Forth, worked equally well on the coast of France. The Germans were so convinced of what their radar screens showed that their coastal batteries actually began hurling 12-inch shells seaward. Inexplicably, not a single German night fighter flew out to reconnoiter the enemy armadas.

Indeed, so few German aircraft appeared at any time, anywhere, on D-Day that the commander in chief of the Allied air forces for the invasion, Air Chief Marshal Sir Trafford Leigh-Mallory, paced his office at headquarters outside London, asking over and over, "Where is the Luftwaffe?"

The answer was that virtually all of the Luftwaffe was in Germany. It had been forced there first by the need to defend the homeland against the massive U.S. bombing raids of previous months, then by preinvasion attacks that had made airfields in France and Belgium unusable. All told, the Luftwaffe only managed some 300 sorties over France on D-Day—one for every 50 by the Allies.

Two of the day's bravest and most futile Luftwaffe sorties were flown by Major Joseph Priller, a fighter-wing commander, and his wingman, Flight Sergeant Heinz Wodarczyk. The pair were alone that morning at the unit's former base near Lille. Under orders from higher up, the rest of Priller's day fighters had recently been scattered to bases around inland France, away from the coastal areas where Priller was certain the invasion was imminent. Priller, an ace with more than 90 combat victories and a reputation for talking back to his superiors, had bitterly protested the dispersal of his unit and then, on the eve of the invasion, had gotten drunk with Wodarczyk.

Early on D-Day, Priller and his wingman, nursing hangovers, raced southwest to Normandy in their FW-190s. They swooped down scarcely 100 feet over the swarming British beachheads, shot up all their ammunition and scurried back to Lille—staggered by the enormity of what they had seen and astonished that they had flown unscathed through the gauntlet of Allied fighters and antiaircraft fire.

Priller and his wingman were among the few German pilots to brave the beaches of Normandy during the daylight hours of D-Day. After dark, a handful of Ju-88s also scattered bombs there. These were the only exceptions to the fulfillment of Eisenhower's confident prediction to his ground forces on the eve of the invasion: "If you see fighting aircraft over you, they will be ours."

AIR SUPPORT FOR THE ARMY

Flying at treetop level, a P-47 Thunderbolt returns after scouting the route ahead of three American tanks advancing along a country road in northern France.

THE ALLIES' WINNING AIR-GROUND TEAM

Tactical air power—the use of planes to support troops in the field rather than for the strategic purpose of undermining the enemy's overall warmaking ability—was pioneered with awesome effect by the Luftwaffe. Thousands of German planes, acting in close coordination with armored and infantry units, lent terrifying potency to the German juggernaut that rolled across Europe in 1939 and 1940. But by mid-1943, the British and Americans had seized the lead in developing tactical air techniques, and their hard-hitting sorties ultimately helped tip the balance in their favor on the battlefields of Western Europe.

The Allies employed tactical air power in a deadly three-stage pattern, throwing into the fray planes of all types—even heavy bombers normally used on strategic missions. First, planes of all sorts ranged well ahead of the ground assault forces, attacking any Luftwaffe planes and bases in the chosen zone to achieve local air superiority—if not total mastery. Then, to isolate the enemy forces in the battle area, bombers and fighters plastered rail lines, highway junctions, truck convoys and trains. Finally, as Allied ground forces moved forward, fighter-bombers hit enemy troops and strong points that stood in the way of the advance. These dangerous operations were executed primarily by airmen of the British Second Tactical Air Force, the U.S. Ninth Air Force and the U.S. First Tactical Air Force, who had received months of special training for the job.

The mightiest—and most successful—tactical air operation supported the Allied invasion of Normandy in June 1944. Tactical air forces operated from England until the beachhead was secured, then moved to hastily built airstrips in Normandy. Thereafter, tactical units were constantly on the move, not only flying several sorties a day but also relocating their makeshift bases to keep up with ground advances. The pace was exhausting, but the pilots thrived on combat. "Our eyes sharpened with each mission," said Lieut. Colonel Norman Holt, commander of the 366th Fighter Group. After a sortie, said Holt, "all of us wanted to get back, refuel, re-arm and get in another sock at the Nazis."

In a sod-floor operations hut in Normandy, P-47 pilots study tactical targets pointed out by their commander, Lieut. Colonel Norman Holt.

Paving the way for a ground attack, two B-26 Marauders leave ruins behind them after a bombing raid on a rail yard and power station at Charleroi, Belgium.

The strafing of three German planes during postinvasion aerial operations is recorded in blurred photos taken by cameras in the wings of Allied fighters. At top, the pilot of a downed Me-110 flattens himself in snow as the attacker makes another pass. In the other low-level strafing missions, parked Ju-52 transports (center) and a Dornier seaplane are riddled by Allied fighter-bombers.

A pall of smoke blankets the Luftwaffe's airdrome at Chateaudun, south of Paris, while two Consolidated B-24 Liberators make their final bombing passes.

HUNTING DOWN THE ENEMY'S PLANES

To gain local air superiority, Allied tactical air forces hit the Luftwaffe relentlessly in the air and on the ground. Their standard attack plan carried a grimly efficient one-two punch. While fighters were engaging Luftwaffe planes in the air, bombers and fighter-bombers dodged flak in order to hit hangars, administration buildings and maintenance revetments. Meanwhile, other planes made strafing runs and dropped 20- to 500-pound bombs on unattended aircraft, runways and dispersal areas.

In tactical operations coordinated with the Normandy invasion, Allied air forces gained control of the air far beyond the beachhead area. The massive and wide-ranging assault knocked out 36 airfields within 130 miles of the assault beaches, denying their facilities to Luftwaffe planes that might have succeeded the hundreds that had been destroyed. By the time the invasion armies broke out of the Normandy beachhead, the Allies' mastery of the skies was so complete that German infantrymen in the combat zone made a bitter joke of their plight. They claimed to have a foolproof method of identifying aircraft overhead: if the plane was silver, it was American; if dark in color, British; if it could not be seen at all, it was German.

Climbing for another pass, a P-38 Lightning flies over a smouldering locomotive. Some German trains carried guns for defense.

Entangled track and

Bombs fall on a vital bridge across the Moselle River north of Trier, Germany, as four B-26s prepare to add their load to the assault.

demolished trains litter the railway marshaling yard near Limburg, Germany. The yard was struck by medium and light bombers of the U.S. Ninth Air Force.

CUTTING OFF AND CUTTING UP THE COMBAT ZONE

After minimizing the Luftwaffe's ability to interfere with ground operations, Allied air units drew a broad circle of destruction around the combat zone. Roads and rail lines were cut, bridges were bombed and enemy shipping disrupted. This prevented supplies and reinforcements from reaching the front—and it also obstructed the German troops who were trying to leave the combat zone and establish new defense lines elsewhere.

The objectives that offered the biggest dividends were railway marshaling yards, where tracks converged and trains were loaded. By knocking out one such clearing point (about 500 tons of bombs would do the job, the Allies calculated), bombers could stop rail traffic over a vast area.

Meanwhile, other aircraft flew tactical missions against enemy transport within the battle zone. Many trains, immobilized by bombed-out rails to the front and rear, were blown to bits by low-flying fighter-bombers. "I had to fly through one of the explosions," an American pilot said. "I saw a box car wheel go up by my wing."

A British Beaufighter (top) fires its rockets
at a ship in the North Sea. Such tactical strikes
claimed uncounted victims, among them
the minesweeper M-37 (bottom), which burned
and sank in the Bay of Biscay in August 1944.

A German truck convoy carrying ammunition and fuel blows up, ignited by .50-caliber tracer bullets fired from the P-47 that took this photograph. The explosion of one truck started a lethal chain reaction that destroyed approximately 90 per cent of the convoy.

A P-47 escapes the inferno of an ammunition truck it has just hit. Many low-flying planes were destroyed when their targets exploded.

Scanning the sky from the hatch of a Sherman tank, a fighter pilot serving as air liaison officer directs support planes to their target by radio. Liaison duty was highly unpopular with most pilots; they were eager to return to their P-47s and P-51s, which they considered safer than tanks.

A P-47 Thunderbolt (upper right) dives and strafes a smoke-shrouded German position outside Couptrain, France, in August 1944. U.S. armored troops watch the action while awaiting orders to proceed toward town. Often, supporting fighters made tactical attacks with surgical precision on enemy strong points only a few hundred yards from Allied ground units.

THE "GUARDIAN ANGELS" OF ALLIED ARMOR

Tactical air units were a natural partner and complement to the fast-moving tank columns that ranged ahead of the infantry. Because success depended on a knowledgeable dialogue between the men in the planes and those on the ground, fighter pilots, thoroughly familiar with the capabilities of close-support aircraft, were assigned to ride as air liaison officers in tank units rigged with aircraft radios. The pilots of the covering planes—usually flights of four P-47s—hit close-in targets at the request of the liaison officer or, free-lancing ahead, struck danger spots and warned the advancing tanks of what to expect.

Tankmen were duly grateful to the fliers, whom they called their "guardian angels." After P-47s had demolished a German position that was holding up an armored unit near Liege, Belgium, in 1944, the exuberant column commander radioed his flight leader: "Great! With support like that we can go all the way to Berlin."

6

Spreading carpets of bombs across Normandy
A colossal gun misfires
No hiding place in a leafy lane
Unexpected gifts from a rookie German pilot
Thousand-plane raids become commonplace
Production chief Speer sees his nightmare materialize
The Germans unveil a plane of the future
Fire storm at Dresden
British second thoughts on strategic bombing

In the summer of 1944, the German soldiers fighting the Allied invaders of Normandy got a bitter foretaste of what would befall their own homeland during the final phases of the air war. Armadas of as many as 2,000 enemy bombers roared over them, disgorging explosives in such enormous quantities that the terrified troops below called them *Bombenteppich*—"carpets of bombs."

For the Allies, carpet bombing had a particular purpose: to help their ground forces break out of Normandy by obliterating certain German strong points that blocked the paths of advance. When artillery alone did not suffice, carpet bombing—concentrated on a few square miles of battleground—reduced the German positions to corpse-strewn debris, literally clearing the way for the Allied soldiers to move on.

Since the opposing forces were sometimes separated by a distance of as little as 1,000 yards, carpet bombing required the utmost precision to avoid Allied casualties. Close coordination with the Allied ground commanders was also essential. Their troops had to be ready to move as soon as the target area was laid waste; otherwise, those Germans who had survived the saturation attack would have time to regroup or call in reinforcements.

The carpet-bombing tactic turned out to be sounder in theory than in practice. On July 7, 1944, when 457 RAF bombers came to the aid of British and Canadian infantry stalled outside Caen by dropping some 2,300 tons of bombs on the northern sector of the city, the infantrymen were able to advance—but the tanks and supply columns were not. The carpet bombing had cratered Caen's streets and blocked them with rubble, making it impossible for any sort of vehicle to get through.

A more serious concern was the bombers' accidental toll of the men they were supposed to be supporting. Allied ground commanders had vigorously expressed their fear of this possibility, insisting that the bombline be no closer to their troops than 1,200 yards. Still, a number of bombs fell short of their intended mark, most notoriously on the 24th and 25th of July, when planes of the United States Eighth and Ninth Air Forces targeted the area around a key highway between Saint-Lô and Périers. The Germans' elite Panzer Lehr Division held one side of the road, and troops of the American First Army held the other side.

THE FINAL ONSLAUGHT

The attack on July 25 employed 1,900 bombers carrying a total of 3,950 tons of bombs. From his side of the road, the panzer commander, Major General Fritz Bayerlein, watched in stupefaction as the monster armada appeared. "The planes kept coming over as if on a conveyor belt, and the bomb carpets unrolled in great rectangles," he recalled. "My flak had hardly opened its mouth when the batteries received direct hits which knocked out half the guns and silenced the rest. After an hour I had no communication with anybody, even by radio. By noon nothing was visible but dust and smoke." Surveying the scene around him, Bayerlein was reminded of a lunar landscape. About 1,000 of his men lost their lives in this carpet bombing; so many others were wounded or numb with shock or babbling insanely that for all practical purposes the Panzer Lehr Division was out of action.

On the other side of the highway, the Americans were also counting their losses: errant bombs had killed 111 men and wounded 490 others. Two days later the U.S. breakout near Saint-Lô took place, creating an opening for the Allied sweep across the rest of France. But the grief visited upon American troops by American planes brought a swift response from Supreme Allied Command headquarters. General Eisenhower, who had previously approved of carpet bombing because of its "most heartening effect upon our own men," now ruled that heavy bombers were no longer to be used for close ground support.

The power of the bombers was brought to bear for another special purpose: the destruction of German installations that were suspected of housing the launching pads and the storage depots for Hitler's "vengeance" weapons. Scores of such sites had been destroyed along France's west coast before the invasion; now the operation was focused mainly on those in northern France. From this area the V-weapons not only had a lesser distance to travel to their projected primary target, London, but also posed a threat to the Allies' newly won positions in Normandy.

To smash the German installations, which were protected by iron-and-concrete domes as thick as 30 feet, required explosives in extraordinary quantities. The British and the Americans came up with separate answers to the problem. The RAF bombers carried a six-ton blockbuster designed by Barnes Wallis, who had devised the huge, spinning bombs used against the Ruhr dams in 1943. The new bomb, 21 feet long, was appropriately dubbed Tallboy. Streamlined to achieve a speed of about 750 miles per hour as it hit the ground, it was capable of boring through dozens of feet of concrete or rock before it was detonated by a delayed-action fuse deep inside the bomb.

The Americans experimented with a different sort of firepower. Expendable battle-worn Flying Fortresses and Liberators were packed with 20,000 pounds of high explosives; then, manned by a pilot and copilot, they were flown toward France. At a point on the English coast, just before the Channel was to be crossed, a fuse would be set and the two men aboard would bail out; a reconnaissance plane overhead would note their landing place so that they could be picked up. Meanwhile, their lethal aircraft roared on toward the target, remotely controlled by radio equipment contained in a conventional "mother" plane that guided the drone into the target.

Seven such missions, given the code name *Aphrodite*, were mounted in August of 1944, some with unhappy results. Several of the drone planes blew up prematurely, killing their pilots. Among the vicitms was a U.S. Navy lieutenant on loan to *Aphrodite*, Joseph Kennedy Jr., the older brother of a future U.S. President.

The bombing of the V-weapon sites turned out to be a case of too much, too late. The four main targets, all in the Pas-de-Calais area, were quickly overrun by Allied troops, and showed no signs of occupancy except by rats and cockroaches. At Hitler's order, the installations had been moved farther eastward.

One of the abandoned sites—at a hamlet named Mimoyecques, near the port of Calais—was found to contain a partially assembled V-weapon previously unknown to Allied intelligence and completely different from the V-1 flying bomb and the V-2 rocket. The V-3 was an enormous gun designed to have 50 barrels, each 416 feet long; one Allied expert described it as "perhaps the most extraordinary weapon of the Second World War, excluding the atomic bomb." The gun was intended to shower London with 300-pound shells hurled at the rate of one every six seconds. Though London was 95 miles away, the V-3's potential range was 100 miles; this remarkable range was to be achieved by the ignition of explosive charges placed at intervals along each barrel. Fortunately for the Londoners, who were already having to cope with the V-1s, the V-3's projectiles had proved unstable in flight. Despite their tremendous velocity inside the barrel, they tended to wobble after leaving the gun, and the increased air resistance reduced the range.

Together, the campaign against the V-weapons and the carpet-bombing missions represented but a fraction of the effort expended by the Allied air forces in aid of the invasion of the Continent. During the summer of 1944, the bombers of the U.S. Eighth Air Force and RAF Bomber Command, in concert with the medium and light bombers and fighter-bombers of the U.S. Ninth Air Force and the RAF's Second Tactical Air Force, supported the advancing troops by flying nearly half a million sorties—pounding rail lines, road junctions, bridges, barges, airfields, supply depots and enemy troops on the run. The flights were not only shorter but far less hazardous than the previous operations over Germany itself had been; on the Western Front, the Allied planes outnumbered the Luftwaffe by about 8 to 1. Predictably, the Allied pilots came to look upon their sorties as mere "milk runs."

As they fled from Normandy, the German troops tried desperately to elude attack from the air by taking advantage of the peculiarities of the local terrain. Carefully avoiding the major roadways, they traveled along lanes lined with ditches, thick hedges and tall, overarching beeches and hornbeam trees that formed natural tunnels; as an added attempt at cover, they stacked the roofs of their vehicles with fresh-cut branches.

But concealment from the sky was not always possible. In mid-August, after the rout of the Germans at Falaise, a British ground observer inspected a one-mile stretch of a lane along which a fleeing enemy column had come under rocket and cannon fire from Typhoons of the RAF Second Tactical Air Force, fighter planes that were especially effective in low-flying attacks. The observer reported:

"Where the retreating Germans had been caught in the open, they lay in irregular swathes mostly in the shallow ditches. Their transport was mixed. Cars of every description, many of them Citroens, Renaults and other French makes, strewed the fields, mingled with horses dead in the shafts of stolen carts and even old-fashioned traps of two generations ago. I noticed one up-to-date limousine painted with the stippled green and brown camouflage affected by the Germans. It contained on the back seat a colonel and his smartly dressed mistress. Each had been shot through the chest with cannon shells. The driver, who had quitted the wheel, lay a yard or two further on in the ditch with a very dead cow for company. At the entrance to the next section of leafy lane a tank, its gun pointing skywards, straddled the road. From the turret hung a German, his bloated face black with flies. . . . In the sunken lane under the semi-darkness of the arching trees in full August leaf the picture of destruction was complete and terrible to the last detail."

In the view of the British and American bomber bosses, Air Chief Marshal Harris and General Spaatz, these missions were diversions from their principal strategic objective— the extinction of Germany's capacity to make war. Harris and Spaatz were impatient to get on with the job. For the first time since the start of the air war, their forces possessed sufficient numbers of heavy bombers—almost 5,000—and the requisite air superiority to strike decisive blows against the German homeland.

Both men thought it might "still be possible," as Spaatz put it, "to beat up the insides of Germany enough by air action to cause her to collapse" by the spring of 1945. But they had sharply differing opinions as to the surest way to bring on the collapse. Spaatz remained wedded to the idea that wrecking Germany's oil industry would speed the end. In pursuit of this unshakable belief, he had already taken advantage of Eisenhower's agreement to let him conduct a limited offensive against the enemy's oil resources, both natural and synthetic, whenever his planes could be spared from missions in Normandy. By summer's end, Rumania's Ploesti oil fields and other German suppliers in Eastern Europe, as well as synthetic-fuel plants in Germany itself, had been hit by Spaatz's airmen.

Harris had grudgingly allotted RAF bombers to join in some of these strikes, but his own idea of how to knock out Germany was the same as it had been in 1942, and no less adamant. He continued to insist that the Reich would collapse when enough of its cities lay in ruins. Harris was certain his bombers could finish the job they had started

NEW PLANES, VAIN HOPES

Toward the end of the War, German engineers produced an assortment of seemingly farfetched military aircraft. Though all of them had technical problems, one epoch-making creation regularly outperformed the Allies' best planes in combat. Following a losing encounter with a jet-powered Messerschmitt-262, a Spitfire pilot worried: "Should the enemy possess reasonable numbers of these remarkable aircraft, it would not be long before we lost the air superiority for which we had struggled." But Germany's bold aeronautical initiatives came too late to do much more than stir the Luftwaffe's yearning for what might have been.

The Me-262, introduced in July 1944, was the first jet plane to fly combat. The 540-mph planes claimed more than 500 Allied aircraft.

The Messerschmitt-163 Komet was propelled by a rocket engine that took off at full throttle, burning up its entire fuel supply in minutes.

The composite Mistel consisted of an FW-190 mounted on an unpiloted, bomb-laden Ju-88 that was guided to the target by radio.

The Dornier-335 was powered by two engines, one pulling from the front, the other set in the tail and pushing from the rear.

The Heinkel-162 jet was simply designed and built of inexpensive materials, but its mass-production potential failed for lack of time.

two years earlier. He had more planes than ever at his disposal; though the U.S. planes outnumbered the British planes by more than 2 to 1, Bomber Command now had round-the-clock capability on its own. Beginning in September the RAF planes could fly missions by day, escorted by U.S. fighters or shorter-range British Spitfires operating from forward bases in liberated sections of France. And at night, Harris' bombers at last had the superiority over the Luftwaffe that had eluded them for so long.

In part, this newly acquired advantage was due to the hard-won advance of the Allied ground forces through France and Belgium. By overrunning German night-fighter bases and ground control stations, the troops knocked out the cornerstones of the Luftwaffe's early-warning network. German night fighters no longer would be able to receive the signals that had alerted them to intercept the British bombers 100 or so miles from their targets, as had been the case during the disastrous RAF mission to Nuremberg in March of 1944.

The RAF's night fliers also benefited from a lucky fluke. In July, a rookie Luftwaffe pilot, thinking he was over a German-held base in Holland, landed his night fighter at an English airfield. Apparently he had been attracted by the glare of oil burners placed on the field to heat the air and disperse the fog over the runways.

The German plane, a Junkers-88 of the latest type, carried two electronic devices, previously unknown to the British, that had enabled the Luftwaffe's night fighters to detect aircraft in the dark. One was the SN-2 airborne radar, which used a long wavelength that could not be jammed by the metal strips of Window; the Germans had made good use of SN-2 against the Nuremberg-bound RAF bombers. The second instrument, which was code-named Flensburg, enabled the Luftwaffe's night fighters to track down enemy bombers by homing in on transmissions from a special radar device aboard the RAF planes. This device, code-named Monica and installed in the tail of a bomber, gave warning of a German fighter's approach from the rear.

By careful study and testing of these unexpected gifts from the rookie German pilot, the British came up with a couple of effective countermeasures. A new type of Window strip, matched to the SN-2's wavelength, made the night fighters' radar susceptible to jamming. And the threat presented by the Flensburg homing device was dealt with simply by removing Monica from the RAF bombers. The Luftwaffe's only technological advantages in the night skies were thus neutralized.

On September 14, 1944, Harris and Spaatz got the go-ahead they had restlessly awaited. Authority over the bombers formally reverted to them under a directive issued by the Combined Chiefs of Staff. Supreme Allied Commander Eisenhower, who had held control over the bombers for the past six months, retained first call on them for emergency tactical missions. But Harris and Spaatz were now free to resume a full-scale bomber offensive against the German homeland. The Combined Chiefs of Staff designated Germany's oil industry as the top-priority target and its lines of communication as the second most important. Without canals and railways and highways to transport fuel and other essential supplies, the German war machine would be stopped dead in its tracks.

In the next seven months, Allied planes were to ravage Germany with more than 800,000 tons of bombs—some 60 per cent of all the tonnage dropped on the Reich in nearly five years of war. Oil targets alone were hit with 220,000 tons, finally reducing the Reich's production to a mere 5 per cent of what it had been before the concentrated attacks began. Raids of 1,000 planes—the number Harris had barely scraped together for his epic mission against Cologne in 1942—became commonplace.

The process of assembling these gigantic armadas had by now been refined virtually to an exact science. Spaatz's Eighth Air Force bombers would take off from their bases in southeastern England at intervals of about 30 seconds. Each plane would fly out to sea on a predetermined heading and for a predetermined length of time. It would then double back toward the English coast to an assigned radio beacon, approach at an assigned altitude and look for its own group. To make the search easier as the sky filled with incoming bombers, each group had a so-called assembly plane, a battle-worn castoff painted with polka dots, zebra stripes or other distinctive markings; some planes had the group letter blazoned 10 feet high on the side and outlined in flashing lights.

Human skill took over from science once the bomber

A B-24 assembly plane, painted with red, yellow and black polka dots to offer maximum visibility, stands ready to serve as an aerial rallying point for bombers forming up prior to a mission over Germany. Bombers used as assembly planes were usually older models no longer fit for combat; after the formation was complete, they retired to home base.

located its group and moved to get into the formation, a maneuver much like hopping aboard a speeding carrousel. An experienced pilot learned how to time his bomber's turn—its turning radius was about five miles—to meet the group formation as it came around on its next circle. Collisions with other planes trying to join the formation were frequent, and even more so on days when vapor contrails hampered visibility.

At a certain time, exact to the minute, the command pilot leading the group would leave the beacon on a given heading and begin to work his way into the main bomber stream. Very gingerly, 1,000 planes would edge into formation and head toward Europe, rising, lowering, tipping, skidding and rocking to stay in position. The strain of the entire exercise showed in odd ways. One copilot of a B-24 recalled: "I've seen the steam rising from the throttle hand of my pilot with the temperature in the cockpit around 50 below."

By October of 1944, General Spaatz's oil campaign was in full swing. He no longer had to concern himself about the Germans' major outside source of oil, Ploesti. The Rumanian oil fields, heavily damaged by his Fifteenth Air Force bombers striking from Italy, had been captured in late summer by the resurgent Russian armies; in their sweep into Eastern Europe, the Russians had also overrun a number of refineries in Poland. The Reich's chief remaining outside supplier was Hungary. While the Fifteenth's bombers raided the oil-rich area around Budapest, Spaatz's Eighth Air Force bombers, flying from England, pounded the Germans' last bastions of oil production—some two dozen synthetic-fuel plants situated inside Germany itself.

Air Chief Marshal Harris, despite his unconcealed preference for bombing the enemy's cities, threw the weight of RAF Bomber Command into the oil campaign. The British planes possessed advantages the American planes lacked: the capacity for carrying bigger bombs, and an improved radar device called GH, which permitted blind bombing of the target through cloud cover and smoke when visual sighting proved futile. But most important, the joint efforts of the bombers of the RAF and the U.S. Eighth and Fifteenth Air Forces made it possible to carry out a systematic attack on the oil installations.

The prospect of just such an attack "had been a nightmare to us for more than two years," Albert Speer later revealed. The Allied raiders were no longer switching from target to target and paying their visits irregularly. Speer, now presiding over all of Germany's war production, knew that it faced strangulation.

He launched an all-out effort to save the oil. Workers—largely slave laborers—ringed the most important parts of the plants with blast walls of thick concrete. They built air-raid shelters inside the plants so that oil crews would lose no time returning to their jobs when the Allied bombers left. After a raid, the workmen toiled to repair and piece together the wreckage so that plants could resume operating as quickly as possible. But the workers were not always cooperative; during one Allied raid, an Italian conscript was caught surreptitiously spreading the fire started by the Allied bombs.

Speer was banking on the usual bad weather of late autumn to slow down the Allied campaign and permit at least partial restoration of production. He was also counting on enemy strategists to display some of their earlier incon-

sistency. "Our one hope," he once remarked to Hitler, "is that the other side has an air force General Staff as scatterbrained as ours."

But throughout the fall and winter of 1944, the Allied air strategists had the right targets in mind, the weather turned out better than Speer had anticipated and the Allied resources were so great that there was no question about follow-up. The bombers were able to return again and again, repeating their attacks until repair efforts became more and more futile.

The most dramatic demonstration of the Allies' new staying power was directed at the giant Leuna chemical-fuel works 100 miles southwest of Berlin, not only the largest producer of synthetic fuel in Germany but also the most heavily defended. It was guarded by the biggest concentration of gun batteries the Germans had yet assembled, and it could be further shielded during a raid by a dense smoke screen produced by the fumes of an acid solution sprayed into the air. In all, the Allies mounted 22 missions against Leuna, 20 by the Eighth Air Force and two by the RAF, reducing its output to a monthly average of 9 per cent of its normal capacity.

By the end of 1944, the Allies' destructive attacks were clearly outstripping Speer's herculean efforts at restoration. On December 16, when Hitler began a last-ditch counteroffensive against the Allies in the Ardennes region of Belgium, his tanks started out with only a five-day fuel supply—and the offensive was literally to run out of gas.

For the Luftwaffe, the oil campaign packed a double punch. As supplies of aviation gasoline dwindled, the interceptors had to be grounded for days at a time. And when they did go up to do combat, they faced unbeatable odds. German fighter-pilot losses were so high that Heinz Knoke, a young commander whose unit of Messerschmitt-109s was sometimes outnumbered by as much as 40 to 1, wrote in his diary: "Every time I close the canopy before taking off, I feel that I am closing the lid of my own coffin."

The Luftwaffe's last great hope—and the Allied air strategists' chief worry—during the closing months of 1944 centered on two new German fighter planes that did not need conventional high-octane fuel. There was, in fact, little that was conventional about either plane. One was powered by a rocket motor; the other was a jet. Both could outspeed and outclimb any plane in the world.

The rocket-powered fighter, the Me-163 Komet, had a short, squat shape, and was dubbed the "powered egg" by the hand-picked pilots who flew it. The Komet had plenty of power. Its top speed was about 590 miles per hour, 100 miles per hour faster than the U.S. Mustang, and it could climb straight up at the rate of 11,500 feet per minute. In one of the plane's first combat trials, during an American raid on Magdeburg in August of 1944, a trio of Komets had easily overwhelmed a formation of Mustang escorts. The German fighters climbed high above the formation, looped and suddenly zoomed down on the Mustangs, scoring three quick hits.

But the Komet also had problems. One was landing. The Komet took off on wheels, but these were jettisoned in flight and the plane had to land—at 120 miles per hour —on a skid fastened to its undercarriage. A more serious problem was the Komet's lack of endurance. The fighter exhausted its 437-gallon fuel supply in four to seven minutes; even if the enemy could be engaged in that short period of time, the pilot would have to cut off combat and glide back to base. This limited the Komet's radius of action to about 25 miles from home.

The worst problem lay in the fuel itself—actually two distinct fuels that burned when they were mixed in the engine. The mixture consisted of a catalyst called C-Stoff, mainly methyl alcohol, and T-Stoff, concentrated hydrogen peroxide. Both were so corrosive that they could dissolve flesh, and the mixture itself was so volatile that a number of Komets simply exploded on the runway.

Only 279 Komets came off the German assembly lines, and perhaps a quarter of them saw combat. Though Komet pilots claimed a total of nine Allied bombers and fighters, the troublesome plane took a much larger toll of the Germans who tried to fly it.

If the Komet proved to be no more than a historical oddity, the Luftwaffe's other new fighter, the jet-powered Messerschmitt-262, represented the wave of the future. It was a bit slower than the Komet, with a top speed of 540 miles per hour, but it could stay aloft for well over an hour. Moreover, the Me-262's twin engines consumed common diesel fuel, which posed none of the dangers of the volatile rocket fuels and which was easier to come by than high-octane aviation fuel.

A few of the Me-262s were sent into combat during the summer of 1944 and quickly took the measure of some of Britain's fast-flying Mosquito reconnaissance planes. At first, the German jets avoided the enemy bomber formations and their fighter escorts. But the very presence of such a formidable new weapon alarmed the Allied air commanders; they were aware that sufficient numbers of jets might well jeopardize their entire bomber offensive. The British had a jet interceptor, the Gloster Meteor, but its range was too short to get it to Germany, and an experimental American jet was more than a year from combat readiness.

Fortunately for the Allies, the Luftwaffe as yet had only a few Me-262s. Hitler had dallied too long in developing the jet. When Germany's aeronautical experts unveiled the world's first model in August of 1939, four days before the start of the War, the Führer was so confident of an early victory in the coming conflict that he paid little attention to the enormous military potential of the jet. By November of 1943, when the Me-262 reached the stage when it could be mass produced and employed as a fighter, Hitler was so obsessed with pressing offensive action against the Allies that he had only one question to ask about the plane: "Can this aircraft carry bombs?" And when his compliant Luftwaffe chief, Göring, answered, "Yes, my Führer, theoretically yes," Hitler ordered the Me-262 put into production—but as a fighter-bomber.

At the time, however, the Me-262 had no fixtures for releasing bombs, and modifying it would have critically delayed deliveries. Hitler's order was quietly disobeyed by Göring's top deputy, Field Marshal Milch. As Director of Air Armament for the Luftwaffe, Milch knew that the jet was desperately needed to fend off the Allied bombers, and he put the plane into production as a fighter. But in May of 1944 the Führer learned that his order had been flouted. Furiously he halted production, called in Milch and demanded an explanation.

Milch compounded his dilemma. "My Führer," he burst out, "the smallest infant can see that this is a fighter, not a bomber aircraft!" A shocked silence filled the room; no one talked to Hitler that way. "Aufschlagbrand" (crashed in flames), one awed witness whispered. Within the month Milch was out of a job, consigned to less prestigious duties within the Luftwaffe.

Hitler thereafter forbade mention of the Me-262 as anything but a "blitz bomber." But some of the men around him, including Speer, dared to keep up the pressure for its full-scale production as a fighter. The most vociferous advocate was Adolf Galland, the Luftwaffe's outspoken fighter chief. Galland had test-flown the Me-262 in 1943 and had found the experience "like flying on the wings of an angel." He declared that he would rather have one jet than five conventional fighters.

In late September of 1944, Hitler finally relented. A second jet plane, the Arado 234, which had been intended from the beginning as a light bomber and reconnaissance plane, was now slowly coming off the assembly lines. Hitler grudgingly made a deal with Galland and the other jet-fighter proponents: for every Arado bomber produced, he would permit one Me-262 to go into action as a fighter.

A week later, on October 3, the Luftwaffe's first jet-fighter unit became operational at two bases near Osnabrück, not far from the border with Holland athwart the main U.S. bomber route to Germany. The unit consisted of about 30 Me-262s commanded by Major Walter Nowotny, an Austrian-born pilot who, at the age of 23, had become the first Luftwaffe ace to be credited with 250 aerial victories. His remarkable total was run up mainly against easier opposition on the Eastern Front, and it also reflected the German practice of giving credit for kills even though the enemy was not seen to crash or bail out (the Allies would list such victories as "probables").

Under Nowotny's enthusiastic leadership, the new unit tackled American bomber formations on the way to their targets in Germany—and the Mustang escorts were soon forced to revise their tactics. Instead of ranging ahead of the bomber formations to seek out the Germans, they had to stick close to their Big Friends to screen off the swiftly darting Me-262s. During the first month of operations, Nowotny's jets shot down 22 enemy bombers and fighters.

But technical troubles and inadequate pilot training in the tactical uses of the Me-262—as well as the overwhelming numbers of American fighters—soon took their toll. Since the jet engines required a complete overhaul after every dozen hours of use, Nowotny could seldom put up more than three or four planes on a given day. Moreover, the takeoffs and landings of the Me-262s—their toughest maneuvers—had to be made through a gauntlet of Mustangs and Thunderbolts patrolling above the jet bases.

On the morning of November 8, Nowotny led a flight of five jets against an American bomber formation. Three Me-262s went down, but Nowotny radioed back to base that he had just claimed his 258th kill. Then one of his engines died. Nowotny was attempting to make a landing with a swarm of Mustangs on his tail when the plane suddenly plunged to earth and exploded.

Among those witnessing the crash was General Galland, who was at the base waiting for Nowotny's return. Galland withdrew the unit from operations; the day's losses had left it with only four serviceable jets. While a new unit was being formed with Nowotny's surviving pilots as the nucleus, Galland fell back on his one remaining hope for a Luftwaffe triumph—a plan that would make use of his conventional fighters.

The scheme called for assembling an armada of 3,000 fighters, then flinging them—all in one day—against a big American bomber mission. All through the autumn Galland had been husbanding his Me-109s and FW-190s. He was prepared to lose as many as 500 fighters if he could bring down as many enemy bombers in one powerful stroke. He called his plan *Der Grosse Schlag*—The Great Blow. Galland believed that if the bombers could be dealt such a blow in one day they would be forced to suspend their campaign against Germany's oil.

However, circumstances chipped away at Galland's plan. The enemy bombers appeared a total of 13 days that November, unloading their highest tonnage ever on the oil targets. The Luftwaffe had to commit reserve planes to fend off the raiders, and in just four days of fierce combat the Germans lost a total of nearly 300 pilots killed or wounded. Then, in mid-November, Hitler took away the remaining fighters Galland had assembled for his Great Blow and sent them to the Western Front in preparation for the big counteroffensive in the Ardennes.

Hitler wanted the fighters to stage a massive surprise strafing attack on Allied forward airfields in Holland, Belgium and France, then provide air cover for his panzers' advance. The panzers moved on December 16, but thick winter fog delayed the Luftwaffe's assault on the Allied air bases. By the time it was launched on the morning of New Year's Day, 1945, the huge German fighter force had been whittled to less than half by Allied strafing and by combat in the skies over the front lines.

The New Year's strike force consisted of nearly 900 Messerschmitts and Focke-Wulfs, practically the entire available strength of the Luftwaffe's fighter arm. Many of the pilots were ill-trained novices, and some of the older hands were hung over after a celebration of what they believed would be their last New Year's Eve. As a result, many pilots never found the Allied bases. But others did, and they caught several of the bases by complete surprise. They destroyed or severely damaged 206 enemy planes, most of them still parked on the ground.

Elsewhere, U.S. and British fighters quickly rose to the defense, and furious aerial combat ensued. At the U.S. base at Asch, in Belgium, a dozen Mustangs were taking off shortly before 10 a.m. when 50 German raiders swooped down. The Mustangs were led by Lieut. Colonel John C. Meyer, deputy commander of the 352nd Group and a fighter ace. Had Meyer followed the official orders for the day, his pilots would have been in their snow-covered tents preparing for a bomber-escort mission to Germany. But earlier that morning, on a hunch that the Luftwaffe might show up over the Ardennes front, Meyer had talked his commanding general into permitting part of his group to remain behind to fly a tactical patrol.

Meyer was leading his Mustangs off the runway when he suddenly looked up and saw an FW-190 coming straight at a nearby transport plane on the field. He quickly pulled up his landing gear, gave the Mustang full throttle and gunned down the intruder. For the next hour, Meyer and his pilots tangled with the Germans while frantically dodging barrages of antiaircraft fire from American gunners around the base. Though Meyer lost a chunk of his wing to his own ground gunners and almost ran out of ammunition, he survived both the flak and the enemy fighters. His Mustangs destroyed nearly half of the 50 raiding planes.

Meyer was credited with two Focke-Wulfs shot down that morning, giving him a total of 24 aerial victories for the War.

A group of three Spitfires, piloted by French exiles serving with the RAF, prepares to make a landing near others on a recaptured airfield at Luxeuil-les-Bains, France, in September 1944. American bombers demolished the hangars and the Luftwaffe plane at left before the Germans retreated.

These kills made him one of the highest-scoring American aces in Europe. That afternoon, Meyer safely flew a tactical patrol mission. Soon afterward, he was grounded for the duration of the War—by injuries suffered in an automobile accident.

Asch was only one of the bases over which the German raiders incurred heavy losses. Of the nearly 900 pilots involved in the New Year's mission, 253 were killed, wounded or taken prisoner. This represented the Luftwaffe's largest loss in a single day of the War, and one the Germans could no longer afford. What had begun as Galland's Great Blow had been transformed—by Allied fighter power and by Hitler's meddling—into the Luftwaffe's last gasp.

Early in 1945, the Allied bombers turned their full fury upon the Reich, now virtually defenseless. Vast carpets of bombs unrolled across its cities, leveling those that had escaped Allied attention and piling rubble upon ashes in those that had not. By then, large parts of most big German cities—those with populations of more than 100,000—lay in ruins.

The champion of the area-bombing policy, Air Chief Marshal Harris, had started in early 1943 with a list of 60 cities he intended to destroy, and he kept ticking them off one by one. He persisted despite intense pressure from his boss, Chief of the Air Staff Portal, to concentrate on the top Allied bombing priorities, oil and communications—targets whose destruction was paying far greater dividends to the Allied cause than were being gained by the wholesale onslaught on the cities.

Portal and his superiors questioned only the effectiveness of the area bombing, not its morality. Portal himself had recently put forward a proposal to stage a massive attack on Berlin, calling for round-the-clock punishment by British and U.S. bombers. The purpose of the operation, code-named *Thunderclap,* was to shatter popular morale so that the Germans would give up and sue for peace. However, the operation had been shelved because the Americans could not provide sufficient fighter escort for all the bombers the plan required.

In any case, General Spaatz opposed *Thunderclap* and,

indeed, the entire concept of bombing cities. The U.S. bomber boss said he did not want to be "tarred" with the aftermath—the recriminations that would surely follow after the War. Despite Spaatz's intentions, however, the distinction between British area bombing and U.S. precision attacks was not all that clear. When bad weather prevented the sighting of a target, the American bombardiers resorted to blind bombing, using newly developed radar devices like those employed at night by the British. Bombs dropped by radar—a method exploited at least in part during about 80 per cent of the American raids in the last three months of 1944—sprayed all over the area, spreading destruction far from the refinery or railway marshaling yard that was the specific target. On the average, fewer than one third of the bombs fell within 1,000 feet of the target.

Moreover, early in 1945, after Hitler's Ardennes offensive had shaken Allied confidence in the likelihood of an early end to the War, there was increasing pressure on Spaatz to come up with some decisive, *Thunderclap*-like blow from the air. In this atmosphere of impatience and frustration, Spaatz abandoned his usual stance. On February 3, 1945, he sent nearly 1,000 bombers against Berlin. The raid was directed at rail yards and other transportation targets, but many of the bombs fell on government buildings at the center of the city. Later, Spaatz admitted that his Fortresses had bombed indiscriminately, "making no effort to confine ourselves to military targets." Perhaps 25,000 Berliners died in that raid.

An even deadlier attack on another city soon followed. On February 13 and 14, British and American bombers raided Dresden, 100 miles south of Berlin. The destruction of Dresden became the symbol of the air war's final months of terror from the sky.

On the hit list kept by Air Chief Marshal Harris, Dresden ranked near the bottom; it was, in fact, the largest German city to have escaped full-scale bombing thus far. It had been touched by bombs just twice—in both instances by American planes that were diverted to Dresden's rail yards after clouds obscured their primary targets, oil installations. Dresden had little else of importance to the Allied strategists. Throughout Germany, it was known for its cultural and historical amenities—parks, museums, an opera house

and buildings, some of which dated back to the 13th Century. The world beyond Germany identified Dresden with the delicate porcelain that was actually produced in a village about 12 miles away.

The initiative for the attack on Dresden came from Prime Minister Churchill, as part of a larger plan to bomb a number of cities in eastern Germany. Churchill's motive was essentially political. He and President Roosevelt were soon to meet with Stalin at Yalta, and neither Western leader had much to show the Soviet dictator in the way of recent Anglo-American ground successes. The British and U.S. armies were stalled at the western approaches to Germany while a massive Russian Army offensive was in progress along the Reich's eastern borders.

Blasting Dresden and other cities in eastern Germany from the air would give Stalin tangible proof of the efforts of the British and the Americans on Russia's behalf. The raids would not only sow confusion among the hundreds of thousands of Germans fleeing the Red Army offensive, but would also hamper the movement of German troops to the Eastern Front. Not incidentally, the raids would also remind Stalin of the awesome air power possessed by Britain and the United States.

The staff planners at RAF Bomber Command showed no great enthusiasm for hitting Dresden. They knew little about the city's defenses and even lacked a standard target map of the area. Harris himself seemed surprised at his new orders. Some of his squadrons expressed their disapproval of the assignment by voting to forgo a customary ritual—the dropping of bottles, bits of concrete and other junk intended as an insult to the Germans.

Otherwise, the manner in which the attack on Dresden was delivered was, by this late stage of the air war, distinctly routine. On the night of February 13, the British sent two separate waves of Lancasters. The first wave, 234 planes, bombed for 17 minutes. The second wave, 538 planes, arrived three hours later and aimed at the fringes of the spreading flames below. Altogether, the British dropped 2,656 tons of bombs, a load by now regarded as unexceptional. About 75 per cent of the bombs were incendiaries, standard procedure for an old city whose wooden dwellings were so flammable. Some 10 hours after the last British bombs fell, the Americans arrived. It was Ash Wednesday,

Atop Dresden's town hall, a sandstone figure gestures with eerie serenity toward the ruins of the city's old quarter, ravaged in a fire storm set off by Allied bombing in February 1945. A British pilot wrote: "For the first time in many operations I felt sorry for the population below."

and shortly after noon the 311 Flying Fortresses bombed by radar, aiming 771 tons at the city's railway stations and marshaling yards.

What made the Dresden attack so extraordinarily destructive was an unusual combination of circumstances. There was virtually no opposition; the city's antiaircraft guns had been removed the previous month and sent to the Russian front, and though a unit of Me-110 night fighters was based only five miles away, the fuel shortage was now so acute that the pilots were forbidden to take off without authorization from division headquarters. The authorization came too late, and the pilots had to sit in their planes on the runway and watch Dresden burn.

Moreover, the weather over Dresden was unusually clear during the night. The clouds covering Germany broke for a few hours, allowing the RAF's Lancasters to concentrate their bombs with an aiming accuracy that had been perfected after five years of trial and error. Most important, Dresden was woefully unprepared for an attack of such dimensions. In all the city there was but one concrete bunker suitable for a bomb shelter—and it was reserved for the local gauleiter. Neither Dresden's officials nor its citizens had wanted to believe that their city would be bombed. Local rumor had it that Dresden would be spared because the Allies intended to relocate Germany's capital there after the War—or because relatives of Churchill's supposedly resided in the city. The lack of preparedness was compounded by the presence of refugees from the Eastern Front, who had swollen the city's population of 630,000 to well over a million. Many of the refugees came from remote country areas and had never heard an air-raid siren.

Dresden burned for a week. The worst fire came within an hour after the British attack, when thousands of separate blazes merged into a howling fire storm of the type created by the RAF at Hamburg in July of 1943. It engulfed some 1,600 acres, practically the whole of old Dresden, generating winds of tornado force, incinerating everything and everyone in its path, and sucking the life out of those who had attempted to seek refuge in the cellars of the city.

A Dresden schoolmaster named Hanns Voigt, who was pressed into service as chief of an emergency agency called the *Abteilung Tote,* or dead-persons department, later described the horror. "Never would I have thought that death could come to so many people in so many different ways," he recalled. "Never had I expected to see people interred in that state: burnt, cremated, torn and crushed to death; sometimes the victims looked like ordinary people apparently peacefully sleeping; the faces of others were racked with pain, the bodies stripped almost naked by the tornado; there were wretched refugees from the East clad only in rags, and people from the Opera in all their finery; here the victim was a shapeless slab, there a layer of ashes shoveled into a zinc tub."

The task of identifying and removing the dead proved so difficult that, to prevent typhus and other epidemics, Dresden's authorities finally cordoned off the center of the city and set up 25-foot-long grills where thousands of the victims were cremated.

Initial estimates of the death toll, ranging as high as 135,000, were later revised downward to 35,000—less than the number of people who had perished at Hamburg in 1943. But the earlier estimates—and an unprecedented barrage of German radio propaganda—served to perpetuate Dresden's tragedy as a symbol of air power gone amok. In the days immediately following the attack, many Americans and Britons became aware for the first time that Allied bombing was not always directed at military and industrial targets—as their governments had led them to believe. On February 17, 1945, an Associated Press dispatch reported that the Allied air chiefs had made the "long-awaited decision to adopt deliberate terror bombing of the great German population centers as a ruthless expedient to hasten Hitler's doom." The dispatch was incorrect in suggesting that the decision was a new one; actually, indiscriminate bombing was by this time an old story—although the Allied chiefs balked at the use of the term "terror bombing."

The Associated Press dispatch was widely published in American newspapers but was suppressed by the British government. Nonetheless, questions about Dresden and area bombing were raised in the House of Commons on March 6. Even Churchill had second thoughts, although he seemed to be less concerned about morality than about Britain's own self-interest.

On March 28, Churchill stated his view in an infelicitously worded memorandum to Chief of the Air Staff Portal. "It seems to me," the Prime Minister wrote, "that the moment has come when the question of bombing German cities simply for the sake of increasing the terror, though under other pretexts, should be reviewed. Otherwise we shall come into control of an utterly ruined land. We shall not, for instance, be able to get housing material out of Germany for our own needs because some temporary provision would have to be made for the Germans themselves."

The reference to "terror" bombing so incensed Portal that Churchill reworded the memorandum. However, indiscriminate bombing was now clearly out of favor with Churchill, Portal and other officials who had originated the policy even before Air Chief Marshal Harris took over its implementation in 1942. When the British Government showered formal honors on its fighting men at the end of the War, Harris and RAF Bomber Command were to be conspicuously ignored. On the first anniversary of the Dresden raid, Harris retired to Rhodesia.

Despite its powerlessness at Dresden, the Luftwaffe fought on. In March of 1945 it managed to send up 40 or 50 jet fighters at a time to try to fend off new attacks by the Allied bombers. One of the new jet units was led by Adolf Galland, who had begun the War as a squadron commander and wanted to end it in the same capacity. Göring, with Hitler's approval, had finally ousted Galland as the Luftwaffe's fighter chief after he had openly ridiculed the Führer's newest pet scheme for winning the air war. This scheme involved a wonder weapon, not yet operational, known as the *Volksjäger*—People's Fighter. It was a small, single-engined jet that, as Hitler envisioned it, would be flown by fanatical 16- to 18-year-old boys after a brief period of training in gliders.

To Galland's new unit flocked the Luftwaffe's last surviving aces. So eager were they to serve under him—and to end the War with honor by flying the world's fastest fighter—that several pilots left their hospital beds to join up. Göring himself told Galland that he would have been happy to serve if "I were a few years younger and less bulky."

Galland and his aces, sometimes taking off from bomb-cratered runways and flying against insuperable odds, succeeded in shooting down nearly 50 Allied planes. Then, one April day, Galland's own jet was badly shot up. He skillfully crash-landed it at 150 miles per hour and was taken to the hospital with shell fragments in his knee.

On the previous day, 318 RAF Lancasters had gone after Hitler himself, bombing the Führer's mountain retreat at Berchtesgaden. Hitler was not there. He was 300 miles away in Berlin, holed up in the bombproof bunker where, five days later, he would take his own life.

The mission to Berchtesgaden was one of the last to be flown by the Allied bombers. By April, they had simply run out of targets. On April 16, with the U.S. and Russian ground forces converging in the heart of Germany, the Anglo-American strategic air offensive was officially ended.

The offensive had been waged at a cost of nearly 160,000 Allied airmen—79,265 American, 79,281 British—and an undetermined number of German fliers. The effectiveness of the bombing, as well as the morality of killing an estimated 305,000 German civilians, would be the subject of endless postwar debate. The bombers did not fulfill the dreams of the early prophets who had predicted that air power alone could win a war. Nor did bombing crack the German will to resist. But the Allied ground armies that were now overrunning the Reich were there in large part because of the devastation that had been wrought at such cost by the bomber offensive.

THE AIRMEN'S ARSENAL

BOEING B-17G FLYING FORTRESS

Power plant: Four 1,200-hp Wright Cyclone radial engines
Wing span: 103 ft. 9 in.
Length: 74 ft. 9 in.
Gross weight: 65,000 lbs.
Range: 1,850 miles with 4,000-lb. bombload
Maximum speed: 302 mph at 25,000 ft.
Armament: Thirteen .50-caliber Browning machine guns; standard bombload, 6,000 lbs.; maximum, 12,800 lbs.
Crew: 10

A B-17G, the most numerous of the six operational Flying Fortress models, bears the red and yellow markings of the Eighth Air Force's 487th Bomber Group.

LEAPFROGGING GAINS IN PLANE MAKING

Throughout the War, Britain, the U.S. and Germany engaged in a technological race to equip their air forces with bombers and fighters that could outfly, outshoot and outlast the enemy's planes. Between them, the aviation industries of the combatants built hundreds of thousands of aircraft in hundreds of different models. Some of the most effective and widely used planes are shown on these pages, along with average specifications for the craft.

The balance of power in the air war shifted repeatedly as one side, then the other, produced new planes—or new models of old ones—that had an edge over enemy aircraft. At the outset of the War, Germany possessed thousands of superior Heinkel-111 medium bombers and Messerschmitt-109 fighters; they spearheaded the swift conquest of Poland, France and the Netherlands, and the subsequent assault on Britain. The British, however, countered with the nimble Supermarine Spitfire, which was instrumental in thwarting the Luftwaffe onslaught. When Britain switched to the offensive, their strategic bombers at first were inadequate. But the advent of the heavy, long-range Lancaster, and later American B-17s and B-24s, gave the Allies the most potent bombing trio of the War. The Luftwaffe took a heavy toll of Allied bombers with its relatively new, deadly Focke-Wulf 190s. But the U.S. quashed this threat by producing the P-47 and P-51, brilliant counterfighter fighters with sufficient range to protect bombers on raids far into Germany.

A few great planes—such as the Me-109 or the sleek Boeing B-17—were admired by friend and foe alike. Several important aircraft had equivocal reputations: for example, the hard-to-handle B-26 Marauder, built at Martin's Maryland aircraft plant, was nicknamed the "Baltimore Whore" because its short, stubby wings gave it "no visible means of support." Yet nearly all of the planes were loved by the men who flew them. "To most pilots," said RAF Group Captain Leonard Cheshire, "the aircraft ceased to be just a machine and became almost another person . . . a being to be cherished and looked after, who in turn would respond to one's own demands to an almost superhuman degree."

FOCKE-WULF 190A-8

Power plant: One 1,700-hp BMW radial engine
Wing span: 34 ft. 5½ in.
Length: 29 ft. 4¾ in.
Gross weight: 10,800 lbs.
Effective operating radius: 942 miles with extra fuel tanks
Maximum speed: 408 mph at 20,670 ft.
Armament: Two 13mm MG 131 machine guns and up to four 20mm MG 151 cannon
Crew: One

Powerful and versatile, the Focke-Wulf 190 was considered Germany's best all-

around fighter. Later models, like this camouflaged FW-190A-8, introduced in 1943, were used primarily to intercept enemy bomber formations over the Reich.

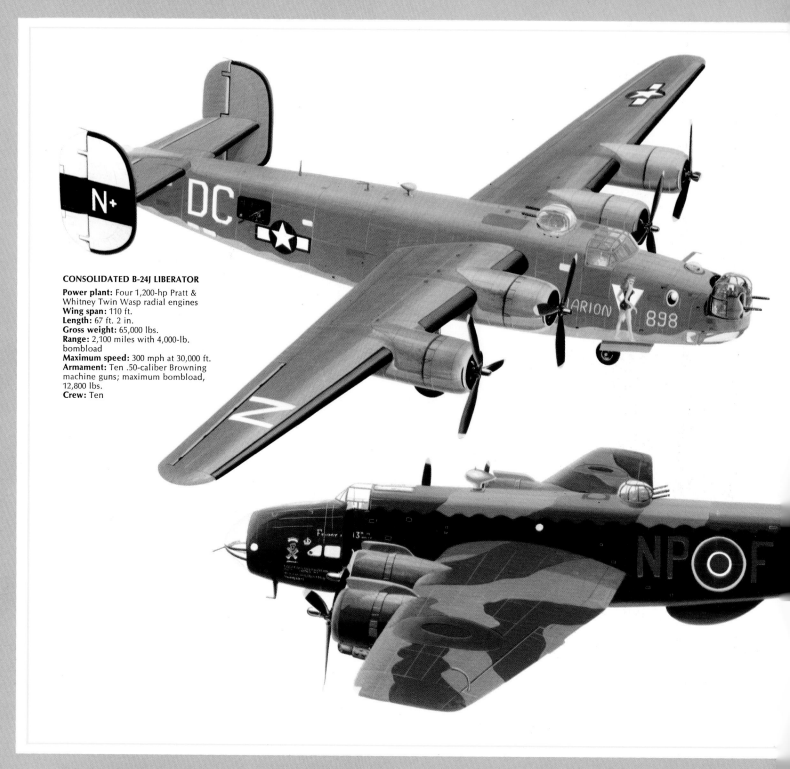

CONSOLIDATED B-24J LIBERATOR

Power plant: Four 1,200-hp Pratt & Whitney Twin Wasp radial engines
Wing span: 110 ft.
Length: 67 ft. 2 in.
Gross weight: 65,000 lbs.
Range: 2,100 miles with 4,000-lb. bombload
Maximum speed: 300 mph at 30,000 ft.
Armament: Ten .50-caliber Browning machine guns; maximum bombload, 12,800 lbs.
Crew: Ten

THE HEAVYWEIGHTS

To hit targets far inside Germany, Britain and the U.S. built several types of long-range, high-altitude heavy bombers. One of the two best British heavyweights was the Handley-Page Halifax, first produced in 1940 and improved steadily in nine subsequent models. The Halifax Mark III, which could carry 13,000 pounds of bombs, was versatile enough to serve as a troop transport, cargo plane, glider tug and antisubmarine patroller.

Overshadowing the Halifax in numbers and performance was the Avro Lancaster, the work horse of RAF Bomber Command. By the War's end, 7,378 Lancasters had flown more than 156,000 sorties to drop 608,612 tons of bombs, more than twice the total load delivered by the Halifaxes.

Of the two U.S. heavy bombers used in Europe, the Boeing B-17 Flying Fortress was more effective, on balance, than the Consolidated B-24 Liberator. But Liberators outnumbered B-17 Flying Fortresses because they were easier to mass produce.

AVRO LANCASTER B. MARK I

Power plant: Four 1,460-hp Rolls-
Royce Merlin engines
Wing span: 102 ft.
Length: 69 ft. 6 in.
Gross weight: 68,000 lbs.
Range: 2,530 miles with 7,000-lb.
bombload
Maximum speed: 275 mph at 15,000 ft.
Armament: Ten .303-in. Browning
machine guns; maximum bombload,
14,000 lbs.
Crew: Seven

HANDLEY-PAGE HALIFAX B. MARK III

Power plant: Four 1,615-hp Bristol
Hercules radial engines
Wing span: 98 ft. 10 in.
Length: 71 ft. 7 in.
Gross weight: 65,000 lbs.
Range: 1,985 miles with 7,000-lb.
bombload
Maximum speed: 282 mph at 13,500 ft.
Armament: One .303-in. Vickers ''K''
machine gun and eight .303-in.
Browning machine guns; maximum
bombload, 13,000 lbs.
Crew: Seven

From 1941 to the end of the War, some
18,400 B-24s were built by five factories in
the U.S.; at Ford Motor Company's half-
mile-long aircraft assembly line at Willow
Run, Michigan, a Liberator could be produced every 50 minutes. Big and boxy, the
B-24 had very long, tapered wings that
made for excellent load capacity, and rate
of climb and range. But Liberator pilots
complained about the bomber's difficult
handling above 20,000 feet. Said one, ''In
the air it was like a fat lady doing a ballet.''

*These three heavy bombers were improved models of old stand-bys. The
B-24J had a new nose turret, revamped fuel lines and a better bomb-
sighting system. The Halifax Mark III, shown here with its nose emblazoned
with bad-luck signs to ward off evil spirits, had more powerful engines
than earlier models. The Lancaster B. Mark I, sporting a painted bomb for
each mission, was a four-engined descendant of the Manchester bomber.*

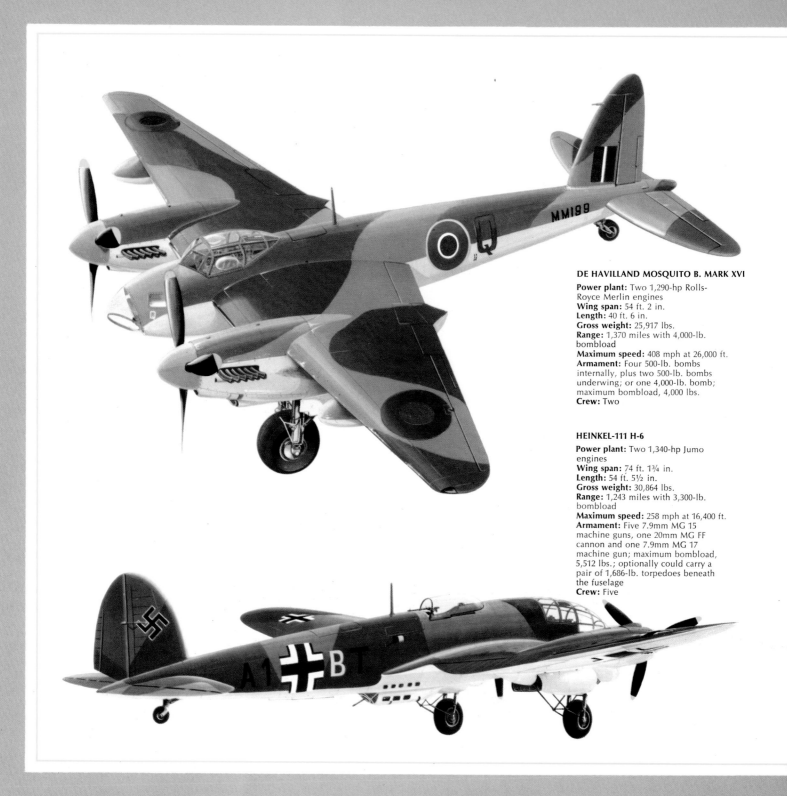

DE HAVILLAND MOSQUITO B. MARK XVI
Power plant: Two 1,290-hp Rolls-Royce Merlin engines
Wing span: 54 ft. 2 in.
Length: 40 ft. 6 in.
Gross weight: 25,917 lbs.
Range: 1,370 miles with 4,000-lb. bombload
Maximum speed: 408 mph at 26,000 ft.
Armament: Four 500-lb. bombs internally, plus two 500-lb. bombs underwing; or one 4,000-lb. bomb; maximum bombload, 4,000 lbs.
Crew: Two

HEINKEL-111 H-6
Power plant: Two 1,340-hp Jumo engines
Wing span: 74 ft. 1¾ in.
Length: 54 ft. 5½ in.
Gross weight: 30,864 lbs.
Range: 1,243 miles with 3,300-lb. bombload
Maximum speed: 258 mph at 16,400 ft.
Armament: Five 7.9mm MG 15 machine guns, one 20mm MG FF cannon and one 7.9mm MG 17 machine gun; maximum bombload, 5,512 lbs.; optionally could carry a pair of 1,686-lb. torpedoes beneath the fuselage
Crew: Five

FOUR FAST BOMBERS

Swifter but smaller than the heavy bombers, with only modest armament and bomb capacity, the medium and light bombers were best suited for short-range tactical air strikes in support of ground troops.

The Germans, who built no successful heavy bombers, believed that large numbers of these fast, agile bombers could do the work of heavyweights, and the Luftwaffe ordered more than 7,000 Heinkel-111s. But the plane, miscast in a strategic role, lacked adequate firepower and armor and proved vulnerable to British fighters. Along with other Luftwaffe light and medium bombers, it failed to do the damage expected of it.

The Allies used their fast bombers in tactical operations and were more successful. The smooth-flying, dependable Douglas A-20G packed six .50-caliber machine guns in its nose, carried 2,000 pounds of bombs and was deadly in ground attacks

MARTIN B-26C-25 MARAUDER
Power plant: Two 2,000-hp Pratt & Whitney engines
Wing span: 71 ft.
Length: 58 ft. 3 in.
Gross weight: 37,000 lbs.
Range: 1,150 miles with 4,000-lb. bombload
Maximum speed: 317 mph at 14,500 ft.
Armament: Twelve .50-caliber Browning machine guns; maximum bombload, 4,000 lbs.
Crew: Seven

DOUGLAS A-20G HAVOC
Power plant: Two 1,600-hp Wright Double Cyclone radial engines
Wing span: 61 ft. 4 in.
Length: 48 ft.
Gross weight: 24,000 lbs.
Range: 1,025 miles with 2,000-lb. bombload

Maximum speed: 339 mph at 12,400 ft.
Armament: Nine .50-caliber Browning machine guns; maximum bombload, 4,000 lbs.
Crew: Three

and light bombing. The Martin B-26 Marauder was an excellent "medium," but the plane was hampered by temperamental flying characteristics. Pilots joked that the Marauder was a "beautiful piece of machinery, but it will never take the place of the airplane."

Of all the medium and light bombers, the most admired was Britain's wooden De Havilland Mosquito; it was so sturdy, versatile and fast—faster than most fighter planes—that Hermann Göring declared, "I wish someone had brought out a wooden aircraft for me." The Mosquito—"Mossie," the British called it—performed best on low-level, high-speed bombing and target-marking runs. Raids by Mosquitoes inevitably came to be known as "Mosquito bites" and, said Adolf Galland, the fighter chief of the Luftwaffe, "like their namesake they became a plague to our command and the population."

Medium and light bombers, such as the Mosquito B. Mark XVI, Heinkel-111 H-6, B-26B and A-20G, were most effective in attacks on troop concentrations, fuel and ammunition dumps, airfields, ships, railroads and bridges.

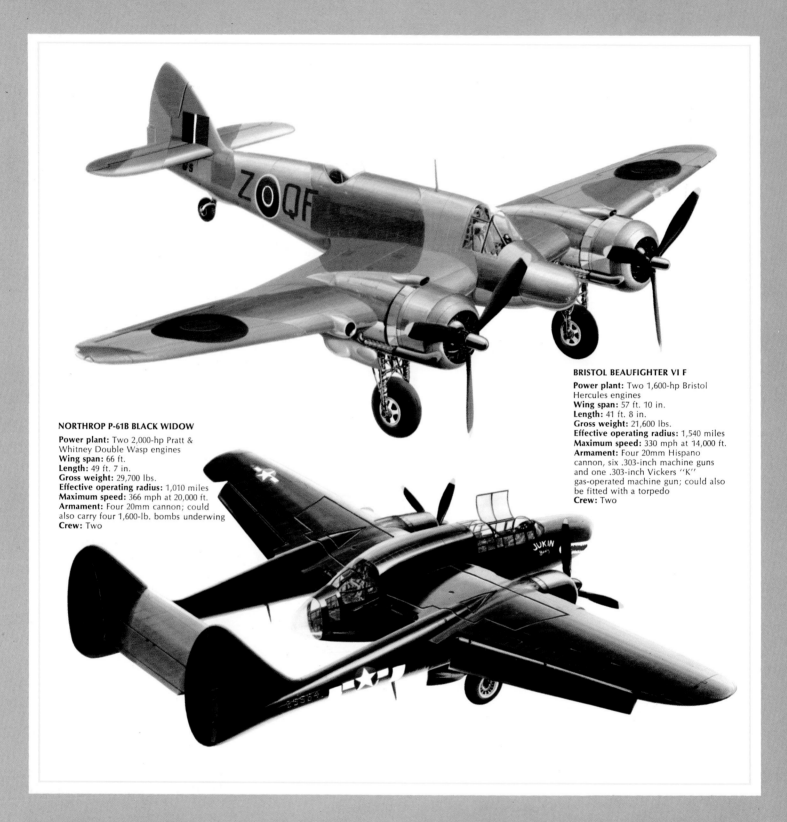

BRISTOL BEAUFIGHTER VI F

Power plant: Two 1,600-hp Bristol Hercules engines
Wing span: 57 ft. 10 in.
Length: 41 ft. 8 in.
Gross weight: 21,600 lbs.
Effective operating radius: 1,540 miles
Maximum speed: 330 mph at 14,000 ft.
Armament: Four 20mm Hispano cannon, six .303-inch machine guns and one .303-inch Vickers "K" gas-operated machine gun; could also be fitted with a torpedo
Crew: Two

NORTHROP P-61B BLACK WIDOW

Power plant: Two 2,000-hp Pratt & Whitney Double Wasp engines
Wing span: 66 ft.
Length: 49 ft. 7 in.
Gross weight: 29,700 lbs.
Effective operating radius: 1,010 miles
Maximum speed: 366 mph at 20,000 ft.
Armament: Four 20mm cannon; could also carry four 1,600-lb. bombs underwing
Crew: Two

SCOURGES OF THE NIGHT

Jolted by the German night blitz of 1940, Britain countered with its radar-equipped night-fighting Bristol Beaufighter. At the time of its debut late that year, the rugged, twin-engined "Beau" was the RAF's only fighter that had the size and power to fly effectively with the bulky Airborne Interception (AI) Mark IV radar gear. The plane was to be a notable success—neutralizing the Luftwaffe's advantage in night attacks.

When the RAF retaliated with strategic bombing of its own, the Luftwaffe hastily modified two of its mainstays, the Junkers-88C and Messerschmitt-110, to serve as night fighters. Both planes were outfitted with primitive radar, whose cumbersome antenna array cut their top speed by 25 miles per hour and significantly reduced their climbing rate and ceiling.

The United States was a late entrant in

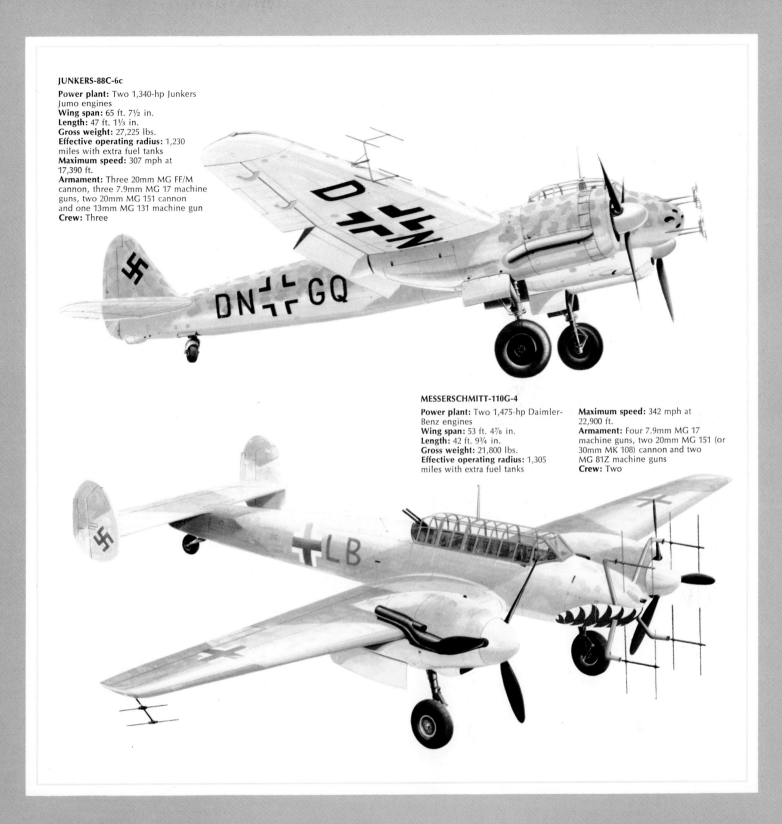

JUNKERS-88C-6c
Power plant: Two 1,340-hp Junkers Jumo engines
Wing span: 65 ft. 7½ in.
Length: 47 ft. 1⅓ in.
Gross weight: 27,225 lbs.
Effective operating radius: 1,230 miles with extra fuel tanks
Maximum speed: 307 mph at 17,390 ft.
Armament: Three 20mm MG FF/M cannon, three 7.9mm MG 17 machine guns, two 20mm MG 151 cannon and one 13mm MG 131 machine gun
Crew: Three

MESSERSCHMITT-110G-4
Power plant: Two 1,475-hp Daimler-Benz engines
Wing span: 53 ft. 4⅞ in.
Length: 42 ft. 9¾ in.
Gross weight: 21,800 lbs.
Effective operating radius: 1,305 miles with extra fuel tanks
Maximum speed: 342 mph at 22,900 ft.
Armament: Four 7.9mm MG 17 machine guns, two 20mm MG 151 (or 30mm MK 108) cannon and two MG 81Z machine guns
Crew: Two

the night-fighter race. However, the twin-fuselage Northrop P-61 Black Widow that was introduced in 1944 was the first airplane designed expressly for night fighting, and it caused a sensation. Two Pratt & Whitney Double Wasp engines, the most powerful motors available, were needed to drive the P-61, whose combat weight of 28,000 pounds made it the heaviest fighter of the War.

Night fighters equipped with radar gear were used almost exclusively as interceptors. The Junkers-88C-6c was the Luftwaffe's most potent night aircraft, while the American P-61B was the Allies' most advanced model.

THE FIGHTERS: DAZZLING AERIAL ACROBATS

The most glamorous performers of the air war were the swift, acrobatic fighters that flew escort and intercepted bombers and staged low-level attacks. The pacesetting early fighters were the RAF's Supermarine Spitfire and the Luftwaffe's Messerschmitt-109. The two remained archrivals throughout the War—the Spitfire relying on unmatched maneuverability, the Me-109 on its superior climbing rate and its performance at high altitudes.

The outstanding American fighters were the heavily armed Republic P-47 Thunderbolt—nicknamed "The Jug" because of its bulky body—and the North American P-51 Mustang, a favorite of pilots. The Mustang's sleek airframe, large fuel capacity and powerful Rolls-Royce Merlin engines combined to produce the high speed, long range and maneuverability that made the P-51 the War's best all-around fighter.

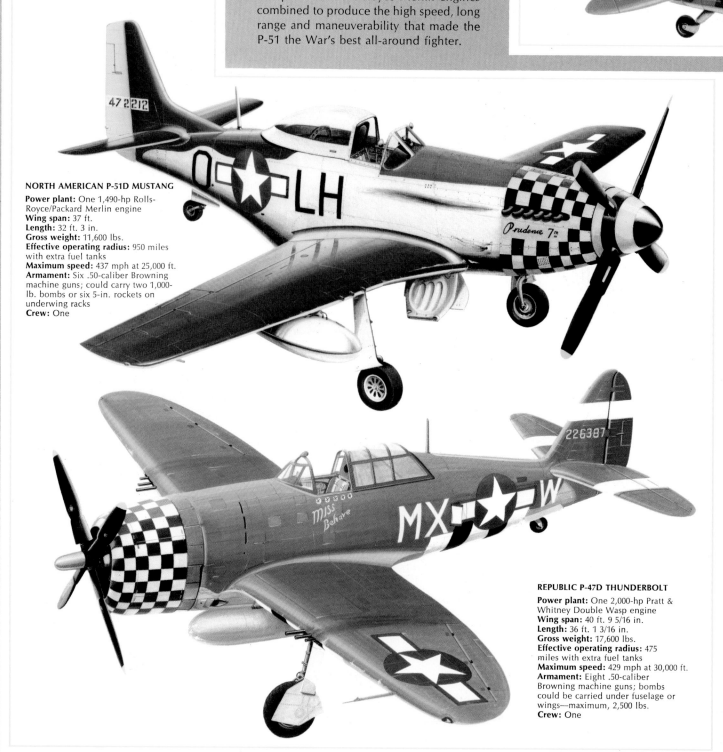

NORTH AMERICAN P-51D MUSTANG

Power plant: One 1,490-hp Rolls-Royce/Packard Merlin engine
Wing span: 37 ft.
Length: 32 ft. 3 in.
Gross weight: 11,600 lbs.
Effective operating radius: 950 miles with extra fuel tanks
Maximum speed: 437 mph at 25,000 ft.
Armament: Six .50-caliber Browning machine guns; could carry two 1,000-lb. bombs or six 5-in. rockets on underwing racks
Crew: One

REPUBLIC P-47D THUNDERBOLT

Power plant: One 2,000-hp Pratt & Whitney Double Wasp engine
Wing span: 40 ft. 9 5/16 in.
Length: 36 ft. 1 3/16 in.
Gross weight: 17,600 lbs.
Effective operating radius: 475 miles with extra fuel tanks
Maximum speed: 429 mph at 30,000 ft.
Armament: Eight .50-caliber Browning machine guns; bombs could be carried under fuselage or wings—maximum, 2,500 lbs.
Crew: One

A P-51D and a P-47D bear checkerboard markings on their noses so that American pilots would not mistake them for the enemy in the heat of battle.

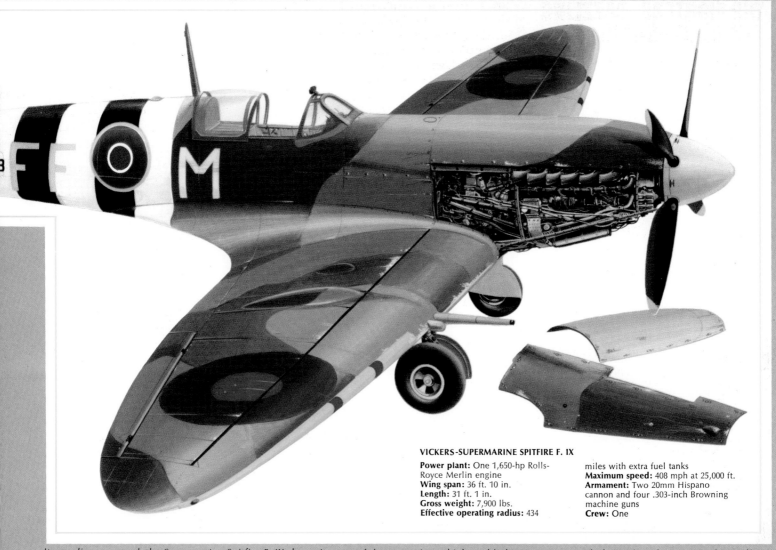

VICKERS-SUPERMARINE SPITFIRE F. IX

Power plant: One 1,650-hp Rolls-
Royce Merlin engine
Wing span: 36 ft. 10 in.
Length: 31 ft. 1 in.
Gross weight: 7,900 lbs.
Effective operating radius: 434

miles with extra fuel tanks
Maximum speed: 408 mph at 25,000 ft.
Armament: Two 20mm Hispano
cannon and four .303-inch Browning
machine guns
Crew: One

Its cowling removed, the Supermarine Spitfire F. IX shows its powerful new engine, which enabled it to compete with the swift and evasive Focke-Wulf 190.

MESSERSCHMITT-109G-6/R6

Power plant: One 1,475-hp Daimler-
Benz engine
Wing span: 32 ft. 6½ in.
Length: 29 ft. 8 in.
Gross weight: 7,491 lbs.
Effective operating radius: 650

miles with extra fuel tanks
Maximum speed: 386 mph at 22,640 ft.
Armament: Three 20mm MG 151
cannon and two 13mm MG 131
machine guns
Crew: One

The Me-109G-6, a late model of the original plane, was equipped with a fuel-injection system that enabled it to dive steeply—a key combat advantage.

203

BIBLIOGRAPHY

Anderson, Wing Commander William, *Pathfinders*. Jarrolds Ltd., 1946.

Andrews, Allen, *The Air Marshals*. William Morrow & Co., Inc., 1970.

Angelucci, Enzo, and Paolo Matricardi, *World War II Airplanes*, Vols. I, II. Rand McNally & Co., 1978.

Arnold, H. H., *Global Mission*. Harper & Bros., 1949.

Barker, Ralph, *The Thousand Plane Raid*. Ballantine Books, Inc., 1965.

Beauman, Wing Commander Bentley, *The Airmen Speak*. Doubleday, Doran & Co., Inc., 1941.

Bekker, Cajus, *The Luftwaffe War Diaries*. Ballantine Books, Inc., 1969.

Bishop, Edward, *The Wooden Wonder*. Max Parrish & Co. Ltd., 1959.

Bombers' Battle: Bomber Command's Three Years of War. Duckworth, 1943.

Bowyer, Chaz, *History of the RAF*. Bison Books Ltd., 1977.

Boyle, Andrew, *Trenchard*. W. W. Norton & Co., Inc., 1962.

Braddon, Russell, *Cheshire V.C.* Arrow Books Ltd., 1966.

Brereton, Lieut. General Lewis H., *The Brereton Diaries*. William Morrow and Co., 1946.

Bridgman, Leonard, ed., *Jane's All the World's Aircraft 1945/6*. David and Charles, Ltd., 1970.

Brookes, Andrew J., *Photo Reconnaissance*. Ian Allan Ltd., 1975.

Brown, Anthony Cave, *Bodyguard of Lies*. Bantam Books, Inc., 1976.

Caidin, Martin:
  Flying Forts. Meredith Press, 1968.
  Me 109: Willy Messerschmitt's Peerless Fighter. Ballantine Books, Inc., 1968.

Campbell, James, *The Bombing of Nuremberg*. Doubleday & Co., Inc., 1974.

Carter, Kit C., and Robert Mueller, *The Army Air Forces in World War II: Combat Chronology 1941-1945*. Office of Air Force History, 1973.

Carver, Field Marshal Sir Michael, *The War Lords*. Little, Brown and Co., 1976.

Cheshire, Squadron-Leader Leonard, *Bomber Pilot*. Hutchinson & Co. Ltd., no date.

Churchill, Winston S.:
  The Second World War. Houghton Mifflin Company.
  Vol. II, *Their Finest Hour*. 1949.
  Vol. III, *The Grand Alliance*. 1950.
  Vol. IV, *The Hinge of Fate*. 1962.

Coffey, Thomas M., *Decision over Schweinfurt*. David McKay Co., Inc., 1977.

Cole, Hugh M., *United States Army in World War II*. Office of the Chief of Military History, 1965.

Craven, Wesley Frank, and James Lea Cate, eds.:
  The Army Air Forces in World War II. The Univ. of Chicago Press.
  Vol. I, *Plans and Early Operations, January 1939 to August 1942*. 1948.
  Vol. II, *Europe: Torch to Pointblank, August 1942 to December 1943*. 1949.
  Vol. III, *Europe: Argument to V-E Day, January 1944 to May 1945*. 1951.
  Vol. VI, *Men and Planes*. 1955.

Divine, David, *The Broken Wing*. Hutchinson & Co. Ltd., 1966.

Dugan, James, and Carroll Stewart, *Ploesti*. Random House, Inc., 1962.

Earle, Edward Mead, ed., *Makers of Modern Strategy*. Princeton Univ. Press, 1944.

Ford, Brian:
  Allied Secret Weapons: The War of Science. Ballantine Books, Inc., 1971.
  German Secret Weapons: Blueprint for Mars. Ballantine Books, Inc., 1969.

Frank, Howard, *The Conquest of the Air*. Random House, Inc., 1972.

Frankland, Noble, *Bomber Offensive: The Devastation of Europe*. Ballantine Books, Inc., 1970.

Freeman, Roger A.:
  The Mighty Eighth. Doubleday and Co., Inc., 1970.
  The U.S. Strategic Bomber. Macdonald and Jane's, 1975.

Galland, Adolf, *The First and the Last*. Henry Holt and Co., 1954.

Gibson, Wing Commander Guy, *Enemy Coast Ahead*. Michael Joseph Ltd., 1953.

Gilbert, James, *The World's Worst Aircraft*. M. & J. Hobbs Ltd. and Michael Joseph Ltd., 1975.

Goddard, Brigadier General George W., USAF (Ret.), *Overview*. Doubleday & Co., Inc., 1969.

Godfrey, John T., *The Look of Eagles*. Random House, Inc., 1958.

Goldberg, Alfred, ed., *A History of the United States Air Force*. Arno Press, 1974.

Green, William:
  Famous Bombers of the Second World War. Doubleday and Co., Inc., 1959.
  Famous Fighters of the Second World War. Hanover House, 1960.
  Warplanes of the Third Reich. Doubleday and Co., Inc., 1970.

Gunston, Bill, *Night Fighters*. Charles Scribner's Sons, 1976.

Hall, Grover C., Jr., *1,000 Destroyed*. Brown Printing Co., 1946.

Hallion, Richard P., *Legacy of Flight*. Univ. of Washington Press, 1977.

Harris, Marshal of the R.A.F. Sir Arthur, *Bomber Offensive*. Collins, 1947.

Hess, William N., *Fighting Mustang*. Doubleday and Co., Inc., 1970.

Higham, Robin, and Abigail T. Siddall, *Flying Combat Aircraft of the USAAF-USAF*. Iowa State Univ. Press, 1975.

IMPACT, Vol. I, 1943; Vol. II, 1944; Vol. III, 1945. United States Air Force.

Infield, Glenn B., *Unarmed and Unafraid*. The Macmillan Co., 1970.

Irving, David:
  The Destruction of Dresden. Holt, Rinehart and Winston, 1963.
  The Rise and Fall of the Luftwaffe. Little, Brown and Co., 1973.

Jablonski, Edward, *Airwar*, Vols. I, II, III, IV. Doubleday & Co., Inc., 1971.

Jones, R. V., *The Wizard War*. Coward, McCann & Geoghegan, Inc., 1978.

Kirk, John, and Robert Young Jr., *Great Weapons of World War II*. Walker and Co., 1961.

Lawrence, W. J., *No. 5 Bomber Group R.A.F.* Faber and Faber Ltd., 1951.

LeMay, General Curtis E., and MacKinlay Kantor, *Mission with LeMay*. Doubleday & Co., Inc., 1965.

Longmate, Norman, *The G.I.'s: The Americans in Britain 1942-1945*. Hutchinson of London, 1975.

Lyall, Gavin, ed., *The War in the Air*. William Morrow & Co., Inc., 1968.

McCrary, Captain John R., and David E. Scherman, *First of the Many*. Simon and Schuster, 1944.

Maurer, Maurer, ed.:
  Air Force Combat Units of World War II. USAF Historical Div., 1960.
  Combat Squadrons of the Air Force, World War II. USAF Historical Div., 1969.

Michie, Allan A., *The Air Offensive against Germany*. Henry Holt and Co., 1943.

Middlebrook, Martin, *The Nuremberg Raid*. William Morrow & Co., Inc., 1973.

Moyes, Philip J. R., *Royal Air Force Bombers of World War II*. Doubleday & Co., Inc., 1968.

Obermeier, Ernst, *Die Ritterkreuzträger der Luftwaffe*. Verlag Dieter Hoffmann, Mainz, 1966.

Olsen, Jack, *Aphrodite: Desperate Mission*. G. P. Putnam's Sons, 1970.

Price, Alfred:
  Battle over the Reich. Charles Scribner's Sons, 1973.
  Instruments of Darkness. Macdonald and Jane's, 1977.
  Luftwaffe: Birth, Life and Death of an Air Force. Ballantine Books Inc., 1971.

Redding, Major John M., and Captain Harold I. Leyshon, *Skyways to Berlin*. Bobbs-Merrill Co., 1943.

Reit, Seymour, *Masquerade: The Amazing Camouflage Deceptions of World War II*. Hawthorn Books, Inc., 1978.

Revie, Alastair, *The Lost Command*. Corgi Books, 1972.

Richards, Denis:
  Royal Air Force 1939-1945. Her Majesty's Stationery Office.
  Vol. I, *The Fight at Odds*. 1974.
  Vol. II, *The Fight Avails*. 1954.

Roseberry, C. R., *The Challenging Skies*. Doubleday & Co., Inc., 1966.

Rumpf, Hans, *The Bombing of Germany*. Holt, Rinehart and Winston, 1961.

Rust, Kenn C.:
  Fifteenth Air Force Story. Historical Aviation Album, 1976.
  The 9th Air Force in World War II. Aero Publishers, Inc., 1970.

Saundby, Air Marshal Sir Robert, *Air Bombardment*. Chatto & Windus Ltd., 1961.

Saunders, Hilary St. George, *Royal Air Force 1939-1945*, Vol. III, *The Fight is Won*. Her Majesty's Stationery Office, 1975.

Saward, Group Captain Dudley, *The Bomber's Eye*. Cassel and Co., Ltd., 1959.

Shepherd, Christopher, *German Aircraft of World War II*. Stein and Day, 1976.

Shores, Christopher, and Clive Williams, *Aces High*. Neville Spearman Ltd., 1966.

Sims, Edward H.:
  American Aces. Harper & Bros., 1968.
  The Greatest Aces. Harper & Row, 1967.

Smith, Constance Babington, *Evidence in Camera*. David & Charles Ltd., 1974.

Smith, Melden E., Jr., *The Bombing of Dresden Reconsidered*. Unpublished manuscript, 1971.

Speer, Albert, *Inside the Third Reich*. The Macmillan Co., 1970.

Tantum, W. H. IV., and E. J. Hoffschmidt, eds., *The Rise and Fall of the German Air Force (1933 to 1945)*. WE Inc., 1969.

Target: Germany—The Army Air Forces' Official Story of the VIII Bomber Command's First Year over Europe. Simon and Schuster, 1943.

Taylor, John W. R., *A History of Aerial Warfare*. Hamlyn Publishing Group Ltd., 1974.

Taylor, John W. R., and Kenneth Munson, *History of Aviation*. Crown Publishers, Inc., 1977.

Tedder, Marshal of the Royal Air Force Lord, *With Prejudice*. Little, Brown and Co., 1966.

Toliver, Colonel Raymond F., USAF (Ret.), and Trevor J. Constable, *Fighter Aces of the Luftwaffe*. Aero Publishers, Inc., 1977.

Tubbs, D. B., *Lancaster Bomber*. Ballantine Books Inc., 1972.

Turner, Lieut. Colonel Richard E., USAF (Ret.), *Big Friend, Little Friend*. Doubleday & Co., Inc., 1969.

United States Army Air Forces, *The United States Strategic Bombing Survey*. 1945.

Vader, John, *Spitfire*. Ballantine Books Inc., 1969.

Verrier, Anthony, *The Bomber Offensive*. The Macmillan Co., 1968.

Weal, Elke Co., compiler, *Combat Aircraft of World War II*. Macmillan Publishing Co., Inc., 1977.

Webster, Sir Charles, and Noble Frankland, *The Strategic Air Offensive Against Germany 1939-1945*, Vols. I, II, III, IV. Her Majesty's Stationery Office, 1961.

Whitehouse, Arch, *The Years of the War Birds*. Doubleday & Co., Inc., 1960.

Wilmot, Chester, *The Struggle for Europe*. Collins, 1952.

Wolff, Leon, *Low Level Mission*. Doubleday & Co., Inc., 1957.

Zuckerman, Solly, *From Apes to Warlords*. Harper & Row, 1978.

PICTURE CREDITS *Credits from left to right are separated by semicolons, from top to bottom by dashes.*

COVER and page 1: U.S. Air Force. 2, 3: Map and legend by Elie Sabban.

FORGING A MIGHTY WEAPON—8, 9: Radio Times Hulton Picture Library, London. 10: Flight International, London. 11: U.S. Air Force. 12: National Air and Space Museum, Smithsonian Institution. 13: National Air and Space Museum, Smithsonian Institution, copied by Charlie Brown; U.S. Air Force—Lockheed-California Company, inset, Wide World. 14, 15: U.S. Air Force; Bildarchiv Preussischer Kulturbesitz, Berlin—John W. R. Taylor, Surbiton, Surrey; National Air and Space Museum, Smithsonian Institution, copied by Charlie Brown. 16, 17: Radio Times Hulton Picture Library, London; U.S. Air Force—National Air and Space Museum, Smithsonian Institution; Pilot Press Ltd., Bromley, Kent. 18, 19: U.S. Navy, National Archives; British Airways—Douglas Aircraft Company; U.S. Navy, National Archives. 20, 21: Flight International, London—United Press International; United Press International—Flight International, London. 22, 23: National Air and Space Museum, Smithsonian Institution, copied by Charlie Brown—courtesy Pan American Airways; U.S. Air Force.

BRITAIN GOES IT ALONE—26: Imperial War Museum, London. 27: Stato Maggiore Aeronautica, Rome. 28: Bruce Robertson, London. 30: Imperial War Museum, London; The Auckland Collection, St. Albans, Herts. 32: Radio Times Hulton Picture Library, London. 34: Flight International, London. 37: Ullstein Bilderdienst, Berlin. 38: Imperial War Museum, London.

HARD TIMES FOR THE RAF—40, 41: Painting by Frank Wootton, courtesy RAF Strike Command Headquarters, High Wycombe. 42: Radio Times Hulton Picture Library, London. 43: Painting by Frank Wootton, courtesy M. Mandall. 44, 45: Painting by Frank Wootton, courtesy RAF Strike Command, 11 Group, Bentley Priory, Stanmore; painting by Frank Wootton—United Press International. 46, 47: Painting by Frank Wootton, owned by the artist and on loan to the National Air and Space Museum, Smithsonian Institution; Imperial War Museum, London—Painting by Frank Wootton, courtesy RAF Strike Command, 11 Group, Bentley Priory, Stanmore. 48, 49: Painting by Frank Wootton, courtesy RAF, Waddington, Lincolnshire—Radio Times Hulton Picture Library, London; painting by Frank Wootton, courtesy RAF Strike Command Headquarters, High Wycombe. 50, 51: Painting by Frank Wootton, courtesy RAF Staff College, Bracknell.

"BOMBER" HARRIS TAKES OVER—54: Imperial War Museum, London. 56: Bob Landry for LIFE. 57: Imperial War Museum, London. 61: Map by Elie Sabban.

ALL-SEEING EYES IN THE SKY—66, 67: Radio Times Hulton Picture Library, London. 69: British Official. 70, 71: U.S. Air Force—Andreas Feininger for LIFE; Radio Times Hulton Picture Library, London. 72, 73: U.S. Air Force, except top right, British Official. 74: Radio Times Hulton Picture Library, London—Imperial War Museum, London. 75-79: U.S. Air Force.

BOMBING ROUND THE CLOCK—82: U.S. Air Force. 84: Courtesy Chaz Bowyer, Norfolk, England. 87: U.S. Air Force. 88: United Press International; U.S. Air Force. 89: Illustration by Martin Caidin from the book *Flying Forts* by Martin Caidin. 91: Imperial War Museum, London. 92: Diagram adapted by John Batchelor from *Allied Secret Weapons: The War of Science*, by Brian J. Ford, © 1971 by Brian J. Ford. Reprinted by permission of Ballantine Books, a division of Random House, Inc. 94: Imperial War Museum, London.

ANATOMY OF A MISSION—96, 97: U.S. Air Force. 98: David E. Scherman for LIFE. 99-103: U.S. Air Force. 104, 105: United Press International, except top left, U.S. Air Force. 106, 107: U.S. Air Force. 108, 109: U.S. Air Force, except top left, David E. Scherman for LIFE. 110, 111: Imperial War Museum, London, inset, U.S. Air Force.

A HAZARDOUS CALLING—112, 113: U.S. Air Force. 114: Wide World. 115: U.S. Air Force. 116: ADN-Zentralbild, Berlin, DDR. 117: U.S. Air Force. 118, 119: U.S. Air Force, except bottom right, Wide World. 120-123: U.S. Air Force. 124: Imperial War Museum, London, except center, U.S. Air Force (2). 125: U.S. Air Force, courtesy United Press International; U.S. Air Force (2)—Imperial War Museum, London (2). 126, 127: Ullstein Bilderdienst, Berlin.

THE LUFTWAFFE FIGHTS BACK—131: Ullstein Bilderdienst, Berlin. 133: U.S. Air Force. 136, 138: Ullstein Bilderdienst, Berlin.

THE LUFTWAFFE'S ELITE—140, 141: Bundesarchiv, Koblenz. 142: Ullstein Bilderdienst, Berlin. 143, 144: Bundesarchiv, Koblenz. 145: Ullstein Bilderdienst, Berlin, except top right, Süddeutscher Verlag Bilderdienst, Munich. 146, 147: Bundesarchiv, Koblenz, except bottom left, Süddeutscher Verlag Bilderdienst, Munich. 148: Bundesarchiv, Koblenz. 149: Bundesarchiv, Koblenz—Ullstein Bilderdienst, Berlin. 150, 151: Bundesarchiv, Koblenz.

SUPREMACY IN THE SKY—154, 156: U.S. Air Force. 159: Courtesy Ernst Obermeier, Munich; Ullstein Bilderdienst, Berlin (2)—Imperial War Museum, London (3)—U.S. Air Force (3). 161, 163: U.S. Air Force.

AIR SUPPORT FOR THE ARMY—166, 167: U.S. Air Force. 168: Radio Times Hulton Picture Library, London. 169-171: U.S. Air Force. 172, 173: U.S. Air Force (2); U.S. Army. 174: Imperial War Museum, London—Crown Copyright. 175: U.S. Air Force—United Press International. 176, 177: U.S. Air Force; U.S. Army.

THE FINAL ONSLAUGHT—181, 183: U.S. Air Force. 187: U.S. Army. 189: Ullstein Bilderdienst, Berlin.

THE AIRMEN'S ARSENAL—192-203: Illustrations by John Batchelor, London.

ACKNOWLEDGMENTS

For help given in preparing this book the editors are especially grateful to Dana Bell, Archives Technician, U.S. Air Force Still Photo Depository, Arlington, Va., and Donald S. Lopez, Assistant Director for Aeronautics, National Air and Space Museum, Washington, D.C. The editors also wish to express their gratitude to Virginia Bader, Virginia Bader Fine Arts, Washington, D.C.; Ian Ballantine, Bantam Books Inc., New York; Denis Bateman, Air Historical Branch, London; Hans Becker, ADN-Zentralbild, Berlin, German Democratic Republic; Carole Boutté, Senior Researcher, U.S. Army Audio-Visual Activity, Pentagon, Arlington, Va.; Chaz Bowyer, Norwich, England; Walter J. Boyne, Curator of Aeronautics, National Air and Space Museum, Washington, D.C.; Jack Bruce, RAF Museum, Hendon, England; Harry E. Calkins, Manager, Editorial Services, Douglas Aircraft Company, Long Beach, Calif.; Contessa Maria Fede Caproni, Museo Aeronautica Caproni di Taliedo, Rome; Alan Cooper, Kent, England; V. M. Destefano, Chief of Research Library, U.S. Army Audio-Visual Activity, Pentagon, Arlington, Va.; Ensign Robert C. Dobson, USN, Naval Air Station, Whiting Field, Milton, Fla.; James N. Eastman Jr., Chief, Research Branch, Albert F. Simpson Historical Research Center, USAF, Maxwell Air Force Base, Montgomery, Ala.; Hans-Joachim Ebert, Messerschmitt-Bölkow-Blohm, Munich; Robert C. Ferguson, Public Relations Photo Coordinator, Lockheed-California Company, Burbank, Calif.; Virginia Fincik, Chief, Research Unit, U.S. Air Force Still Photo Depository, Arlington, Va.; Frederic G. Fleming, Port Washington, N.Y.; Ulrich Frodien, Süddeutscher Verlag, Munich; Adolf Galland, General (Ret.), Bonn-Bad Godesberg, Germany; Amy Geoghegan, Archives Technician, U.S. Air Force Still Photo Depository, Arlington, Va.; Marylou Gjernes, Curator, Center of Military History, Department of the Army, Alexandria, Va.; Robert L. Griffin, Colonel, CAF, Director of Operations, Confederate Air Force, Harlingen, Tex.; David O. Hale, Woodbridge, Va.; Gerard E. Hasselwander, Historian, Albert F. Simpson Historical Research Center, USAF, Maxwell Air Force Base, Montgomery, Ala.; Dr. Matthias Haupt, Bundesarchiv, Koblenz, Germany; Werner Haupt, Bibliothek für Zeitgeschichte, Stuttgart; William Holland, Meridale, N.Y.; Colonel Peter Jungmichel, Air Attaché, Embassy of the Federal Republic of Germany, Washington, D.C.; Dr. Roland Klemig, Bildarchiv Preussischer Kulturbesitz, Berlin; William H. Leary, Archivist, National Archives, Still Photo Branch, Washington, D.C.; Rolf-Ole Lehmann, Lütjenburg, Germany; Library of the New York State University Agricultural and Technical College at Delhi, N.Y.; Margaret B. Livesay, Chief, U.S. Air Force Still Photo Depository, Arlington, Va.; Robert B. Meyer Jr., Curator of Aero-Propulsion, National Air and Space Museum, Washington, D.C.; Ernst Obermeier, Munich; Janusz Piekalkiewicz, Rösrath-Hoffnungsthal, Germany; Dominick A. Pisano, Reference Librarian, National Air and Space Museum, Washington, D.C.; Mrs. Alice Price, Administrator, Air Force Art Program, U.S. Pentagon, Washington, D.C.; Hans Ring, Übersee-München, Germany; David Schoem, Chief, Support Division, Headquarters USAF, Office of Air Force History, Washington, D.C.; Axel Schulz, Ullstein Bilderdienst, Berlin; Mindy K. Small, Archives Technician, U.S. Air Force Still Photo Depository, Arlington, Va.; Melden E. Smith Jr., Boston State College, Boston; Virginia Smith, Archives Technician, U.S. Air Force Still Photo Depository, Arlington, Va.; Jay P. Spenser, Research Assistant, National Air and Space Museum, Washington, D.C.; Lieut. Colonel Roy M. Stanley II, USAF, Fairfax, Va.; Stato Maggiore Aeronautica, Rome; James Stewart, Dayton, Ohio; Richard L. Thurm, Archivist, National Archives Still Photo Branch, Washington, D.C.; James H. Trimble, Archivist, National Archives Still Photo Branch, Washington, D.C.; Alison Uppard, RAF Museum, Hendon, England; Ann White, Public Relations, Pan American Airways, New York; Paul L. White, Archivist, National Archives Still Photo Branch, Washington, D.C.; Alan Williams, Imperial War Museum, London; Marjorie Willis, Radio Times Hulton Picture Library, London.

The index for this book was prepared by Nicholas J. Anthony.

Printed in U.S.A.